By the same Author

THE MODERNIST MOVEMENT IN THE ROMAN CHURCH

A PLAIN MAN'S GUIDE TO CHRISTIANITY

GOD'S JUDGMENT ON EUROPE

SECULAR DESPAIR AND CHRISTIAN FAITH

CHRIST'S STRANGE WORK

THE ORB AND THE CROSS

A NORMATIVE STUDY IN THE RELATIONS OF CHURCH AND STATE WITH REFERENCE TO GLADSTONE'S EARLY WRITINGS

BY

ALEC R. VIDLER, B.D.

Warden of St Deiniol's Library, Hawarden

LONDON
SOCIETY FOR PROMOTING
CHRISTIAN KNOWLEDGE
NORTHUMBERLAND AVENUE, W.C.2

When you see this Orb set under the Cross, remember that the whole world is subject to the power and empire of Christ, our Redeemer. For He is the Prince of the Kings of the earth; King of Kings and Lord of Lords. So that no man can reign happily who derives not his authority from Him, and directs not all his actions according to His laws.

THE CORONATION SERVICE OF QUEEN VICTORIA.

It was the question, it is the question, and it will be the question to the ending of the world, whether the magistrate have any power at all [in matters of religion], and what that power is.

COL. SIR HARDRESS WALTERS AT THE WHITEHALL DEBATES, 1648.
(See A. S. P. Woodhouse, *Puritanism and Liberty*, p. 136.)

The problem of the relations of Church and State . . . raises topics which go down to the root of all political philosophy, and forces us to face the whole problem of the true nature of civil society and the meaning of personality.

J. N. Figgis, *Churches in the Modern State*, p. 170.

In an age which inclines to secularise the State, and ultimately to curtail or overthrow civil liberty by the subtraction of its religious guarantees, to declaim against intolerance becomes a secondary duty, and it is infinitely more important, and as it seems to me more rational, to plead earnestly for those great ethical laws under which we are socially constituted, and which economical speculations and material interests have threatened altogether to subvert.

W. E. Gladstone, *The State in its relations with the Church*, p. viii.

The relation of the spiritual and the secular power is, like that of speculation and revelation, of religion and nature, one of those problems which remain perpetually open, to receive light from the meditations and experience of all ages, and the complete solution of which is among the objects, and would be the end, of all history.

Lord Acton, *The History of Freedom and other Essays*, p. 191.

"He takes up a most interesting position", continued the Father Librarian. "As far as Church jurisdiction is concerned he is apparently quite opposed to the separation of Church from State".

"That's interesting. But in what sense?" Father Zossima asked Ivan.

Dostoevsky, *The Brothers Karamazov*, Book II, chap. 5.

THIS BOOK IS PRODUCED IN COMPLETE CONFORMITY WITH THE AUTHORISED ECONOMY STANDARDS

FIRST PUBLISHED 1945
REPRINTED 1946
MADE IN GREAT BRITAIN

TO MY FATHER

who taught me to delve into the past

PREFACE

Part of the material included in this study was used in a course of four lectures on "Christianity and Statesmanship", which the writer gave at University College, Bangor, in March, 1941. He takes this opportunity of expressing his gratitude for the invitation and for the hospitable welcome which he received during his visit. He is also indebted to a considerable number of friends with whom he has discussed various aspects of the subject.

The title of the study was suggested by a sentence in *The State in its relations with the Church* (4th ed., i. 131):

> By the element . . . of religion, entering into the work of government, . . . its connection is maintained with its origin from above, and public men may see that the orb is still at the foot of the cross.

It is styled a *normative* study, because its purpose is to discover norms or standards, rather than to investigate a past theory for its own sake or to recommend a policy for the present.

A. R. V.

CONTENTS

ABBREVIATIONS

Carlyle = R. W. and A. J. Carlyle, *A History of Mediæval Political Theory in the West*, 6 vols. (1903–36).

CCR = D. C. Lathbury, *Correspondence on Church and Religion of William Ewart Gladstone*, 2 vols. (1910).

CP = W. E. Gladstone, *Church Principles considered in their results* (1840).

Morley = John Morley, *The Life of William Ewart Gladstone*, 3 vols. (1903).

SDL = St Deiniol's Library, Hawarden.

SRC = W. E. Gladstone, *The State in its relations with the Church*, 2 vols. (4th ed.; 1841).

Troeltsch = Ernst Troeltsch, *The Social Teaching of the Christian Churches*, 2 vols. (English Translation, 1931).

CHAPTER ONE

INTRODUCTION

The only subjects worth a wise Man's serious notice, are RELIGION, and GOVERNMENT; such Religion and Government, I mean, as exclude not (which too often they do) MORALITY and POLITICKS; and these are subjects that, at the same time, most need his attention.—Bishop Warburton, Dedication of the 1748 edition of *The Alliance between Church and State.*

I always admired Mrs Grote's saying that politics and theology were the only two really great subjects.—W. E. Gladstone to Lord Rosebery, September 16, 1880. Morley, iii. 4.

"Religion and science" and "the Bible and the higher criticism" as popular subjects of theological debate have, at any rate for the time being, yielded pride of place to "the Church and the world" or "Christianity and the social order". The relation between Christianity and politics (in the large Aristotelian sense of the word[1]) is engaging the attention of theologians to-day to an extent that it has not done for a century or more, and in a way that it has never done before.[2] The conference on "Church, Community and State", which was held at Oxford in 1937, afforded evidence of this fact. But, in spite of all that has been

1. "To Aristotle man is a 'political animal', but when St Thomas Aquinas expressed the same thought for the thirteenth century he had to say, Man is a '*social* and political animal'."—C. H. McIlwain, *The Growth of Political Thought in the West* (1932), p. 5.

2. "If the present social situation is to be controlled by Christian principles, thoughts will be necessary which have not yet been thought, and which will correspond to this new situation as the older forms met the need of the social situation in earlier ages."—Troeltsch, ii. 1012.

"Humanity is now seeking desperately for new answers to this question of the end and the means in political life, and in so doing is urged forward by an instinctive feeling that any valid solution must arise out of religious depths, out of some kind of faith. . . . It is therefore scarcely surprising that a growing number of people within the Churches are deeply convinced that the whole traditional doctrine concerning politics requires a fundamental re-examination and a courageous reformulation."—Nils Ehrenström, *Christian Faith and the Modern State* (1937), p. 38f. This book contains a useful bibliography of recent literature on the subject.

written and said on the subject in recent years, it is doubtful whether much progress has been made towards agreement among Christians as to the definition of the main questions. They certainly seem to be a long way from agreement as to the answers.

This is partly because "the political action of Christianity" is, as Lord Acton said, "perhaps the most complex and comprehensive question that can embarrass a historian".[1] But if the study of Church history, however plain its lessons on other subjects, is calculated here to embarrass the inquirer who seeks for plain answers to simple questions, he is already embarrassed, before he turns the pages of the past, by the strange and unpredictable changes that are taking place in religion and politics to-day. To this sense of embarrassment Sir Fred Clarke has given pointed expression, as one who is concerned with the task of national education.

> In a world such as this and the prospect being what it is, what are we going to teach our growing boys and girls in the critical years of adolescence? There is something almost terrifying about such a question, if we put it quite starkly, and grasp its implications imaginatively. Indeed, some of the older generation may well say, "Who are we that we should attempt to answer it at all"?[2]

For several years I have found that my own reading and studies gravitated inevitably towards this subject, and that I must at least attempt to formulate the main questions. At first I thought that I should do this best by concentrating on some general idea, such as that of "Natural Law"; for it would surely be futile to wander aimlessly about the field. But I found that inquiries into the history and meaning of the conception of "Natural Law" were less fruitful than I had hoped.[3] Or it may be that they pointed me to too ambitious an undertaking; I still consider that we badly need a full treatise on that conception, which will deal both with old traditions and with new conditions, by someone who is competent to provide it. Anyhow, while I was

1. *The History of Freedom and other Essays* (1907), p. 99.
2. *The Spectator* (August 20, 1943), p. 166.
3. See my "Inquiries concerning Natural Law" in *Theology* (February, 1942), pp. 65–73.

uncertain how to proceed, I had occasion to read for the first time Gladstone's book, *The State in its relations with the Church.* I had expected to find it both dull and dead.[1] It cannot be said to be exciting on the surface; but it seemed to me at once to raise questions which, if not alive in the sense of being much discussed, ought to be alive in that sense,—questions in fact of permanent, and to-day of peculiar, interest.

Thus it was not long before I decided that the most useful thing I could do was to study these questions with reference to the context in which Gladstone wrote, and to use his book as a doorway into the general subject of the relations of the State with the Church. This has of course involved a considerable limitation of my original purpose, but I think that there is need for studies which focus attention on certain aspects of the relation between the Church and the world, instead of opening them all up simultaneously. Moreover, when full allowance has been made for the novelty of our present social environment and of contemporary political conditions, it remains true that the history of the past has a great deal to teach us, especially those parts of it in which men of great moral and intellectual stature were engaged. In some respects also questions of first principle can be better studied in relation to a past situation. Fuller information about it is available, and a more balanced perspective is possible. Our judgment should be comparatively unaffected by the passions and hopes and fears that distort our estimate of current affairs. "Those who sit in judgment", said St Thomas Aquinas, "judge of things present, towards which they are affected by love, hatred, or some kind of cupidity; wherefore their judgment is perverted".[2]

Further, although Mr Gladstone was a man of his own time or rather of his own times, yet those times are not so remote from our own as present fashions of speech often suggest. Our own present situation in this country has arisen out of the past which was

1. "Gladstone's works are unread to-day. No one defends them, and judgment seems to go against them by default."—D. C. Somervell, *Disraeli and Gladstone* [2] (1938), p. 291.

"If some of his books continue to be read, it will be rather because they are his than in respect of any permanent contribution they have made to knowledge".—James Bryce, *Studies in Contemporary Biography* (1903), p. 479.

2. *Summa Theol.*, iia. Q. 95. A. 1.

present to him, whatever new factors may have arisen meanwhile. I hope to show also that Gladstone was much more than a man of his own times; that he had prophetic qualities; and that, most notably as a young man, he had a rare sensitiveness to the past and future, as well as to the present, not only of Britain and Europe, but of all that goes under the names of Christianity and civilisation.[1] The biographer of Samuel Wilberforce said of him that "no man ever realised more thoroughly the fact that social institutions are a portion of the providential order of things, and that the spiritual and the so-called secular ought to be reciprocally strengthened and benefited by mutual connection and alliance";[2] this can be said, with at least equal truth, of Gladstone.

Finally, I may recall Troeltsch's description of him as "the great modern representative of Christian politics".[3] This alone suggests that even a partial study of his teaching and career will bring us near to the heart of the main problem. This problem is in fact a permanent one; it is inveterate in the history of the world. Whatever particular manifestation of it we choose to examine, we shall be led on or led back, led out or led up, to the general principles at stake.[4]

I found myself very soon led back to the history of political theory, especially since the beginning of the Christian era. It was necessary to discover what lay behind Gladstone's theory. His own account of earlier theories of the relation of Church and State is severely restricted in its range, though he may have read and known more about them than he betrays. But in any case he had not at his disposal the comprehensive works which to-day

1. "Gladstone was both European and religious in a sense in which those terms could not be applied to any of his contemporaries."—J. L. Hammond, *Gladstone and the Irish Nation* (1938), p. 62.

2. A. R. Ashwell, *Life of Samuel Wilberforce* (1880), i. 139. Gladstone marked the passage in his copy of this book (*SDL*).

3. Troeltsch, ii. 675. I also observe that Dr Carnegie Simpson describes Gladstone as "the greatest Anglican of his generation" in *The Church and the State* (1929), p. 203.

4. There is a further personal reason which may be allowed to justify me in studying the subject with special reference to Gladstone. I have the privilege of being the Warden of his library. While I do not think that this circumstance gives me a bias towards exaggerating his greatness, it does indicate a certain duty and a special opportunity to study his teaching and to reflect upon his career.

introduce a student to all the complexities of the past;[1] he was an inheritor of more than he could know. I have read as much as I could of the history of political theory with special reference to the relations of Church and State, and in the next chapter I present what is no more than a bird's-eye view or a summary interpretation of that historical background which is an indispensable preliminary to a profitable study of the subject either as it stood in Gladstone's time or as it stands in our own. In this summary interpretation I emphasise and annotate such points as seem to me to be either most significant or insufficiently familiar.

I then proceed to give an account of the argument of Gladstone's book, *The State in its relations with the Church*, at least of those parts of it which are of more than topical or temporary interest, and which raise big, permanent questions. In the succeeding chapters I try to elucidate the significance of these questions: What is the nature of the State? What is the nature of the Church (with reference to Gladstone's *Church Principles*)? What is the normative idea of the right relations between them? The last chapter contains some reflections on Gladstone's career.

This is therefore an essay in Church history, political theory, and ecclesiology. I have little to say about economics, although I am aware that, since the time of Karl Marx, there is no excuse for failure to recognise the ways in which political action and theory are economically conditioned. The recent tendency, however, almost to subsume political theory under economics needs to be corrected. I agree with the late Miss Ruth Kenyon that recent discussions "show that thinking about the relations between the Church and politics is even more inchoate than thinking about the Church and economics".[2]

I cannot better conclude this introduction than by making my

1. Notably, R. W. and A. J. Carlyle, *A History of Mediæval Political Theory in the West*, 6 vols. (1903–36); Ernst Troeltsch, *The Social Teaching of the Christian Churches*, 2 vols. (English translation, 1931); C. H. McIlwain, *The Growth of Political Theory in the West* (1932); G. H. Sabine, *A History of Political Theory* (1938); J. W. Allen, *A History of Political Thought in the Sixteenth Century* (1928) and *English Political Thought* 1603–1660 (1938); W. K. Jordan, *The Development of Religious Toleration in England*, 3 vols. (1932–8); Douglas Nobbs, *Theocracy and Toleration; a study of the disputes in Dutch Calvinism from* 1600 *to* 1650 (1938); Luigi Sturzo, *Church and State* (English translation, 1939); the works of J. N. Figgis, Ernest Barker, Christopher Dawson, *et al.*

2. *Christendom* (June, 1941), p. 75.

own the words of Mr T. S. Eliot in the preface to *The Idea of a Christian Society* (1939):

> As I have chosen to consider such a large problem, it should be obvious that the following pages can have but little importance by themselves, and that they can only be of use if taken as an individual contribution to a discussion which must occupy many minds for a long time to come.

CHAPTER TWO

HISTORICAL BACKGROUND

I

Whether or not the New Testament adumbrates, or lays the foundations of, a Christian doctrine of the State, it certainly contains no indications of a doctrine of *a Christian State*,—notwithstanding all that has been written apropos of St Paul's Epistle to the Romans, chapter xiii. 1–7.[1] No one in New Testament times envisaged or anticipated a situation in which the State, *i.e.*, the Roman Empire, would consist of Christians, would be governed by Christians, or would be run on Christian lines.

> It was hardly thought possible in New Testament times that Emperors and other rulers might actually be converted to Christianity . . . and the changes which imperial conversion might entail, not alone in the Christian attitude towards the Emperor, but in the whole ecclesiastical polity, were not envisaged in the most ambitious Christian speculation of the first and second centuries.[2]

The New Testament perspective is not that of an indefinite historical development, nor of a gradually expanding Christian mission to the world, nor of the progressive realisation in history of the kingdom of God. The perspective of the New Testament is eschatological.[3]

1. The following remark of J. W. Allen with regard to the sixteenth century, in spite of its pungent exaggeration, is justified, and could be more widely applied: "The thirteenth chapter of the Epistle to the Romans contains what are perhaps the most important words ever written for the history of political thought. Yet it would be a gross mistake to suppose that men, at any time, took their political opinions from St Paul."—*Political Thought in the Sixteenth Century*, p. 132. Cp. what J. N. Figgis says about the use made of Holy Scripture by mediæval and Reformation political theorists, in *The Cambridge Modern History*, iii. 740.
2. K. M. Setton, *Christian Attitude towards the Emperor in the Fourth Century* (1941), p. 17.
3. Carlyle's chapter on "The Political Theory of the New Testament" in vol. i of *A History of Mediæval Political Theory in the West* (published in 1903) contains no allusion to eschatology nor suggestion of its bearing on the subject, and is consequently very wooden. The same is true of G. H. Sabine who, writing at a later date, has less excuse.

The Christ is represented as having said: "My kingdom is not of this world" (John xviii. 36). This kingdom, the perfect reign or rule of God over His own people, was about to come; it was already nigh at hand; indeed it had begun to come. The mighty works of the Messiah, His death and resurrection, His exaltation to the right hand of God and the outpouring of the Holy Spirit, His imminent return in glory—these events, which are already in motion, signify the end of the present age. The mission of the Church is to tell all who have ears to hear—as many as possible and as rapidly as possible—that these final things are already happening. That is the good news. They must be summoned to repent and believe the gospel, and, if they do, they will be received into God's people, His *ecclesia*, which is not of this world, but is here and now coming into being, is in the making, and is shortly to be consummated.

That—with of course varieties of emphasis and detail—is the New Testament perspective. From such a perspective concern for a doctrine of the State or with the tasks of statesmanship will evidently have a very subsidiary place.[1] Nevertheless, the State, the administration of order and good government, mattered, although it was not going to matter for long.[2] It mattered because it provided and secured the conditions in which the Church could carry out its eschatological mission; and it was important to treat the State with respect, because only so could it be expected to tolerate the propagation of the Christian mission.[3]

1. It is because he overlooks the eschatological perspective that Dr H. M. Relton is able to write: "A spiritual society of such a character thus inaugurated and thus placed as the leaven in human life, destined to leaven the whole lump, *naturally from the start* had to define its relationship to the world in which it had been placed by its Head."—*Religion and the State* (1937), p. 16. (Italics mine.)

2. "César n'avait aucune place dans la future Jérusalem, et si l'Evangile n'était pas une invitation à la révolte contre Rome, c'était une prédiction, au moins implicite, du renversement prochain de sa puissance."—A. Loisy, *A propos d'histoire des religions* (1911), p. 243.

3. J. Weiss describes the Pauline attitude to the State as one of cool indifference. See *The History of Primitive Christianity* (English translation, 1937), ii. 590. Contrast E. Brunner, *The Divine Imperative* (English translation, 1937), who reads back his theological prepossessions into the outlook of the primitive Church: "It is absolutely wrong to ascribe to Primitive Christianity either indifference or hostility towards the State. . . . The assertion that Christianity only gradually acquired a more positive attitude towards the State is pure

Such toleration was plainly advantageous, if it could be obtained without essential compromise. But behind this consideration was the conviction that all power in heaven and on earth had been given to the risen Christ (Matthew xxviii. 18), and that therefore the actual government of this world was under the divine providence and designed to serve the interests of the messianic kingdom.

The attitude to the State which is prescribed in the New Testament seems, however, to be based primarily on practical or pragmatic considerations. It would be misleading to say that the New Testament deliberately adumbrates, or lays the foundations of, a *Christian doctrine* of the State. No doubt the references to the subject, notably in the Epistle to the Romans and the First Epistle of St Peter, have theoretical or doctrinal implications. When Christian teachers had occasion to stress the duty of obedience to the civil government, they adopted and adapted for their purpose precepts which were more or less commonplaces in the Hellenistic world.[1] These precepts, if one cares to go into the matter thoroughly, may be held to imply a definite doctrine of the State, but hardly a specifically Christian doctrine.[2] In any

imagination. What Irenæus says about the State (*adv. hær.* v. 24) is as much in accordance with the fundamental ideas of Paul, and of Primitive Christianity, as it is with those of the Reformation" (p. 684).

1. "The early Christian teachers used ethical material already prepared by the Pagan instructors. Hellenistic Judaism may well have mediated this type of teaching, but the Christian teachers must themselves have come into direct contact with it when the Church began to spread in the Hellenistic world. . . . Of course to everything that was borrowed there was given a definitely Christian tone and flavour."—J. W. C. Wand, *The General Epistles of St Peter and St Jude* (1934), p. 5. But, as T. R. Birks said (*Church and State*, p. 2), "simple maxims of duty towards heathen rulers could not resolve the questions that must inevitably arise, when kings and princes obey the Gospel, and take their place within the Church of Christ. The claims and rights of Church rulers, of civil governors, and of the private Christian, would then need to be reconciled to each other".

On the relation between N.T. teaching and current Hellenistic ideas see Carlyle, *loc. cit.*, and Sabine, *op. cit.*, chap. x.

2. Cp. A. J. Carlyle, *The Christian Church and Liberty* (1924), p. 59: "It is well to recognise that St Paul is here (*sc.* in Romans xiii) only expressing the fundamental judgment of all the great political thinkers of the ancient world both of the centuries before him and of those who were more or less his contemporaries. . . . We do not therefore need to look for the origin of St Paul's phrase in any ideas or circumstances which were specifically Christian. St Paul is only here throwing into the terms of Christian theology the common doctrine of the civilised world".

case, the point is that the early Christians did not care to go into the matter. (There is no reason to suppose that the New Testament gives a false impression of the place that was occupied by this interest in the early Church.) They were occupied with matters that put the question of the State into the shade. And very soon, when the Lord's parousia took place, the State would pass out of the shade, for it would pass out of existence.[1]

In point of fact, however, the Lord's parousia did not take place, as had been expected, and the State did not pass out of existence. It passed out of the shade, but in the opposite direction. It began to loom larger and larger, and it began to occupy a prominent place in the concerns of the Church. For, on the one hand, the State did not continue to tolerate the Church; persecution, of which there is early evidence in the New Testament itself, entered upon an ascending scale. And, on the other hand, as the expectation of the near end of the world faded, the Christians had to acquire a more definite attitude to its government and affairs.

In other words, they had to acquire a doctrine of the State as a guide for their conduct, and the natural way to do this was to appropriate more fully the doctrine that was current in the Roman Empire, since that seemed satisfactory enough. As Professor Sabine says,

> In the beginning, the rise of Christianity did not carry with it a new political philosophy. Christianity itself and its ultimate establishment as the legal religion of the empire were the consummation of social and intellectual changes that had long been at work and which affected almost equally thinkers who never

1. Cp. Lord Acton, *The History of Freedom, &c.* (1907), pp. 27f.: "Going forth to all nations, in many stages of civilisation and under almost every form of government, Christianity had none of the character of a political apostolate, and in its absorbing mission to individuals did not challenge public authority. The early Christians avoided contact with the State, abstained from the responsibilities of office, and were even reluctant to serve in the army. Cherishing their citizenship of a kingdom not of this world, they despaired of an empire which seemed too powerful to be resisted and too corrupt to be converted, whose institutions, the work and the pride of untold centuries of paganism, drew their sanctions from the gods whom the Christians accounted devils, which plunged its hands from age to age in the blood of martyrs, and was beyond the hope of regeneration and foredoomed to perish".

embraced the new faith. So far as political ideas are concerned, those of the Fathers were for the most part those of Cicero and Seneca.[1]

Only when the Church triumphed over persecution and assumed a dominant place in the Roman Empire, did the question how there could be a Christian State become actual, and the full implications of the question were by no means understood at once;[2] indeed it may be doubted whether they are fully understood now. Still, the need to discover the right relation between the kingdom *not of* this world and the kingdom *of* this world became more and more insistent as it became apparent that the latter was likely to last indefinitely and to be composed, largely if not exclusively, of Christians.

What had happened was really this: there had come into existence in the Roman Empire, which was a vast *communitas communitatum*, a new community possessed by, and possessing, a principle of unity and a sense of inherent and ultimate authority more powerful than the unity and authority of the Empire itself. It came into existence not through the deliberate design of the first Christians who, as we have seen, never imagined that they were launching a movement which in the course of centuries would permeate and subdue the Empire itself. It did so almost in spite of itself. What had happened was, as Christians believe, the act of God. He had, through His Son Jesus Christ and the power of His Holy Spirit, founded *in* this world a new community which, although it consisted of sinful men, was mightier, morally and spiritually, than any community *of* this world, because its principle of unity, the source of its authority, and its inherent dynamic, were derived from that eternal order of being which is above and beyond this world.

Nevertheless, the kingdom of God did not become and could not become identical with a kingdom of this world, although men

1. *Op. cit.*, p. 161. Cp. pp. 17f. *infra.* On the absence of a theory of the relations of Church and State during the early centuries, see P. Carnegie Simpson, *The Church and the State* (1929), pp. 37, 54, 59, 64.

2. *E.g.*, see the illuminating account of the ill-considered and unprincipled attitude which Christians assumed towards Constantine and his immediate successors, in K. M. Setton's *Christian Attitude towards the Emperor in the Fourth Century* (1941).

in their pride have been continually tempted to bring about this identification. The early Christians were quite right when in effect they said that the acts of God in His Christ and through the Holy Spirit, by which He had saved His people and was bestowing on them final blessedness, were not yet complete and could not be completed in this world or in this age. They were to be completed by the parousia or the second advent of the Lord. Where the first generation of Christians was mistaken was in supposing that the second advent—the final act in which God would bring His kingly rule to consummation—would occur within a short time. It is not an event that will occur within time at all.[1] The second advent is God's act at the end of time, by which He gathers up time into eternity. It is the counterpart of His act in creation.

The Christians were quite right in affirming the second advent of the Lord as an essential dogma of their creed, and its inclusion as a permanent element in the Church's mythology was, or should have been, a safeguard against any idea that a kingdom of this world, albeit an ecclesiastical kingdom, can ever become identical with the kingdom of God. The safeguard has acted imperfectly, since, both in the medieval and modern periods, Christians have in different ways succumbed to such an ambition. Sooner or later, however, it is exposed and broken up by the forces that really make history, and that will be operative till the end of time.

Man's sin, Christian man's sin, his pride and egotism, were not finally eliminated by the incarnation of the Christ and by the outpouring of the Holy Spirit. What had happened was that a new factor had descended into history which both revealed the nature of man's sin, the curse that is upon him, and his incapacity to save himself, and which also revealed that God had wrought and provided in Christ that justification for man that he could never by himself deserve or achieve. Here and now all who repent and trust in Him for their justification are incorporated into Christ, made members of His mystical body, and receive the first fruits of the Spirit and new possibilities of a sanctified common life. Thereby they enter into the beginnings or a foretaste of the final blessedness of God's kingly rule.

1. See Reinhold Niebuhr, *Beyond Tragedy* (1938), pp. 21–24; and *The Nature and Destiny of Man* (1943), vol. ii, chap. 10.

> The Kingdom of God is already established. The Kingdom is God's order, and is complete in God's will. This we perceive in faith, which is the response to the word spoken in the Son. The Kingdom of God is independent of all world-history, all movements of men, backwards, forwards, up, down, or in the dreary circle of human independence and arbitrary self-willed rebellion. The Kingdom of God does not depend on men's efforts: it awaits their faith in its King. It is in this sense that the Kingdom of God is here and now, because it is in Christ; in this sense too that it is never here and now, but always summoning men, and only at the end of time will judge the works of men, because it is the perfection of Christ's being in creation.[1]

In history only the beginnings, only a foretaste, only the first-fruits, are received. For history is still a scene of conflict, and it retains a tragic character. Not only does sin continue to exercise its hold over unregenerate or unbelieving men; but the regenerate, the believers, themselves are still sinners. What distinguishes them is not sinlessness or perfection, but the knowledge that they have been justified and are being sanctified, not by their own works, but by the grace of God.

> We have to remember that the Kingdom of Christ on earth will never be realised, and also that it is always being realised; we must remember that whatever reform or revolution we carry out, the result will always be a sordid travesty of what human society should be—though the world is never left wholly without glory.[2]

The measure of man's sin is shown in his capacity to pervert, corrupt and prostitute to his own glory and egoistic purposes the very gifts of God—the Scriptures, the ordained ministry, the sacraments—by means of which God wills to deliver him from sin and to sanctify him. The Church, though it is in principle the new community founded by God in Christ through the Holy Spirit, and is the kingdom of God in the making, is in history made

1. R. Gregor Smith on "The Kingdom of God To-day" in *The Evangelical Quarterly* (October, 1943), pp. 276f.
2. T. S. Eliot, *The Idea of a Christian Society* (1939), p. 59.

up of persons who have power, and use their power, to turn every good thing into its opposite.[1]

II

The kingdom of God, then, can never be "of this world", and the history of Church and State from approximately the time of Constantine through the Middle Ages, and again after the Reformation, is one long illustration of this truth. It was a prolonged attempt, at times a magnificent attempt, in one way or another, to unite the kingdom of God with the kingdom of this world, or to realise the ideal of the Church-State. In the Middle Ages an attempt was made to realise this ideal in the whole of Western Europe on a unitary basis.[2] After the rise of the sovereign national States and the break-up of the medieval Church, attempts were made to realise the ideal in terms of national Church-States. *Cuius regio eius religio.* The ultimate emergence of the tolerant State was mainly due to weariness in the pursuit of an unattainable ideal, a disgusted and relieved turning away from an endeavour which had been a source of perennial conflict and of wars of religion.[3]

1. "This is the irony of history—when the very success of an idea creates the conditions that belie it, smother it, and replace it. Catholicism becomes the Papacy. The care for truth turns to the Inquisition. The religious orders, vowed to poverty, die and rot of wealth. A revival movement becomes a too, too prosperous and egoistic Church. Freedom as soon as it is secured becomes tyranny."—P. T. Forsyth, *The Justification of God* (1916), p. 214.

2. Cp. P. Carnegie Simpson, *op. cit.*, p. 65. As to how far this development was prescribed or foreshadowed by St Augustine's *De civitate Dei*, see J. N. Figgis, *The Political Aspects of S. Augustine's "City of God"* (1921), who says: "Augustine (how ever you interpret him) never identified the *Civitas Dei* with any earthly State. But he had prepared the way for other people to do this" (p. 84).

3. *E.g.*, John Locke: "No peace and security, no, not so much as common friendship, can ever be established or preserved among men, so long as this opinion prevails, 'that dominion is founded in grace, and that religion is to be propagated by force of arms'". "A Letter concerning Toleration", *Works* (1823 ed.), vi. 20. C p. A. J. Carlyle, *The Christian Church and Liberty* (1924) p. 116: "It is . . . probably true to say that in the main it was the obviou, failure of the Anglican to suppress the Puritan, and of the Puritan to suppress the Anglican, which ultimately compelled people to acquiesce in the principles of toleration". See also W. K. Jordan, *The Development of Religious Toleration in England*, i. 33, *et passim*; iii. 263.

For our present purpose, the significance of this protracted experiment, which also of course had its noble aspect, is that neither in the Middle Ages nor as a direct outcome of the Reformation was there developed a doctrine of the State as a society separate or separable, distinct or distinguishable, from the Church.[1] For this reason, however it may be with the underlying ideas, the actual teaching of the medieval and Reformation theologians and political theorists cannot be applied to a Europe organised in sovereign national States, independently of the Church. In much the same way the teaching of Plato and Aristotle became formally out of date for later political theory, because they took for granted the Greek city State as the self-subsistent political unit.

As J. N. Figgis said, in the Middle Ages "churchmanship was co-extensive with citizenship . . . Church and State as two competing societies did not exist; you have instead two official hierarchies".[2] That is to say, while there was what is called a Church and State conflict throughout the Middle Ages, it was a conflict not between two separate societies, but in one society between two bodies of officials, the temporal and the spiritual, or the secular and the sacred; and in the Middle Ages "the liberty of the Church" did not mean what it does to modern ears, but the

1. As Carlyle (iv. 395) points out, the principle of the relation between the two, as it was generally accepted, is nowhere better expressed than in the following words of Stephen of Tournai: "In eadem civitate sub eodem rege duo populi sunt, et secundum duos populos duae vitae, secundum duas vitas duo principatus, secundum duos principatus duplex iurisdictionis ordo procedit. Civitas ecclesia; civitatis rex Christus; duo populi duo in ecclesia ordines, clericorum et laicorum; duo vitæ, spiritualis et carnalis; duo principatus, sacerdotium et regnum; duplex iurisdictio, divinum ius et humanum. Redde singula singulis et convenient universa".

What was new, by comparison with the pre-Christian empire, was the principle that human society was governed by two powers, the temporal and the spiritual; see *ibid.*, iv. 385.

2. *Churches in the Modern State* [2] (1914), p. 190. Cp. *From Gerson to Grotius* (1907), pp. 49, 73, 77; Sabine, *op. cit.*, p. 225; Luigi Sturzo, *Church and State* (1939), pp. 68, 72. Nor were the functions of the two hierarchies purely secular, on the one side, and purely sacred, on the other; there was no essential novelty in the rule exercised by kings in the Church after the Reformation. See R. W. Church, art. on "Church and State" in the *Christian Remembrancer* (April, 1850), pp. 471–516.

liberty of the ecclesiastical hierarchy as against the secular rulers.[1]

This remained the case for some time after the Reformation also, except that now the Church-State was organised on a national basis,[2] and the balance of power between the two official elements in it was substantially altered. The following passage from Hooker illustrates this point, but it should be remarked that by this time and afterwards the Church in Roman Catholic countries depended a good deal more upon the power of the civil rulers than the bishop of Rome desired.[3]

> I conclude: First, that under dominions of infidels, the Church of Christ, and their commonwealth, were two societies independent. Secondly, that in those commonwealths where the bishop of Rome beareth sway, one society is both the Church and the commonwealth; but the bishop of Rome doth divide the body into two diverse bodies, and doth not suffer the Church to depend upon the power of any civil prince or potentate. Thirdly, that within this realm of England the case is neither as in the one, nor as in the other of the former two: but from the pagans we differ, in that with us one society is both the Church and commonwealth, which with them it was not; as also from the state of those nations which subject themselves to the bishop of Rome, in that our Church hath dependency upon the chief in our commonwealth, which it hath not under him.[4]

In England, as Figgis said, "both the Laudian and the Puritan

1. Figgis, *Churches in the Modern State*, pp. 77f. Cp. C. H. McIlwain, *The Growth of Political Thought in the West* (1932), p. 205. It is thus misleading to modern minds to use the term "State" with reference to the medieval controversies, unless the change in its meaning is made clear. This is a defect in M. Jean Rivière's otherwise valuable book, *Le problème de l'Eglise et de l'Etat au temps de Philippe le Bel* (1926); he exaggerates the extent to which modern theology is "en présence des mêmes données" (*op. cit.*, p. 380).

2. Cp. P. Carnegie Simpson, *op. cit.*, pp. 112f.

3. Cp. J. W. Allen, *Political Thought in the Sixteenth Century* (1928), pp. 355, 483.

4. *Of the Laws of Ecclesiastical Polity*, ed. J. Keble, VIII. i. 7; cp. William Warburton, *The Alliance between Church and State* (*Works*, 1811 ed. vii. 50ff.). For Hooker's view of the Church and commonwealth as one society, see *Eccl. Pol.*, VIII. i. 2, 4, 5.

party were medievalist; they believed in a State which was also a Church, and were essentially theocratic".[1]

Thus it came about that, although from the time of the establishment of the Church in the Roman Empire there was a vast amount of political theorising done by Christians, conditions were not present in which a specifically Christian doctrine of the State as a distinct society could be developed (except in the case of the sects). Christian political theory had consisted for the most part in the assimilation and application of doctrines which had been adumbrated in ancient Greece and Rome, and in working out a synthesis between these and the teaching of Scripture in such a way that the result was adapted to the actual condition of affairs.

> The scholars of all churches had the same stock of ideas, a rich and varied body of thought extending continuously back to the eleventh century and embodying a tradition which carried it back to antiquity. The logical dependence of any part of this political tradition upon any particular theological system was loose, as it had always been in the Middle Ages. Protestants could select from it, as Catholics had always done, according to their purposes and circumstances. Consequently the Reformation produced no such thing as a Protestant political theory, any more than the Middle Ages produced a Catholic one. . . . Similarity of political conviction depended more on circum-

1. *Churches in the Modern State*, p. 217; cp. *From Gerson to Grotius*, p. 73; and J. W. Allen, *Political Thought in the Sixteenth Century* (1928), p. 134, and *English Political Thought* 1603–1660 (1938), i. 186. This applied to political conceptions in general, *i.e.*, Catholics and Protestants had much more in common with one another and with the medievalists than with the moderns. Even where their political conceptions differed, these differences did not correspond to, but cut across, religious differences. See, *e.g.*, Carlyle (vi. 326): "It is at first sight a curious thing to find a Scottish Protestant like George Buchanan expressing almost the same judgments in political theory as the Spanish Jesuit Mariana; but the fact is that the difference of religious belief, as such, had little or no relation to political conceptions".

There were, however, in the Middle Ages and at the time of the Reformation certain anticipations of modern political theories, *e.g.*, by Marsilio in *Defensor Pacis*, though the novelty of Marsilio's ideas is commonly exaggerated, and C. E. Hudson in *The Church and the World* (ii. 45f.) ought not to have reproduced Professor Laski's remarks on this subject without question; see Carlyle, vi. 9, 44. For a real case of anticipation, see Carlyle, v. 85 (the modern theory of sovereignty).

stances than on theology, and political differences resulted rather from the varying situations in which the churches found themselves than from theological differences.[1]

Although the great formal conceptions which controlled the terms of political thought through the Middle Ages, and even until the end of the eighteenth century, came to the Middle Ages primarily through the Christian Fathers, yet, as Carlyle said, "they were not distinctively Christian conceptions, but rather the commonplaces of the later philosophical schools, and the Fathers learned them in the schools and universities where they were educated. The forms of the political theory of the Middle Ages represent therefore an inheritance from the Stoics and other philosophical schools of the Empire".[2] For example, the idea of natural law, derived from the Stoics, was brought into relation with the Mosaic law, and given a Christian complexion.[3]

As regards the medieval conception of the State, Carlyle summed up as follows:

> The judgment of the Middle Ages was clear and continuous that while the coercive political authority of man over his fellowmen was made necessary by sin, it was appointed by God as a remedy for sin. The State was a divine institution, whose purpose and function it was to maintain righteousness or justice.[4]

Obviously, this does not tell us very much about the nature of the State as such, *i.e.*, as a society distinct from, but in relations with, the Church, although it implies that the State or those who exercise political authority are both capable of acknowledging moral truth and are bound to do so. This was in fact taken for granted. There was no occasion, therefore, to inquire into the implications of this assumption. From our point of view, as Figgis said, the conception of the State in the Middle Ages was "very in-

1. Sabine, *op. cit.*, p. 354.
2. Carlyle, iii. 5f. For a summary of the doctrines of the Fathers, see *ibid.*, i. 174, and of the Middle Ages, v. pt. 3.
3. See my "Inquiries concerning Natural Law" in *Theology* (February, 1941). Cp. Joseph Dalby, *The Catholic Conception of the Law of Nature* (1943); Troeltsch, i. 188ff.
4. Carlyle, v. 25.

choate".[1] Indeed, "the real State of the Middle Ages in the modern sense—if the words are not a paradox—is the Church".[2]

It is true that new elements entered into medieval political theory with St Thomas Aquinas, largely owing to the recovery of Aristotle's works;[3] up till then post-Aristotelian conceptions had been determinant. Nor of course must it be supposed that there was anything like complete unanimity in the Middle Ages about political theory any more than about other matters. In addition to differences between the Church-State theologians, notably the Investiture Controversy, there were heresies and schisms in regard to the whole Church-State idea. (Troeltsch has emphasised the fact that the sect-type of Christian society—*i.e.*, of an uncompromising, unworldly, nonconforming community—arose in the Middle Ages and was not, as is vulgarly supposed, a product of the Reformation.)[4] The great Reformers, however, held firmly to the Church-State idea; they did not believe that a Church should be a sect alongside of, or within, a State.[5] They gave a new turn to the idea, but fundamentally it was the same idea.

It is only in retrospect that the Reformation appears as a stage in the gradual break-down of the Church-State idea. In any case, this break-down was as much a consequence of the Renaissance as of the Reformation. It was the Renaissance that released into European history anthropocentric and secular forces which ultimately led to the dissolution of those theocentric

1. *Churches in the Modern State*, p. 190.

2. *From Gerson to Grotius*, p. 16; cp. pp. 4 and 11.

3. But on the limited effects of this, see A. J. Carlyle, *Political Liberty* (1941), p. 133: "Under the influence of Aristotle St Thomas Aquinas had to some extent passed beyond the post-Aristotelian tradition, but in spite of his immense influence he had only superficially affected the thinkers of the later Middle Ages, and those of the sixteenth and seventeenth centuries": cp. p. 182. Contrast H. J. Laski in *The Cambridge Medieval History*, viii. 627, who writes of "the *Politics* of Aristotle—which Aquinas had made an essential part of the medieval tradition"; cp. p. 631.

4. Troeltsch, ii. 461, 714; cp. J. W. Allen, *Political Thought in the Sixteenth Century*, p. 37; and F. Gavin, *Seven Centuries of the Problem of Church and State* (1938), pp. 101f.

5. "Luther, Zwingli and Calvin alike desired to establish inclusive churches and to support them with civil power, to make admission a matter of form and law and even to enforce membership."—Allen, *ibid.*, p. 41. Cp. J. N. Figgis in *Our Place in Christendom* (1916), pp. 126ff. W. K. Jordan, *op. cit.*, *passim.* This principle was at first applied in the American colonies; see E. B. Greene, *Religion and the State; the making and testing of an American tradition* (1941), chap. iii.

and theocratic assumptions which had as firm a hold on the Reformers as on the men of the Middle Ages.

> The contrast between the medieval spirit and that of the Renaissance lay in this, that the one was absorbed in the scheme of divine providence and man's eternal destiny, the other, in his life on earth, recognised as a scene of intrinsic value, and pronounced, as by God on the creation morning, a thing that was very good. The other worldliness of the Middle Ages had yielded place to the desire to know man in his relation to nature, and nature in its relation to man.[1]

The subsequent development of the independent, secular State, which was first tolerant and then in tendency neutral or indifferent in matters of religion, offered a challenge to Christian theologians to work out a Christian doctrine of the State as such; but they were slow to take it up. It was easier for the theologians to fight a rearguard action for the undermined Church-State idea. It was left chiefly to philosophers and political theorists to work out a new doctrine of the State,[2] and, though most of them were professing Christians, they did not do so on a basis of Christian dogma but of secular conceptions, such as the secularised natural law. Religion was to be kept separate from politics.[3]

1. W. G. de Burgh, quoted by Hudson and Reckitt, *The Church and the World*, ii. 137.

2. "We have now a variety of philosophic theories regarding Church and State, but in effect no Christian theory."—C.O.P.E.C. Commission Report (vol. x) on *Politics and Citizenship*, p. 19.

3. John Locke, whose "Letter concerning Toleration" is, as it were, the charter of the Whig or Liberal State, could hardly state the case more strongly: "The church itself is a thing absolutely separate and distinct from the commonwealth. The boundaries on both sides are fixed and immovable. He jumbles heaven and earth together, the things most remote and opposite, who mixes these societies, which are, in their original, end, business, and in every thing, perfectly distinct, and infinitely different from each other".—*Works* (1823 ed.), vi. 21. "If each of them (the church and the state) would contain itself within its own bounds, the one attending to the worldly welfare of the commonwealth, and the other to the salvation of souls, it is impossible that any discord should ever have happened between them."—*Ibid.*, vi. 54. On Locke, see Troeltsch, ii. 637.

For a wider consideration of the modern secularisation of politics and economics, see R. H. Tawney, *Religion and the Rise of Capitalism* (1926).

On the development of ideas of toleration and democracy among the English Puritans, see *Puritanism and Liberty: being the Army Debates* (1647–9) *from the Clarke Manuscripts with supplementary documents*, ed. by A. S. P. Woodhouse (1938).

The theory of the secular State, as in principle it was expounded by Locke and was maintained and developed by the Whigs and Liberals, depended on the view that the State was properly concerned with temporal welfare and material interests only. Religion was concerned with spiritual and other-worldly interests, and Churches were voluntary societies for the promotion of those interests. It might or might not be expedient for the State to enter relations with a Church; that depended on circumstances and on the State's convenience. According to this theory, whatever connexion there is between Church and State in any particular country, they are in principle separate.[1]

It is therefore true to say that the idea of Church and State as two separate societies occurs only, so far as the main tradition goes, in the primitive period of Church history and again in the modern period.[2] But in the modern period the problem of their relation is different and more complicated both because, instead of one Empire, we have national States of anything but uniform or stable character, and because of the divisions in the Church. I do not propose to use the term "the Modern State", for in any case the word "modern" is of only temporary application to a changing phenomenon; and in the present case it would conceal the important difference between the Liberal or *laissez-faire* State, which flourished in the nineteenth century, and the Collectivist or planned State, by which it is being succeeded in this century.

By the Liberal State [3] I mean the broad type of State which was atomistic or individualistic in economics and politics and, in tendency, tolerant or indifferent in regard to religion, but at bottom secular or naturalistic, though it might on grounds of expediency concede privileges to religious institutions. Its atti-

1. Luigi Sturzo, *Church and State* (1939), p. 292, writes: "The Church no longer integrated the State as in the Middle Ages. It was not absorbed by the State, as in Lutheranism. It did not form with the State a single spiritual complexus, as in Calvinism. But it fell within the orbit of the State as simply an activity of individuals, who could freely meet together to that end, so long as they did not conflict with the ends, activity and responsibility of the public power". Cp. pp. 52ff. *infra*.

2. Figgis, *Churches in the Modern State*, p. 215.

3. On the various forms of political liberalism, see Christopher Dawson, *The Judgement of the Nations* (1943), pt. i, chap. iv; Viscount Morley, *Recollections* (1921), i. 19f.

tude to religion, as well as to economics, was *laissez-faire*.[1] With the Liberal State I contrast the Collectivist State, which is characterised not only by economic planning but also by the profession of a more or less definite faith, which may be religious or anti-religious but has so far tended, in either case, to be intolerant and anti-liberal. "There cannot be", said Troeltsch, "a real social coherence at all without the unity of the world-view".[2] The Collectivist State becomes "totalitarian" when it seeks to guide the whole community according to its own will, and to extend its control over culture, the national ethos and philosophy of life, suppressing dissentients.[3] The move towards collectivism and away from liberalism is giving the question of the relation of the Church and the State a new form,[4] for which Christians are very ill-prepared, since they had not really worked out the consequences of the Church's existence in the Liberal State.

1. F. R. Hoare rightly points out that "the States were Liberalised in very different degrees. Moreover, in one case one aspect, in another case another aspect of their civic life was especially affected, so that no general formula adequately describes them all."—*The Papacy and the Modern State*, p. 225.

For a comparison between *laissez-faire* in economics and religion, see Thomas Chalmers, *Select Works* (1857 ed.), xi. 136–155, who speaks of "what has been termed the system of Free Trade in Christianity" (p. 122).

Ernest Barker writes: "Laissez-faire means on the one hand, and in domestic politics, a restriction of governmental activity to the bare minimum: on the other hand, and in foreign affairs, a policy of free trade and of friendship between nations".—*Political Thought in England from Herbert Spencer to the Present Day* (1915), p. 19; cp. *ibid.*, p. 196.

A. L. Smith in *The Cambridge Modern History*, vi. 820, speaks of the change from "medieval views of the paternal and religious duties of the State" to "the *laissez-faire* view and the reduction of the State to a policeman".

2. Troeltsch, ii. 833.

3. Nils Ehrenström, *Christian Faith and the Modern State* (1937), p. 228; cp. A. Keller, *Church and State on the European Continent* (1936), p. 118.

4. As regards the U.S.A., Professor E. B. Greene writes in *Religion and the State* (1941): "Here, too, *laissez-faire* liberalism has—for better or worse—been weakened, governmental functions have expanded, and nationalism is little less intense than it is across the water. As our government extends its control over the economic activities of its citizens, are we sure that this increasingly powerful modern state may not enlarge its control over other social concerns? How far, for instance, may the state go in molding the ideas of youth, without coming into conflict with other corporate loyalties, including those of the churches?" (pp. 2f.).

III

Gladstone began his career at a time when the transition from the Church-State to the Liberal State was already occurring and was in fact far advanced, whereas we appear to-day to be involved in a reversionary transition from the Liberal to the Collectivist State. Before his career closed, "the progressive political thought of the day was moving", as D. C. Somervell says, "in the direction of Collectivism, whereas Gladstone's Liberalism was of the old individualistic school".[1] Gladstone was destined to live in the great age of political liberalism. He was indeed largely instrumental [2] in bringing the Liberal State into being in this country,—that is, in so far as it was brought into being by the conscious acts of statesmen as distinguished from the instrumentality of impersonal economic and social forces. For these reasons, he is commonly regarded as the great example of a Liberal statesman, and it is supposed that he was by deep conviction the advocate, the author, and the administrator of the Liberal State as the best sort of State in the best of all possible worlds.

It is known of course that he began his career as a Conservative —"the rising hope of those stern and unbending Tories"; so Macaulay described him.[3] But this circumstance is readily accounted for as the youthful aberration of an immature mind which had not yet discovered where its real genius lay. The book, in which at this period he enunciated his political convictions, *The State in its relations with the Church*, is looked upon as a curiosity of literature,[4] which can be ignored by anyone who

1. *Disraeli and Gladstone*, p. 274. As regards Gladstone's liberalism, see however pp. 145–8 *infra*.

2. D. C. Somervell aptly remarks that "the new Liberalism . . . found in Gladstone its instrument rather than its prophet".—*Op. cit.*, p. 159; cp. *ibid.*, p. 308. See also p. 157, n. 1 *infra*.

3. *Critical and Historical Essays* [5] (1848), ii. 430.

4. "We concede to the modern that *Gladstone on Church and State* may well be numbered among the literary remains of the early Victorian age which are best forgotten." So writes an "ardent Gladstonian" in an article in *Theology* (November, 1939), p. 363. "Probably few living people have read through it 324 solid pages, and it is remembered to-day only through Macaulay's critical essay."—G. T. Garratt, *The Two Mr Gladstones* (1936), p. 16. Mr Garratt himself does not seem to have been aware of the fact that the fourth edition of Gladstone's book, which was in two volumes, contained 750 pages.

The Church and the World by Hudson and Reckitt, the third volume of which

wants to discover what Gladstone's political faith really was. The book merely shows (so it has been assumed) what Gladstone might have been if he had not been called out of darkness into light; and so it is hardly worth reading.

The argument of the present essay goes to show that this assumption is a mistake. I am not daunted by the fact that Gladstone himself did a good deal to encourage it. The reasons for that will become evident, before we have finished. I hold that the later and famous part of his career needs to be interpreted in the light of the earlier and obscured part and of the changing conditions of the age. I shall indeed go so far as to say that *The State in its relations with the Church* is a profound and prophetic book, and that Gladstone became a Liberal statesman and an author of the Liberal State in this country, not because of innate conviction, nor because this was the logic of his faith as a Christian, of which at first he did not see the implications, but because the conditions of the age in which he lived determined that it was in that way that he could most effectively take a positive and active part in the political administration and leadership of the country.

has as its subject "Church and Society in England from 1800", not only contains no reference to this book by Gladstone even as a curiosity, but contains no reference whatever to Gladstone himself except a brief quotation on the state of church services early in the nineteenth century, reproduced from S. C. Carpenter's *Church and People*.

A. F. Robbins, writing in 1894, says: "Everyone, however partially acquainted with his career, has heard of, few have seen, fewer still have read, his work upon the relations between the Church and the State".—*The Early Public Life of William Ewart Gladstone*, p. 296.

Even Viscount Gladstone in *After Thirty Years* (1928)—a stalwart defence of his father's memory—betrays a very casual acquaintance with the book, since he refers to it as *The Church in its Relations with the State* (p. 69); Mary Drew does the same twice in her *Catherine Gladstone* (1919), pp. 7, 63; so does Goldwin Smith in *My Memory of Gladstone* (1904), p. 11; so does the Marquess of Crewe, art. on "Mr Gladstone" in *The Quarterly Review* (October, 1932), p. 196; and also my predecessor as Warden of St Deiniol's Library, Dr G. C. Joyce, in a sermon preached on Founder's Day, 1934, and subsequently printed. I see no reason to doubt that all these more or less intimate Gladstonians gave the book a wrong title independently of one another, probably owing to the facts that the words "Church" and "State" are commonly conjoined in that order, and that "Gladstone on Church and State" was the title of Macaulay's review.

Doubtless, his Christian sense of duty to God and to the service of the Church impelled him to embark on, and continue, a political career. But he was also impelled by a love of power, and we are not in a position to pass a final judgment on his motives. G. W. E. Russell said of Gladstone:

> If we assign the first place in Gladstone's character to his religiousness, we must certainly allow the second place to his love of power. . . . From his youth up Gladstone had been conscious of high aims and great abilities. He earnestly desired to serve his day and generation, and he knew that he had unusual capacity for giving effect to this desire. In order that those powers and that capacity might have free scope, it was necessary that their possessor should be in a position of authority, of leadership, of command.[1]

He would not have been able to follow the high aims nor to use the great abilities, with which he had been entrusted by God, nor would he have been able to serve his day and generation in the political sphere, to any immediate effect, if he had remained (to use his own expression) "the last man on the sinking ship" [2] of the Church-State. It was the destined day of political liberalism and of ecclesiastical sectarianism, and he must do his work in that day if he was to do it at all. "The country was committed to *laissez faire* and liberty", said J. A. Froude, "and no reversion to earlier principles was now possible until *laissez faire* had been tired (*sic*) out and the consequences of it tasted and digested." [3] Gladstone was bound to accept these conditions, if he was to engage in politics. But though he may have appeared subsequently to pigeon-hole the principles, to which he had committed himself at the beginning of his career, and to which he gave carefully considered expression in *The State in its relations with the Church*, he never disowned them, nor did he think out or commit himself to another set of principles. It will, however, be more appropriate to enlarge upon this question, after his ideas have been expounded and discussed; we shall therefore return to it in the concluding chapter.

1. *William Ewart Gladstone* (Everyman ed.), p. x; cp. pp. 134f.
2. *A Chapter of Autobiography* (1868), p. 25.
3. *The Earl of Beaconsfield* (Everyman ed.), p. 147.

CHAPTER THREE

GLADSTONE'S THEORY

I

The State in its Relations with the Church was published in December, 1838; by 1841 it had run into a fourth edition. This fourth edition, according to Morley, "fell flat".[1] It is, however, the fourth edition of which I am going to make use; it is a considerably enlarged and revised version of the first edition.[2] The alterations and additions were designed not to change the original argument, but to give it a clarification which reviews of the book had shown to be necessary.[3] Gladstone claimed that not a single sentence or expression had been added in the fourth edition of the book, "which at the time of its first publication I should have been inclined to disavow" (p. x).[4] My own examination of the matter leads me to believe that he was quite justified in saying that. I use the fourth edition, therefore, because it presents the argument in its most clear and complete form.

On April 6, 1842, Gladstone wrote to his publisher, Mr Murray:

> As to the third edition of the "State in its relations", I should think the remaining copies had better be got rid of in whatever summary or ignominious mode you may deem best . . . With regard to the fourth edition . . . my idea is, that it is less defective both in the theoretical and in the historical develop-

1. Morley, i. 181.
2. Gladstone wrote to Manning on November 13, 1840: "I am busy recasting my former book, and have now, I hope, done the substantial part of it. It will have grown, I think, about 50 per cent. in bulk, and will have much more pretension to method and to making known its own meaning . . ."—*CCR*, i. 47.
3. Gladstone, wrote Walter Bagehot, defended his theory, "as was said, mistily—at any rate, he defended it in a manner which requires much careful pains to appreciate, and much preliminary information to understand; he puzzled the ordinary mass of English churchmen".—*Biographical Studies* (1881), p. 107.
4. References, except where otherwise stated, are to the fourth edition.

> ment . . . that it would really put a reader in possession of the view it was intended to convey, which I fear is more than can with truth be said of its predecessors.[1]

The fact that three years after the first publication Gladstone had not found reason to change or abandon the argument, and indeed thought it worth while to present it again in a much expanded form, confirms, what is otherwise evident, that it is the outcome of a protracted and mature process of thought.[2] There is no justification for treating the book as a hurriedly prepared and blundering attempt at juvenile pamphleteering, which is an impression

1. G. W. E. Russell, *op. cit.*, pp. 56f. Cp. Gladstone, *A Chapter of Autobiography*, p. 14: "The book entitled 'The State in its Relations with the Church' was printed during the autumn of 1838. . . . Three editions of it were published without textual change; and in the year 1841 a fourth, greatly enlarged, though in other respects little altered, issued from the press".

The MS. in the course of its preparation had been submitted to, and criticised in detail, by his friend J. R. Hope, who also corrected the proofs as Gladstone was then abroad. Some of the letters containing his criticisms are included in R. Ornsby's *Memoirs of James Robert Hope-Scott*, vol. i (1884).

H. J. Laski, in his *Studies in the Problem of Sovereignty* (1917), p. 93n., says that Gladstone's book was "mainly influenced by" James Hope and W. Palmer of Worcester. Palmer's *Treatise on the Church of Christ* (1838) was certainly greatly appreciated by Gladstone (see *e.g. CCR*, ii. 174), though its influence is more evident in *CP* than in *SRC*; indeed, Hope recommended Gladstone to read Palmer's book when the first draft of *SRC* was already written. Coleridge was a more important influence in the case of *SRC*. As regards Hope's influence see *CCR*, i. 12f.; Morley, i. 162; M. MacColl in *The Life of William Ewart Gladstone* (ed. by Sir Wemyss Reid), pp. 256f. Gladstone said to MacColl: "I worked out my views on Church matters chiefly alone".

2. Lathbury, *CCR*, i. 18, writes as though Gladstone had begun to change his mind almost as soon as the book was published. "The process of emancipation had already begun, and henceforward it was to go on without further interruption." It is quite true that scarcely had his work issued from the press when he found himself "the last man on a sinking ship" (at least so it seemed to him thirty years later); it is also true that he had told Pusey in the summer of 1838 that he thought his "own church and state principles within one stage of being hopeless as regards success in this generation" (Morley, i. 170). But in 1841 he still believed in those principles, however improbable it seemed that under existing conditions they could be successfully applied.

Bishop Charles Wordsworth was nearer the mark when he wrote that, *from 1845*, Gladstone "virtually discarded his original theory, and set himself to move, not all at once, but gradually and surely, in the direction of the opposite extreme"; *Public Appeals in behalf of Christian Unity* (1886), p. 22. This remark, however, errs in exaggerating the extent to which Gladstone eventually did abandon his original theory.

that has sometimes been given.[1] The original manuscript was indeed written in the course of a few months and "with uncommon vigour and persistency",[2] but in it he said:

> For the last six years (the writer) has watched the subject in its practical as well as its speculative forms with the deepest earnestness, and has endeavoured to give his whole mind to the lessons with which they have abounded.[3]

During the previous decade the relations of Church and State had been a subject of constant public debate, and Gladstone had had every incitement to reflect seriously concerning them.

It is the former or more abstract part of the book that will

1. *E.g.*, "His book *The State in its Relations to* (sic) *the Church*, published in 1839 (*sic*), was his adolescent attempt to apply his Evangelical ideal to politics".—Osbert Burdett, *W. E. Gladstone* (1927), p. 44.

George Edinger and E. J. C. Neep describe the publication of the book as Gladstone's "first big blunder"; *The Grand Old Man: a Gladstone Spectrum* (1936), p. 85.

Nor was the book merely a piece of special pleading for the maintenance of the Irish Church establishment, which is what R. H. Murray seems to suggest in his *Social and Political Thinkers of the Nineteenth Century* (1929), i. 271.

E. Halévy wrote in *A History of the English People* 1830–1841 (English translation, 1927), p. 214: "The youthful Gladstone published a treatise on the relations between Church and State, and the fact that the book seems a poor performance to-day only makes its success when it first appeared the more significant". Halévy refers only to the first edition.

G. C. Joyce in a sermon, that was subsequently published, on Founder's Day, 1934, at Hawarden, said: "We bear in mind . . . that this book was written before the author had reached the age of thirty, and that he himself in later life profoundly modified his earlier views. Indeed, we learn his mature mind much more fully in other ways. On this high theme he expressed himself in action, and in correspondence, rather than in the set words of literature".

On the other hand, the book was much more justly appraised by the anonymous, orthodox dissenter, who wrote *The Ultimate Principle of Religious Liberty* (1860), p. 93: "The fundamental elements of the theories of Hooker, Coleridge, Burke and Arnold, are embodied or implied in Mr Gladstone's system. He, moreover, is the only one of these great writers who has really argued out the doctrine and its implications".

2. Morley, i. 172.

3. First edition, p. 322. In the fourth edition he wrote: "For nearly nine years past the subject, in its practical and its speculative forms, in all the impressive lessons with which the period has abounded, has been continually in my view, and has tasked my mind to the uttermost" (ii. 403). For confirmation of this see Gladstone's letters to Manning in *CCR*, vol. i, chap. 1.

engage our attention, since that deals with general principles and is of permanent interest.[1] The part, in which he tried to show that his general principles justified and even required the maintenance of the actual relations between Church and State that existed in 1838, not only in England and Wales, but also in Scotland and Ireland,[2] we need not consider, although that part of the book is remarkable enough in its way, since it proves that at this early stage in his career Gladstone possessed an astonishing aptitude for defending an impossible case with a full armoury of moral fervour and intellectual ingenuity,[3]—an aptitude which was always to elicit the admiration of his supporters and the exasperation of his opponents.

While I believe that Gladstone's discussion of general principles is of permanent importance, I freely admit that his attempt to apply them to the United Kingdom of 1838 was anachronistic. It was this attempt which he himself saw to be out of date almost as soon as the book was published. It is symptomatic of the way in which the book has been treated by posterity that, after the initial excitement, the feature by which it was chiefly remembered was its incidental, though certainly original, defence of the Church-establishment in Ireland, and also that the only time when it again caught public attention was when, thirty years later, the Irish Church Disestablishment bill was before Parliament. It

1. I can make my own the words of the author of *The Ultimate Principle of Religious Liberty*, p. 96: "We do not propose anything like a complete review of the entire contents of these volumes, embracing, as by the author's treatment they do, almost every branch of the controversy; but simply to engage our attention upon the great fundamental idea or argument of the work, taking some notice of secondary points falling within our prescribed scope of discussion".

2. A rigorous episcopalian, he had to justify the maintenance of the presbyterian establishment in Scotland; and also on grounds of moral and spiritual principle the maintenance of the anglican establishment in Ireland! Thirty years later, he justly pointed out that his work had used "none of the stock arguments for maintaining the Church of Ireland". "My doctrine was, that the Church, as established by law, was to be maintained for its truth; that this was the only principle on which it could be properly and permanently upheld; that this principle, if good in England, was good also for Ireland . . ."—*A Chapter of Autobiography*, pp. 22, 19.

3. In *A Chapter of Autobiography*, pp. 46–56, Gladstone gives his account of the circumstances which led him to form "a completely false estimate of what was about to happen".

then provided a happy hunting-ground for the more obdurate Tory politicians.[1] I hope that it will at least be agreed that the book deserved a better fate than that.

II

In the introductory chapter Gladstone gives some account and appraisal of what he calls "prevalent theories" of the relations of the State with the Church, ruling out the extreme opinions of Hobbes, on the one side, and of Bellarmine and ultramontane Romanists, on the other, since those are theories not of connexion between State and Church, but of the derivation of one from the other. According to Hobbes the Church is "a mere creature of the State"; according to the ultramontane Romanists: "the temporal power is wholly dependent and subordinate" (i. 31). "These views are not avowed among ourselves". A third extreme opinion is that "the magistrate has no concern with religion"; and it is against this opinion that Gladstone's general argument is directed (*ibid.*).[2]

The first theory to be closely regarded is that of Hooker. This Gladstone praises because it involved "the great doctrine that the state is a person, having a conscience, cognisant of matter of religion, and bound by all constitutional and natural means to advance it" (i. 14). On the other hand, while Bishop Warburton, whose theory, propounded in the "Alliance of Church and State" (*sic*), is next considered, "taught that civil society, being defective in the controul of motives and in the sanction of reward, had in all

1. See what Gladstone says in *A Chapter of Autobiography*, p. 14: "All interest (in the book) had . . . long gone by, and it lived for nearly thirty years only in the vigorous and brilliant, though not (in my opinion) entirely faithful picture, drawn by the accomplished hand of Lord Macaulay. During the present year (1868), as I understand from good authority, it has again been in demand, and in my hearing it has received the emphatic suffrages of many, of whose approval I was never made aware during the earlier and less noisy stages of its existence".

Liddon, in his preface to the reprint (1869) of Keble's review of the book, speaks of "that work of Mr Gladstone's earlier years which has of late been quarried so largely with a view to furnishing *ad hominem* arguments" (p. iv).

2. Gladstone notes that Stahl has observed that " the first of these schemes has been the peculiar danger of Lutheranism, the second of Romanism, and the third of Calvinism" (i. 31 n.).

ages called in the aid of religion to supply the want",[1] and recog-

1. In a footnote Gladstone remarks that "there is a much nobler and purer statement of the inadequacy of the State, taken alone, to fulfil its purposes, in No. IX of Letters to a Member of the Society of Friends . . . by the Rev. F. Maurice" (see *The Kingdom of Christ*, 1838, vol. iii); he also refers to Maurice's Lectures on National Education, *i.e. Has the Church, or the State, the Power to Educate the Nation?* (1839).

Maurice's teaching on the relation of Church and State had much in common with Gladstone's, though the latter seems to have appreciated this fact more than the former. Both founded their teaching in theology; both taught that the State has a conscience, and maintained a high doctrine of its duty to the Church. But whereas, as we shall see, Gladstone held that the State is capable of taking cognisance of, and has a duty to acknowledge, theological truth, Maurice denied this and based the State's duty to recognise the Church and "give it free scope to educate the people" on the State's incapacity to do so, though it can see that for its own well-being the people must be educated (*The Kingdom of Christ*, iii. 213f.). Maurice's theory was, as he himself owned (*ibid.*, iii. 2ff.), little more than a working out of Coleridge's, and his method was primarily historical, where Gladstone's was primarily analytical.

On February 12, 1839, Maurice wrote to R. C. Trench: "Gladstone's book has disappointed me more than I like to confess, but he seems to be an excellent and really wise man".—F. Maurice, *Life of Frederick Denison Maurice* [2] (1884), i. 257. (This of course refers to the first edition of Gladstone's book; no record appears to have survived of Maurice's opinion of the fourth edition, unless the reference, *ibid.*, i. 437, is to the fourth edition: "I do not feel that the theories set forth in Mr Gladstone's book, though most honestly and elaborately contrived, as it seems to me, for the purpose of checking the evil tendencies of this time, are adequate to counteract them".)

In a note appended to *Has the Church, or the State, the Power to Educate the Nation?* Maurice refers to Macaulay's criticism of Gladstone's book in the *Edinburgh Review* (see p. 48 *infra*), and suggests that Gladstone's and Macaulay's views of the relation of Church and State are not necessarily incompatible with one another, and in fact can be reconciled. "If a nation has no security for the lives and property of its people, unless it can provide some means for improving their moral condition; and if the support of Christianity be that means, then Mr Gladstone's doctrine and the reviewer's (*i.e.* Macaulay's) become identical. At the same time it seems to me very advisable that the reviewer's principle should be distinctly understood and asserted, as well as Mr Gladstone's. It should be distinctly felt, the state as a state, has a commission only to deal with the bodies and properties of men. If anything beyond this is found to be necessary that this function may not be abortive, some other body must be found, which has a special commission for that other work" (*op. cit.*, pp. 303f.). But Maurice's characteristic zest for reconciling contraries, and distinguishing his own thought from both (cp. R. W. Church's essay on "Maurice's Theological Essays" in vol. ii of his *Occasional Papers*), here betrayed him into overlooking the strength of Gladstone's position and the weakness of Macaulay's. It would be truer to say that Maurice's own theory could be

nised that Church and State were distinct and separate societies,[1] yet his doctrine of the State was morally defective, since he held that civil government had to do only with the body and bodily goods, and he based the adoption of a national Church on public utility and not on the State's capacity for acknowledging truth (i. 16–20).

Paley's utilitarianism was even more blatant. Burke [2] and Coleridge, on the other hand, are referred to with approval, the latter especially; but their theories had not been sufficiently worked out,[3] and were wrought by painters rather than anatomists. Last but not least, Dr Chalmers, whose lectures in London in the spring (April 25 to May 12) of 1838 had provoked Gladstone to set pen to paper,[4] is praised for his "profuse and brilliant eloquence", and Gladstone obviously regarded his teaching sympathetically, since it bore a considerable resemblance to his own.[5] He suggests that Chalmers' arguments were more open to criticism than his conclusions, and writes of him:

> It is painful even to indicate points of difference from a most distinguished and excellent man, who has done his subject and his country permanent service by his lucid and powerful

reconciled with Gladstone's, and required to be complemented and corrected thereby. Cp. what Gladstone says about Coleridge's views (*SRC*, i. 27).

For Maurice's doctrine of the respective and complementary tasks of Church and State, see also *The Patriarchs and Lawgivers of the Old Testament*, Sermon XIV, and his letter to Ludlow in the *Life of Maurice*, ii. 7–10. On Gladstone's relations with Maurice, see also p. 84, n. 4 *infra*.

1. Gladstone might have noted that Herbert Thorndike had maintained this strongly: see *The Rights of the Church in a Christian State*, chap. i, section 42, *et passim*.

2. Cp. for Burke's influence on Gladstone's "youthful mind", A. Tilney Bassett, *Gladstone's Speeches* (1916), p. 358.

3. Mr M. B. Reckitt surely makes a slip when he says with reference to Coleridge's *Constitution of Church and State* that "Coleridge's whole thesis is very thoroughly (*sic*) worked out": *The Church and the World* (1940), iii. 12. Contrast what Reckitt himself says, *ibid.*, iii. 46.

4. For the extraordinary enthusiasm with which these lectures were received see William Hanna, *Memoirs of the Life and Writings of Thomas Chalmers* (1852), vol. iv., chap. 3. They were republished in *Select Works of Thomas Chalmers*, ed. by William Hanna (1857), xi. 117–220.

5. Contrast Maurice's unfavourable remarks about Chalmers' Lectures in *The Kingdom of Christ*, iii. pp. ix-xiv.

explanations of the machinery of a religious establishment (i. 31).[1]

Having thus indicated his attitude to those whom he regarded as his chief predecessors [2] in this field of thought, Gladstone proceeds to the exposition of his own theory.

III

He specifies four principal methods by which the subject may be investigated, namely, (i) by direct appeal to Scripture, (ii) by an analytic examination of the nature of the State, (iii) consequentially or, as we should now say, pragmatically, by inquiring what works, and (iv) by appeal to historical testimony or to common consent.[3] Gladstone proposes chiefly to follow the second of these methods, that is, analysis of the nature of the State. For, he says, there can be no direct appeal to Scripture in this matter, since the Hebrew commonwealth differed in many points of importance from any that concerns us now,[4] and since

1. Mr G. Kitson Clark in *Peel and the Conservative Party* (1929) says with regard to Dr Chalmers' Lectures that "Gladstone listened disapprovingly for he realised that Chalmer's (*sic*) hazy and enthusiastic mind glozed over the difficulties of the position" (p. 441). This statement, which presumably is based on Morley, i. 170ff., is not quite just either to Gladstone or to Chalmers. For Gladstone's view of Chalmers, see also G. Barnett Smith, *Thoughts from the Writings and Speeches of William Ewart Gladstone* (1894), pp. 130f.

2. The introductory chapter concludes with a more summary allusion to others, and with a list of recently published books on the subject. See also ii. 405, where Gladstone sums up: "All who have touched this subject have illustrated some of its aspects: for example, Hooker, the national unity of life; Warburton, the distinction of sanctions; Paley, some of the exterior evils which a public religion obviates; Chalmers, the physical anatomy of a national establishment; Coleridge, the moral analysis of a State".

3. These four courts of appeal may be represented by these formulas: "It is written; it is natural; it is expedient; it is customary" (i. 38).

4. In a footnote Gladstone quotes without comment a long extract from Keble's review of first edition of *SRC*, dealing with the bearing of Old Testament prophecy on the theory of Church and State. This review appeared in the *British Critic*, October, 1839 (not *September*, as Gladstone says); it was republished separately in 1869 with a preface by H. P. Liddon.

The Reformers and the divines of the seventeenth century had made great play with arguments based on the Old Testament dispensation. Gladstone rightly regards them as indecisive. Church and State in the old Israel were one society; the Old Testament bears testimony that civil as well as ecclesiasti-

"the Scriptures of the New Testament were written at a time when there was no case of a nation of persons professedly Christian" (i. 40).[1] The argument from consequences is indecisive and tends to be amoral. The appeal to common consent may be decisive up to date, and show that all nations have hitherto professed a religion, but it is encountered by the objection that a new age of enlightenment has recently dawned, and "having exploded the axioms of former times, we must no longer argue from their practice" (i. 44).

There remains the examination of the law of nature.[2]

The most authentic, the most conclusive, the most philosophi-

cal government is under God's ordinance, but it does not distinguish the functions of Church and State, which are now seen to be distinct societies. Cp. Acton, *The History of Freedom, &c.*, p. 205; and J. W. Allen, *Political Thought in the Sixteenth Century*, pp. 55, 302.

1. For a bold and well-argued exposition of a theory of the relations of the State with the Church, which is similar in its conclusions to Gladstone's theory, but founded on a direct appeal to the Scriptures, see T. R. Birks, *Church and State; or, National Religion and Church Establishments considered with reference to Present Controversies* (1869). Birks was vicar of Holy Trinity, Cambridge. The book has a preface by Bishop Christopher Wordsworth.

For an opposite theory, based on the appeal to Scripture as well as on the effects of a union of the Church with the State, and purporting to controvert Gladstone, see Baptist W. Noel, *Essay on the Union of Church and State* (1848). Noel misses the point of Gladstone's distinction between the appeal to Scripture and to the moral nature of the State (*op. cit.*, pp. 3f.). In 1849 he abandoned the ministry of the Church of England for nonconformity.

2. In view of the ambiguity that surrounds the concept of the law of nature, and in spite of the fact that Gladstone speaks of "resorting to an argument distinct from that of Divine Revelation" and of God's having already "by the light of nature . . . when revelation was unknown, imparted sufficiently the grounds and proofs of the principle of public religion, together with those of other elementary truths and duties" (i. 43f.), it must be said that he did not really regard the law of nature in abstraction from Divine Revelation, as is shown by the way his argument begins (see the next paragraph in the text).

It was in the light of Divine Revelation that he defined the law of nature, which he supposed all men could or ought to discern by natural reason (see *SRC*, i. 65, 329). He had to acknowledge that this was so when, on June 20, 1849, in the course of a speech on a Deceased Wife's Sister bill, he spoke as follows:

> What was the law of nature? Would it be contended that the law of nature was a fixed and definite code, independent of the laws of religion? He would wish to know when the law of nature had been developed in that form. . . . How was the law of nature cherished and developed except by

cal, and, in the absence of literal and undisputed precept from Scripture, also the most direct method of handling this important investigation, is that which examines the moral character and capacities of nations and rulers, and thus founds the whole idea of their duty upon that will which gave them their existence (i. 45).

Gladstone adds that "this province is one almost untrodden",[1]

the law of religion? The law of nature depended on the law of Christianity. They could not keep the law of nature and get rid of the law of religion. It was Christianity which showed what were the demands, the capacities, the obligations of nature, and therefore the answer to the question, "What was the law of nature"? depended on the answer to the question, "What was the law of Christianity"? (Hansard, col. 631).

Cp. what he says about "natural religion" in *SRC*, ii. 384: "From certain truths, stolen out of Christianity, has been compiled a structure, under the name of natural religion, which Nature did not discover, but which, now that they have been established for her, she can sometimes receive and appreciate". He also speaks of "natural religion (as it is falsely called)"; *ibid.*, ii. 367.

Gladstone can scarcely have wished to disguise the fact that his political philosophy rested on theological assumptions. In 1840, in a speech in the House of Commons, he said: "My belief . . . is, that not, indeed, at any given place or time, but ultimately and permanently, the study of theology is the only adequate and firm foundation on which the successful pursuit of all other studies can be followed".—*Speech of W. E. Gladstone, Esq., M.P., in the House of Commons, Monday, June* 29, 1840, pp. 20*f.* See also p. 129 *infra.*

1. It may not be without interest to remark that Machiavelli made a similar claim as regards his method and used the same metaphor: "I have resolved to open a new route, which has not yet been followed by anyone, and may prove difficult and troublesome".—*Discourses*, English translation by E. E. Detmold (1882), ii. 93. Cp. also what Dante says in the first chapter of his *De Monarchia*: "Inasmuch as amongst other unexplored and important truths the knowledge of the temporal monarchy is most important and least explored, and (for that it stands in no direct relation to gain) has been attempted by none; therefore am I minded to extract it from its recesses" (Temple Classics ed., p. 128).

The truth of Gladstone's claim is confirmed by a study of Carlyle's six volumes and of J. W. Allen's *Political Thought in the Sixteenth Century* from which it becomes clear that the questions with which Gladstone was most concerned had not been worked out in patristic, medieval or Reformation times. Answers to some of them were doubtless presupposed, *e.g.* that the State is capable of acknowledging, and acting with reference to, theological truth. "That it is one of the principal parts of that duty which appertains to a Christian King", wrote James I, "to protect the true Church within his own dominions and extirpate heresies, is a maxim *without all controversy*" (quoted by Allen, p. 234; italics mine). See also the passages quoted from Keble, Hooker and Jewel, pp. 106f. *infra*. Gladstone (*SRC*, ii. 156), interpreting an Act of Henry VIII, writes: "The collective power and responsibility, the moral personality of

and that "it lies in a region of abstraction to which the temper of the age, and the prevailing pursuits of this country, are averse" (*ibid.*).[1]

The argument then begins with what are really theological foundations. "The universe everywhere bears testimony to oneness of life and action, to absolute and invariable dependence on a centre, as the characteristic law of its nature, and therefore also the condition of its well-being" (i. 46). This theocratic order was, however, deranged by the Fall of man, which caused there to be "as many new centres, as many rebellious and divided systems of action, as there should be human beings; atomic

nations (*a principle not then drawn into precise theory, perhaps for the very reason that it was assumed as not only fundamental but unquestionable,*) in its own nature evidently requires to be associated with the profession of religion" (italics mine). When Locke and his successors had denied this conclusion, the attempt to controvert them had hitherto been based mainly on arguments from utility (*e.g.* Warburton and Paley) or from Scripture, not on the ground of the moral nature of the State, so that this province was still almost untrodden.

1. With this we may compare Bishop Creighton's well-known remark: "An Englishman is not only without ideas, but he hates an idea when he sees it".—*Life and Letters*, ed. by Louise Creighton, ii. 504. Cp. "Unfortunately the English mind has no grasp of ideas, and no sense of proportion. Indeed the Englishman has no mind at all, he only has an hereditary obstinacy" (*ibid.*, ii. 366). Most Englishmen agree with Lord Selborne in preferring "practical to theoretical arguments": see his *Defence of the Church of England against Disestablishment* (1886), p. 72.

Gladstone's statement makes allowance for the fact that this English characteristic is sociologically conditioned (though he would not have put it so!), and is not the result of innate disability. Cp. *SRC*, ii. 404: "The weakness of England has for some time lain in its inadequate appreciation of the speculative life. Our active habits have been overwrought, and have absorbed some portion of the energies due to contemplation". (How far, later on, did this become true of Gladstone himself? See pp. 144f. *infra.*)

That this was so in general is illustrated by the effect of Gladstone's book on English churchmen; see the remark of Bagehot, p. 26, n. 3 *supra.* Contrast the enthusiasm with which Baron Bunsen received it. On December 13, 1838, he wrote to his wife: "Last night, at eleven, when I came from the Duke (of Lucca), Gladstone's book was on my table, the second edition having come out at seven o'clock. It is the book of the time, a great event—the first book since Burke that goes to the bottom of the vital question; far above his party and his time. I sat up till after midnight, and this morning I continued until I had read the whole. . . . Gladstone is the first man in England as to intellectual power, and he has heard higher tones than anyone else in this island."—*A Memoir of Baron Bunsen* (1868), i. 489f. For some qualification of this enthusiasm see, however, *ibid.*, i. 493f.

centres of limited and petty influence, but without subordination to Him from whom they had derived even the power to rise in revolt against Him" (i. 48).[1] In other words, because of the Fall cosmos became chaos.

If the consequences of man's self-centred rebelliousness had been left uncontrolled, at length every vestige of truth and love would have been destroyed, and earth would have reached "the riper wickedness of hell". But God in His mercy did not leave these consequences to take their course;[2] He designed man's final redemption, and to that end ordained an intermediate or preliminary system of discipline.

> While . . . it pleased the mercy of God to design a provision for the redemption of mankind by His Son, to be accomplished when the fulness of time should have come; so He likewise

1. Gladstone of course identified the Fall of man with the event narrated in the Book of Genesis, but his argument retains its force for all who believe that the dogma of original sin has not been discredited by our incapacity any longer to affirm the historical or pre-historical character of that event. See appended note on "The Doctrine of the Fall and History" in my *Christ's Strange Work* (1944), pp. 68f.

F. J. A. Hort, in a letter (January, 1886) dealing with difficulties suggested by the Thirty-Nine Articles, wrote as follows about Article IX:

> The authors of the Article doubtless assumed the strictly historical character of the account of the Fall in Genesis. The assumption is now, in my belief, no longer reasonable. But the early chapters of Genesis remain a divinely appointed parable or apologue setting forth important practical truths on subjects which, as a matter of history, lie outside our present ken. Whether or not the corrupted state of human nature was preceded in temporal sequence by an incorrupt state, this is the most vivid and natural way of exhibiting the truth that in God's primary purpose man was incorrupt, so that evil in him should be regarded as having a secondary or adventitious character. Ideal antecedence is, as it were, pictured in temporal antecedence.—A. F. Hort, *Life and Letters of Fenton John Anthony Hort* (1896), ii. 329.

Cp. Mary C. Church, *Life and Letters of Dean Church* (1897), pp. 294f.

2. Gladstone does not here refer to Bishop Butler (one of the four authors to choose as guides of life; see Mary Gladstone, *Diaries and Letters*, 1930, p. 286), but we may compare the opening sentence of Butler's sermon "Upon the Forgiveness of Injuries": "As God Almighty foresaw the irregularities and disorders, both natural and moral, which would happen in this state of things; he hath graciously made some provision against them, by giving us several passions and affections, which arise from, or whose objects are, those disorders".

> ordained certain conditions of the human existence, which, as intermediate expedients, and instruments of a secondary discipline, should both check the progress of selfishness, so far, at least, as to prevent the disease from arriving at its crisis, by establishing a counteracting principle, and should likewise prepare men to recognise the higher truths taught in Divine revelation, and supply them with real though partial approximations to the true law of their being (i. 50).

These expedients or instruments of discipline, which God ordained, were various, but their pervading character was that of a common life, for example, in the family, the tribe, the nation.[1] In these ways the individual's self-centredness is repressed and restrained; duties to be done to others are set before us; and within certain bounds one law for all is established. Moreover, our affections are thus intertwined one with another, and conditions of disinterestedness are provided. The incorporation of individual human beings in associations of this kind "establishes an αἴδως, a sense of honour and shame, a responsibility, one to another, among the partners in that common life which it has created" (i. 60).[2]

1. It should be noted that Gladstone does not allow for the distinction between the "orders" of creation and the "orders" of preservation, concerning which see Marc Boegner in *Church and Community* (1938), pp. 70f.

2. We may again compare the words of Bishop Butler in his sermon before the House of Lords on June 11, 1747: "In aid to this general appointment of Providence, civil government has been instituted over the world, both by the light of nature and by revelation, to instruct men in the duties of fidelity, justice, and regard to common good, and enforce the practice of these virtues, without which there could have been no peace or quiet amongst mankind. . . . For if we could suppose men to have lived out of government, they must have run wild, and all knowledge of divine things must have been lost from among them. But by means of their uniting under it, they have been preserved in some tolerable security from the fraud and violence of each other; order, a sense of virtue, and the practice of it, has been in some measure kept up. . . . So that I make no scruple to affirm, that civil government has been, in all ages, a standing publication of the law of nature, and an enforcement of it; though never in its perfection, for the most part greatly corrupted, and I suppose always so in some degree".

Cp. also Irenæus, *Adversus Hæreses*, V. xxiv. 2: "Ad utilitatem ergo gentilium terrenum regnum positum est a Deo; sed non a diabolo, qui nunquam omnino quietus est, imo qui ne ipsas quidem gentes vult in tranquillo agere; ut timentes regnum hominum, non se alterutrum homines vice piscium consumant, sed per legum positiones repercutiant multiplicem gentilium iniustitiam".

These corporate institutions, however, are not in themselves an unmixed blessing. While collective life is designed to produce good results, it also produces evil. It brings "into existence a new power which may itself be greedy, unjust, and aggressive, and may perpetrate for the community more and grosser evils than would have been committed by the feebler means of its members as individuals" (i. 60f.; cp. ii. 38). Combination enlarges the power of the creature man, increases his liability to be affected by conduct which he cannot control, and impairs and obstructs his sense of moral responsibility, since "where many unite to do wrong, the conscience is staggered as by an appearance of authority, and we are tempted to believe it right, or to insist less upon its wrongfulness" (i. 62).[1]

We thus see the need for some further remedy for the increased dangers and abuses to which collective life in general gives rise. This further remedy is supplied by collective religion, which is not merely another institution on the same plane as the family, the nation, etc., but the application of "a consecrating principle" to all forms of moral agency, whether individual or collective, and the means whereby the truth that all power is the rightful property of God and can be exercised rightly only in accordance with His laws is established and made effective in human life.

Does it then follow that a specific profession of religion is directly necessary to all forms of human combination?[2] This does not follow. The forms of human association may be divided into those that are primary and those that are secondary, accord-

1. Cp. Coleridge's saying: "Multitudes never blush": *Church and State* (1830), p. 119; also L. B. Namier, *Conflicts* (1942), p. 91: "As members of a group-personality most people enjoy greater freedom from moral scruples and inhibitions, and readily do things which they would hesitate to do for their own benefit".

2. Macaulay, in his review of the second edition of Gladstone's book, had said that the argument, as there stated, required that all the following combinations should profess a religion: "banks, insurance offices, dock companies, canal companies, gas companies, hospitals, dispensaries, associations for the relief of the poor, associations for apprehending malefactors, associations of medical pupils for procuring subjects, associations of country gentlemen for keeping fox-hounds, book societies, benefit societies, clubs of all ranks, from those which have lined Pall-Mall and St James' Street with their palaces, down to the Free-and-easy which meets in the shabby parlour of a village inn".—*Critical and Historical Essays*, ii. 445. Gladstone, in the fourth edition of his book, has expanded the argument to meet this objection.

ing to the nature and degree of their personality as societies. (This question of the personality of societies will be considered in the next chapter.) The characteristics of the primary class of human association, for example the family and the nation, are as follows:

> Those combinations . . . which are general, and belong to man as such; which are natural, and so come upon him as parts of the dispensation into which he is providentially born; which are permanent, and so run parallel to his entire existence; which are manifold in their functions and unlimited in their claims upon him; above all, those which, in concurrence with all the foregoing conditions, are moral in such respects as these: that they require in a high degree moral motives and restraints for the right discharge of the obligations subsisting under them; that they distinctly contemplate moral ends; that they exercise manifold, pervasive, subtle, potent, moral influences (i. 94).

Forms of association, in which these conditions are absent or are "only in a slight degree discernible"—such as clubs, commercial companies, and sporting associations—fall into the secondary class.[1]

The two forms of universal association, to which the primary conditions manifestly apply, are the family and the nation or the State.[2] Not only is each of these forms of association capable of

1. Gladstone does not himself use this distinction between "primary" and "secondary" classes; but it serves to make his meaning clearer.

2. "Nation", "State" and adjacent terms are often used interchangeably, or, where they are used with distinct meanings, different authors define them differently. Cp. E. Barker, *Political Thought in England* (1915), pp. 66f.; Introduction to Gierke's *Natural Law and the Theory of Society* (1934), pp. xxiif.; Essay in *Church and Community* (1938), pp. 21ff.; and *Reflections on Government* (1942), pp. xivf. Gladstone is careful to define the distinct senses in which he uses these terms. "When we speak of a multitude, we indicate mere number; when we speak of a people, we separate the governed from the governors; when we speak of a nation, we contemplate them together, but we merge the governors in the governed; when we speak of the state, we contemplate the same personal subjects, but wholly and singly in respect of their partnership in the national life and order, not as individuals" (*SRC*, i. 77).

Thus what Gladstone generally means by the State is what Dr Barker defines as follows: "The State is the members of the nation regarded as living a regulated life, in a single legal association under rules of law declared and enforced

having one religion, but it is necessary to its well-being that it should have one. We must pass over what Gladstone says about family religion, though we must not forget that he regards the family as being, with the State, the twin basis of man's true social life.

But we must pay close attention to the argument about the State, and first we must see how, according to Gladstone, the State satisfies the conditions that have just been specified. He says that the State,

> like the family . . . is of universal, or, at the least, general application. Its agency is permanent and annexed to the whole of our life. It is natural, as opposed to what is spontaneous and conventional. There is no limit of quantity to the obligations of the individual towards it. It is moral, and not merely economical, inasmuch as its laws and institutions, and the acts done under them, are intimately connected with the formation of our moral habits, our modes of thought, and the state of our affections, and inasmuch as its influences pervade the whole scheme and system of our being . . . inasmuch as that which we are individually, we have come to be, in a very considerable degree, through and by means of what we are nationally (i. 86).[1]

What is specially to be noted here is the contention that the State is, properly and according to its nature, moral. By this not only does Gladstone mean that there must be such things as public faith and justice, if political society is to be in the least

by a government which represents the whole of the association"; see his *Britain and the British People* (1942), p. 26, and cp. p. 63, n. 2 *infra*. "The state", said Gladstone, "is the self-governing energy of the nation made objective" (*SRC*, i. 78). Thus he also sometimes uses the term "the State" in a narrower sense as meaning the governing body, see i. 274, 276.

J. N. Figgis in *From Gerson to Grotius* suggested that the constant use of the word "State" (*status*), instead of "Commonwealth" (*respublica*) in modern political speech and writing, is due to the influence of Italy and especially of Machiavelli (*op. cit.*, p. 241). On State and Nation, see also E. Brunner, *The Divine Imperative* (English translation, 1937), pp. 441, 454ff.; E. H. Carr, *Conditions of Peace* (1942), pp. 39, 62; and Lord Morley on "Politics and History" in *Works* (1921 ed.), iv. 50ff.

1. Cp. i. 84: The State "is a main instrument and an absolute condition of (each individual man's) culture, as it is also that comprehensive and overreaching form of the natural human life which includes and harmonises all its other forms, under which they must fall, and to which they must adjust themselves".

degree tolerable; but he means that the State as such is subject to an objective moral law, that it is capable of making and acting upon moral judgments, and that it must needs be fruitful of influences that are moral or immoral. That is to say, it cannot be morally neutral.

He grants, however, that the statesman is not purely concerned with morals, *i.e.* with the intrinsic quality of the acts of the State, since the State has to serve certain lower purposes, such as the establishment of order and the security of property, "without the regular attainment of which he cannot proceed to such as are higher" (i. 87).[1] As regards these lower purposes, which are "first in time and necessity", the State has to be guided by a calculation of the consequences of its acts, and not simply by a moral judgment as to their intrinsic quality. What Gladstone is in effect contending against is the utilitarian or secular theory of the nature of the State, according to which its proper concern is *only* with the body and bodily goods,[2] and not directly with truth or morality at all.

1. Cp. i. 116: "These lower ends of the State are first in time and necessity; and without their attainment in some tolerable measure, it cannot so much as itself exist to contemplate the higher, because civil society is virtually dissolved". And i. 325: "The well-being of a State presupposes and requires its being. Therefore, in order to be capable of realising a spiritual, it must actually have realised an animal life" (see the whole passage to p. 328, and pp. 332f.).

2. The theory, for example, of Bishop Warburton: "The genuine end of civil society . . . is no other than SECURITY TO THE TEMPORAL LIBERTY AND PROPERTY OF MAN" (*Works*, 1811 ed., vii. 42). For Warburton's utilitarianism, see also *ibid.*, pp. 91, 187, 273, 282, 287. The theory that the end of the State is strictly temporal was not of course peculiar to Warburton, though Gladstone appears to have had him chiefly in mind. For the same view as maintained by Machiavelli, see J. W. Allen, *Political Thought in the Sixteenth Century*, part IV, chap. ii, section 6; by William Barclay, see Hudson and Reckitt, *The Church and the World*, ii. 99. Locke's famous statement that "Government has no other end but the preservation of property", which is quoted by Hudson and Reckitt, ii. 117, needs to be qualified by the large meaning that Locke gave to "property", as G. H. Sabine points out in *A History of Political Theory*, p. 528; see also W. Stark, *The Ideal Foundations of Economic Thought* (1943), p. 18, n. 1. A more adequate idea of Locke's view is conveyed in the following passage from "A Letter concerning Toleration":

"The commonwealth seems to me to be a society of men constituted only for the procuring, preserving, and advancing their own civil interests.

"Civil interest I call life, liberty, health, and indolency of body; and the possession of outward things, such as money, lands, houses, furniture, and the like."—*Works* (1823 ed.), vi. 9f.

It is an essential part of Gladstone's thesis that the State has a conscience, and he points out that the language that is habitually used about it implies so much. We speak of the duty of a State; we predicate of it many moral qualities and their opposites. In doing so, we imply something quite beyond the virtue or the guilt of the individual statesmen who may have been the instruments of this or that policy. The conscientious statesman too apprehends that, in entering upon his duties as a statesman, he becomes subject to a wider and deeper range of moral obligations than those to which he is subject as an individual.

It is the moral responsibilities of the State, and the fact that "it requires in a pre-eminent degree moral restraints and motives in its subjects and its agents" (i. 95), that both qualify it, and require it for its well-being, specifically to profess and to promote a religion, and to offer, through its appropriate organs, notably its governing body, and to maintain everywhere, "that worship which shall publicly sanctify its acts" (i. 105).

If this obligation cannot be applied in the same degree to the lesser or secondary forms of human combination, this is due to the infirmity and not to the strength of our nature, and the life of society would be better if in all its departments it could be equally sanctified.[1] But this limitation makes it more and not less needful that religious obligation should be applied where it can be applied, that is, that it should be acknowledged and acted upon by the State as such. Of the inferior combinations, such as gas companies and hospitals, it may be said either that they do not require moral restraints and motives to anything like the same degree, or that they presuppose them (see i. 96).

The extent to which the principle of national religion can be

1. "If the mind and conscience of our own time were sufficiently harmonised and enlightened to admit of adequate securities for uniformly annexing a provision for religious ordinances to the schemes of temporal enterprise and pecuniary aggrandisement, we should probably avoid many kinds of evil which are now engendered among us, on a fearful scale, by the separation of the two, as respects a large proportion of our population" (i. 104). Gladstone cites as an analogy the case of an individual man, who cannot, on account of the infirmity of his nature, refer all his actions distinctly, palpably, and deliberately, to the glory of God, but the more he can do so the better. "That the dedication of the whole life may be real and cordial, it is required that it be as specific as possible; and therefore that at least all the leading and more arduous functions of our condition be hallowed by religious worship" (i. 100).

applied depends on the circumstances of particular nations. In federations of States and in Empires with diverse colonies, the principle can be practically applied to a smaller degree than in single homogeneous States, but "the principle of national religion is rather subjected to limitation in its scope and sphere of action by these diversities of circumstance than to any essential change. . . . Quantity rather than quality is affected" (i. 109).

Gladstone also observes in this connexion that

> while the stringency of the obligations (of this principle) may vary according to the closeness of the political and economical relations in each case, it is desirable to avoid attempting to tighten the bonds of a merely secular connection wherever it has been found impracticable to cement and dignify the union by a true brotherhood in the Christian faith (i. 109).

The course of the argument has now prepared us for the inference that the State should not only recognise a specific religion (since a vague religiosity would be valueless for the purpose), but also that it should recognise only one religion. Two inconsistent religions cannot both be true, and by hypothesis the State can, and ought to, acknowledge truth and therefore theological truth. Not indeed that the State is qualified to decide upon the fine points of theology; it can recognise a specific religion as generally authoritative, while leaving the determination of its particular forms to the religious authorities.[1] Also, since the State cannot, like an individual, be "a discerner and a balancer of particular points in theology" and modify accordingly its support of this or that religious institution, it must commit itself to one institution, and refuse to recognise others, or else it will be unable to draw a line anywhere. This does not, however, require or justify a refusal to *tolerate* other religions. (The difference between the recognition and the toleration of religion will engage our attention later; see pp. 46, 99f., 115–9. *infra.*)

The obligations of the State in regard to religion will be analogous to those of the individual person, namely (*a*) to acknowledge God by worship and prayer and to seek His guidance in all its acts; (*b*) to regulate its conduct by the commandments of God; and (*c*) to provide for the diffusion of religion throughout the

1. Cp. *SRC*, i. 308f.

body of the nation.[1] At all events, says Gladstone, "Christianity is a principle of life intended to govern and pervade the whole of human life. Further, it is a principle of common life; must it not therefore govern and pervade our human common life, our association in the family and in the State?" (i. 115).

But while, on these grounds, the State ought to recognise the Church (we are postponing till chapter five consideration of the question: What is the Church that claims this recognition?), and while the ends of Church and State are "reciprocally inclusive" and coordinate, yet Church and State differ both as to the ends for which they are ordained by God and as to the means by which they are bound to pursue those ends. Thus Gladstone writes:

> The State and the Church have both of them moral agencies. But the State aims at character through conduct: the Church at conduct through character; in harmony with which, the State forbids more than enjoins, the Church enjoins more than forbids. The Church brings down from heaven a divine principle of life, and plants it in the centre of the human heart to work outwards and to leaven the whole mass: the State out of the fragments of primeval virtue, and the powers of the external world, constructs a partial and elementary system, corrective from without, and subsidiary to the great process of redemption and spiritual recovery which advances towards it from within (i. 115f.).[2]

1. i. 110f. For a fuller enumeration of the ways in which the State can lend aid to religion, see i. 244f. See also T. R. Birks, *op. cit.*, pp. 5ff., where "the maxims on which the duty of National Religion is based, in its true and Scriptural idea", are stated in the form of seven propositions, which are then developed in detail.

2. Cp. i. 134: "They represent the two leading processes of Divine government, the one of which works upon what is inward by means of what is outward, the other upon what is outward by means of what is inward; and they integrate one another". We may once more compare Bishop Butler's remarks at the end of his sermon preached before the House of Lords on January 30, 1740–1: "Civil government can by no means take cognisance of *every work*, which is good or evil; many *things* are done in *secret*; the authors unknown to it, and often the things themselves: then it cannot so much consider actions, under the view of their being morally *good* or *evil*, as under the view of their being mischievous or beneficial to society: nor can it in any wise execute *judgment* in rewarding what is *good*, as it can and ought and does, in punishing what is *evil*".

It is interesting also to compare Bishop Creighton's remarks on the same subject: "There is a divergence of function between Church and State: one is

IV

Before we go on to consider some of the main questions that are raised by this theory of the relations of the State with the Church, a preliminary indication may be given of the way in which, according to Gladstone, dissidents from the national religion should be treated. The objection that is most often and most plausibly made against the State's exclusive recognition of one religion on the ground of its truth is that such recognition involves naturally and logically the persecution or oppression of dissenters, or at least the denial to them of equal civil rights and privileges.

In a speech in the House of Commons in 1835, Gladstone had spoken of "combining the efficient maintenance and energetic promotion of the creed believed to be true, with pure and perfect toleration".[1] It is essential to bear in mind the contrast between religious toleration, on the one hand, and religious indifference, neutrality or impartiality, on the other. They are now commonly confused; but originally and properly a doctrine of religious toleration presupposes that the agency that exercises toleration recognises the authority of beliefs with which those that are to be tolerated are at variance. Thus the *New English Dictionary* defines toleration in this sense as "allowance (with or without limitations), by the ruling power, of the exercise of religion otherwise than in the form officially established or recognised" (*s.v.* "Toleration", 4).

To be contrasted with this is the doctrine that the State ought to be indifferent in matters of religion.[2] This doctrine, it need hardly be said, has never been formally adopted by the English

the inspirer, the other the executor, of man's endeavours for the improvement of common life. . . . It is the office of the State to protect rights and to define them; to maintain justice as the binding link of society; to forbid and to punish injuries, 'bearing not the sword in vain'. It appeals to men's sense of order, and operates on the will through the body. The Church inspires the power to fulfil duties. It enjoins love as the fruit of that knowledge which comes through faith. Its injunctions are willingly accepted because they appeal to the whole nature of man. It has no weapon save conviction."—*Persecution and Tolerance* (1895), pp. 78f.

1. Speech on the Irish Church Surplus Revenue, March 31, 1835. In this speech the main theme of *SRC* is anticipated.

2. On this, cp. Lamennais' *Essai sur l'indifférence en matière de religion* (4 vols). The first volume only was translated into English by Lord Stanley of Alderley (1895).

State, but it would be hard to estimate to what extent its practice and public opinion in England have been affected by an implicit acceptance of it. Except by the small number of militant secularists, it may be seldom advocated in so many words, though the following statement from a book by an anonymous author, entitled *The Ultimate Principle of Religious Liberty: the philosophical argument with a review of the controversy on grounds of reason and expediency, in the writings of Locke, Warburton, Paley, Dick, Wardlaw, Gladstone, Martineau, and Miall*, published in 1860, is definite enough:

> What is justice in the matter of religious belief and practice? We answer, that nothing short of the absence of any creed or worship prescribed by civil authority, or of any pecuniary exaction for religious purposes, can leave intact the individual rights of every citizen. Even a simple official declaration in favour of certain views or forms would be an unfair use of the *prestige* of civil authority and influence, not to be tolerated by those members of the community who may dissent from the doctrine and worship proclaimed (*op. cit.*, p. 24).

It is also presupposed by such a statement as that of Mr A. L. Rowse in *Horizon* (June, 1941): "The proper place for churches in the modern community is as free and voluntary associations for those who want that sort of thing, and those who want it paying for it" (p. 388).

When he wrote *The State in its relations with the Church* Gladstone held that the State ought to recognise and support the Church on the ground of truth, but that "the State ought not to use coercion for the propagation of religious truth, or for the repression of erroneous opinion, because the employment of force by man upon man is essentially inappropriate for such a purpose" (i. 310). "In general, even a parent would, it is obvious, decline the attempt to force the religion of his child; and the moral authority of the State over the private person, and its responsibility for his full training, are far less determinate" (i. 312). Further, Gladstone regarded "the corrupting influence of coercive power in religion upon those who wield it" as a consideration "entitled to great weight" (i. 315).

The question of the consistency of Gladstone's theory with religious liberty is, however, one that will be dealt with more fully at a later point.[1]

1. See chapter six, *infra*.

CHAPTER FOUR

IS THE STATE A "MORAL PERSONALITY"?

In the remainder of this study I propose to examine certain main questions that arise out of Gladstone's theory of the relations of the State with the Church. It is not intended to examine every detail in his formulation of the theory; it is obvious that, if such a theory were restated to-day, many details could and would be modified without affecting the main position. The present chapter will deal with questions that arise out of his theory of the nature of the State. For this purpose it will be an advantage to have before us the sketch of a contrasted theory, in fact of the theory against which Gladstone's general argument was specially directed (see *SRC*, i. 31). At the time when his book was published, Macaulay constituted himself the defender or proponent of such a theory. To pay at this point some attention to Macaulay and his criticism of Gladstone's theory will be in accord with the historical reference of the present study, and will conveniently introduce the subject of this chapter.

I

Macaulay's essay, "Gladstone on Church and State", was published in the *Edinburgh Review* for April, 1839, and was republished in the second volume of his *Critical and Historical Essays*.[1] Macaulay had of course no serious standing as a theologian,[2] nor was

1. References here are to the fifth edition of 1848, but the pagination of earlier editions is the same.

2. Sir George Trevelyan asserted that Macaulay had a decided and strong taste for theology: *Life of Macaulay* (1876), ii. 462. Gladstone, in his review of Trevelyan's book, rightly challenged this: "As respects theology, the ten volumes of (Macaulay's) published works do nothing to bear out the assertion of Mr Trevelyan."—*Gleanings* (1879), ii. 285. Cp. *ibid.*, ii. 284: "There are passages which suggest a doubt whether he had completely wrought the Christian dogma, with all its lessons and all its consolations, into the texture of his mind." This is to put the case very mildly.

Charles Macaulay said of his brother: "He was very fond of discussing psychological and ethical questions; and sometimes, but more rarely, would lift the veil behind which he habitually kept his religious opinions."—Trevelyan

there much originality or depth in his ideas. His interest for us lies in the fact that he candidly expresses views which may be taken as representative of those of a great many English people then and now. Describing Macaulay in his note-book, Thomas Carlyle once exclaimed: "These be thy Gods, O Israel!"[1] Lord Morley went so far as to say: "It is one of the first things to be said about Macaulay, that he was in exact accord with the common average sentiment of his day on every subject on which he spoke."[2]

Gladstone himself, when in 1876 he reviewed Sir George Trevelyan's *Life* of his uncle, said that Macaulay "was the child, and became the type, of his country and his age".[3] The two men's minds were cast in as different moulds as possible. Macaulay was a Whig, a child of the age of Reason and Enlighten-

op. cit., ii. 95. Writing to Napier on March 19, 1839, about the proofs of the article in the *Edinburgh Review,* Macaulay said: "Some parts of the subject are ticklish. I have taken the trouble to turn over the Apostolical fathers, Ignatius, Clemens, Hermas, in order to speak with some knowledge of what I was talking about"; see *Selections from the Correspondence of the late Macvey Napier, Esq.* (1879), p. 289.

1. D. A. Wilson, *Carlyle on Cromwell and Others* (1925), p. 381.

2. Lord Morley on "Macaulay" in *Critical Miscellanies* (1921 ed.), p. 185.

3. *Gleanings,* ii. 286; cp. ii. 272: Macaulay, "who as speaker and writer seemed above all others to represent the age and the world. . . . He, for whom the mysteries of human life, thought and destiny appear to have neither charm nor terror, and whose writings seem audibly to boast in every page of being bounded by the visible horizon of the practical and work-a-day sphere . . ."

Cp. Coventry Patmore, *The Rod, the Root, and the Flower* [2] (1923), p. 80: "A man may read Plato without clearly comprehending much of what he means. He cannot read him without becoming, in some degree, a changed man. But he may read and understand every line that Lord Macaulay ever wrote, without any other profit than that of having extended his acquaintance with historical facts, and having become, perhaps, a clearer writer and speaker."

What Dr A. J. Carlyle said of Cicero might almost be said of Macaulay: "Cicero is a political writer of great interest, not because he possesses any great originality of mind, or any great power of political analysis, but rather because, in the eclectic fashion of an amateur philosopher, he sums up the commonplaces of the political theory of his time."—Carlyle, i. 3.

F. D. Maurice wrote of Macaulay in *Macmillan's Magazine* (February, 1860), p. 247: "He did all that he undertook to do perfectly. He has left no germs of thought to be developed hereafter. He defended no truths which were disputed in his own time, and which the experience of after-times may vindicate." See also *Life and Letters of Dean Church* (1897), p. 29; Leslie Stephen, *Hours in a Library,* ii. 347.

ment,[1] and although Gladstone was in time to work together with Whigs, he never came near to being one himself.[2] Macaulay was brilliant but superficial, sensible but not sensitive. His attitude to both Church and State was characteristically Whig. This attitude may be inferred from some of his sayings, gathered from Trevelyan's *Life*.

I have read Augustin's Confessions. The book is not without interest; but he expresses himself in the style of a field-preacher (1837; *op. cit.*, i. 465).

(Gibbon's) opinion of the Christian fathers is very little removed from mine (1838; ii. 39).

There seems to be a most pernicious disposition to mix up religion with politics (1838; ii. 58).

I am surrounded by the din of a sort of controversy which is

1. The anonymous author of *The Ultimate Principle of Religious Liberty* (1860) calls him "the recognised exponent of prevailing Whig churchmanship" (p. 136); W. F. Monypenny calls him "the very genius of triumphant Whiggery", *Life of Disraeli* (1912), ii. 78.

F. D. Maurice, in *The Kingdom of Christ* (1838), iii. 116f., writes as follows about the "modern Whig school" and the *Edinburgh Review*: "No one who will take the trouble of reading the political articles in the organ and oracle of this party, need be at the trouble of answering this question (*i.e.* whether they have a new principle to offer). Every one knows that the great object of its writers is not to establish a principle, but to prove that no sensible statesman will ever think of following one. To keep the boat well trimmed, to observe the cross-currents and avoid them, to sail with the wind,—these are the rules of modern statesmanship, which the Edinburgh Review enforces by a thousand arguments." See also D. A. Wilson, *Carlyle to the "French Revolution"* (1924), p. 280.

2. Sir George Leveson-Gower tells how Mr Gladstone once said to him: "I suppose it is hopeless. You are an Erastian, as all you Whigs always have been and always will be".—*Years of Content* (1940), p. 64. Cp. J. L. Hammond in *Gladstone and the Irish Nation* (1938) on the Whig attitude to politics: "The Whig noblemen who sat round (Gladstone's) table (in the 1880 Ministry) looked on government as the intelligent and economical administration of a world that was happy under their rule, and needed little in the way of change or reform" (p. 183); "the typical Whig . . . looked on politics as a field of duty for his class, in which a man needed above all things the reasonable habits of mind that come from a life of leisure and ease. The problems of government had to be met as they arose" (p. 391).

H. Scott Holland in *Personal Studies* (1905), p. 51: "In all his passage from Toryism to Radicalism (Gladstone) was never for one moment a Whig. That is exactly the temper towards Religion which he abhorred."

See also J. Bryce, *Studies in Contemporary Biography* (1903), p. 469.

most distasteful to me. "Yes, Mr Macaulay; that is all very well for a statesman. But what becomes of the headship of our Lord Jesus Christ"? And I cannot answer a constituent quite as bluntly as any one else who might reason after such a fashion (Edinburgh, 1841; ii. 92).[1]

Then he paid me the highest compliment that ever was paid me in my life; for he said that nobody who knew the world could fail to see that I was what the English call a gentleman, "homme comme il faut" (ii. 46; Gladstone in his copy of Trevelyan's *Life* (*SDL*) wrote against this passage *ma*, which was his way of registering emphatic dissent).

I love a little of the Epicurean element in virtue (ii. 272.)

To me a book which is not amusing wants the highest of all recommendations (ii. 273).

These sayings show well enough not only how Macaulay was characteristically Whig, and a typical Englishman of his age, but also how little natural sympathy there could be between him and Gladstone.

And so we may turn to his review of Gladstone's book. At first sight it is devastating; and it is evident that the writer relished his task.[2] He fastened on all the weakest and most obscure points in Gladstone's argument and demolished them in sparkling style. Actually, several of his thrusts were parried by Gladstone in the fourth edition of his book. Nevertheless, at the time and for long

1. Macaulay "wished all the world to know", says Trevelyan, "that, however much the people whom he represented might regard ecclesiastical matters from the standpoint of the Church, he regarded them, and would always continue to regard them, exclusively from the standpoint of the State".—*Ibid.*, ii. 178.

2. On February 8, 1839, he wrote in his diary: "I bought Gladstone's book: a capital shrovetide cock to throw at. Almost too good to mark" (Trevelyan, ii. 49). And on February 13: "I read, while walking, a good deal of Gladstone's book. The Lord hath delivered him into our hand. I think I see my way to a popular, and at the same time gentlemanlike, critique. . . . In two or three days I shall have the whole in my head, and then my pen will go like fire" (*ibid.*, ii. 49f.). On February 26 he wrote to Napier, the editor of the *Edinburgh Review*: "I can now promise you an article in a week, or ten days at the furthest . . . I find the subject grow on me. I think I shall dispose completely of Gladstone's theory. I wish that I could see my way clearly to a good counter theory; but I catch only glimpses here and there of what I take to be the truth" (*ibid.*, li. 50; *Correspondence of Macvey Napier*, p. 288).

afterwards and even to this day, Macaulay's main thrust will to most readers have seemed fatal. Mr Gladstone's book, he wrote, "is the measure of what a man can do to be left behind by the world. It is the strenuous effort of a very vigorous mind to keep as far in the rear of the general progress as possible".[1] This fatal verdict came to be accepted as a literary commonplace.

Perhaps, however, it was not so much Macaulay's attack as the impending fruition of the age of liberalism that was at the time fatal to the force of Gladstone's argument. In due course Gladstone himself was compelled to admit that this was so; in fact he had suspected that it might be so, even before the book was published.[2] But what if the age of liberalism were to prove a fruit that ripened only to rot? In that case Macaulay's triumph would be ambiguous, and his assumption about "general progress" would come to wear a different complexion, more fatal to itself than to Gladstone's argument about first principles.

It was easy enough in the circumstances of the time to make fun of a high Church-and-State doctrine. Macaulay noted, indeed, that Gladstone rested his case for the maintenance of the existing order "on entirely new grounds"; but whatever the grounds adduced in support of it, the conclusion could easily be shown to be absurd. Now that those circumstances no longer hold, Macaulay's attack may seem less devastating in its effect. The weakness of his position comes out in the theory which he advocates or assumes as an alternative to Gladstone's.[3]

Macaulay's view of the nature of the State was simple and confident. The proper ends of civil government are purely temporal.

> That it is designed to protect our persons and our property, that it is designed to compel us to satisfy our wants, not by rapine, but by industry, that it is designed to compel us to decide our differences, not by the strong hand, but by arbitration, that it is designed to direct our whole force, as that of one man,

1. *Critical and Historical Essays*, ii. 467.
2. See p. 27, n. 2, *supra*.
3. He was not unaware of this weakness himself, so far as the relations of the State with the Church were concerned (see n. 2 on the preceding page), but he does not seem to have had any misgivings about his theory of the nature of the State and of the ends of civil government.

> against any other society which may offer us injury, these are propositions which will hardly be disputed (ii. 437).
>
> We consider the primary end of government as a purely temporal end, the protection of the persons and property of men . . . We think that government should be organised solely with a view to its main end; and that no part of its efficiency for that end should be sacrificed in order to promote any other end however excellent (ii. 493; cp. i. 269).

In his view society is purely atomistic. Societies are merely collections of individuals who combine for one purpose or another.

> Nothing seems to us more beautiful or admirable in our social system than the facility with which thousands of people, who perhaps agree only on a single point, can combine their energies for the purpose of carrying out that single point (ii. 447).

Theological truth, which is the province of religion, has nothing to do with the end of government.

> It passes our understanding to comprehend what connexion any (constitution of government) has with theological truth (ii. 454).[1]

As for the Church of England, Macaulay, as a true Whig, supposed it to have been founded at the time of the Reformation (ii. 484, 500), and that its genius was to be as latitudinarian as possible (ii. 489).

What then of the relation between Church and State? It depends on circumstances; it is a matter of expediency. Where circumstances admit of its doing so, a government may pursue other than its primary, temporal ends, provided that the other ends are useful for the achievement of the primary ends or in no

1. Cp. Macaulay's *Essays*, i. 296f. This was of course the Lockian theory. "The business of laws is not to provide for the truth of opinions, but for the safety and security of the commonwealth, and of every particular man's goods and person."—John Locke, "Letter concerning Toleration", *Works* (1832 ed.), vi. 40.

On the other hand, as regards this question, Dr Arnold was in warm agreement with Gladstone. See Arnold's *Fragment on the Church* [2] (1845), p. 224, and Stanley's *Life of Arnold* [2] (1844), ii. 147.

way interfere with their achievement. That is to say, a government may, and indeed should, make use of religion and morality in so far as these things are of temporal assistance.

> The education of the people, conducted on those principles of morality which are common to all forms of Christianity, is highly valuable as a means of promoting the main object for which government exists, and is on this ground well deserving the attention of rulers (ii. 495).[1]

In the case of the Church of England, a statesman who takes a very low view of the religious claims that are made by some of its members (not to say, by its formularies)

> may think that she teaches more truth with less alloy of error than would be taught by those who, if she were swept away, would occupy the vacant space. He may think that the effect produced by her beautiful services and by her pulpits on the national mind, is, on the whole, beneficial. He may think that her civilising influence is usefully felt in remote districts. He may think that, if she were destroyed, a large portion of those who now compose her congregations would neglect all religious duties; and that a still larger portion would fall under the influence of spiritual mountebanks, hungry for gain, or drunk with fanaticism. . . . He may be of opinion that an institution, so deeply fixed in the hearts and minds of millions, could not be subverted without loosening and shaking all the foundations of civil society. . . . In this way, we conceive, a statesman might, on our principles, satisfy himself that it

1. In *A Chapter of Autobiography* (1868) Gladstone summed up Macaulay's theory as follows: "Government is police. All other functions, except those of police proper, are the accidents of its existence. As if a man should say to his friend when in the country, 'I am going up to town; can I take anything for you'? So the State, while busy about protecting life and property, will allow its officer of police to perform any useful office for the community, to instruct a wayfarer as to his road, or tell the passer by what o'clock it is, provided it does not interfere with his watching the pickpocket, or laying the strong hand upon the assassin" (p. 57).

Goldwin Smith said of Macaulay's rejoinder to Gladstone: "The Reviewer . . . ends with a defence of religious establishments really weaker than anything in Gladstone. The State, according to Macaulay, though religion is not its business, has some time and energy to spare which it may usefully devote to the regulation of religion."—*My Memory of Gladstone* (1904), p. 8; cp. *The Nineteenth Century* (October, 1891), p. 526.

would be in the highest degree inexpedient to abolish the Church, either of England or of Scotland (ii. 500ff.).

The contrast between Macaulay's teaching and Gladstone's about the first principles of politics is fairly plain. Further aspects of it may be brought out by one or two passages in Macaulay's essay on Machiavelli. Macaulay, no more than other English statesmen, was likely to acknowledge that he was a faithful disciple of Machiavelli, but his essay is marked by an extreme indulgence. While paying lip-service to conventional morality, in effect he sets Machiavelli on a pedestal,[1] and it is significant that he describes his great, if not his only, fault as follows:

> There are errors in these works (*The Prince* and *The Discourses*). But they are errors which a writer, situated like Machiavelli, could scarcely avoid. They arise, for the most part, from a single defect which appears to us to pervade his whole system. In his political scheme, the means had been more deeply considered than the ends. The great principle, that societies and laws exist only for the purpose of increasing the sum of private happiness, is not recognised with sufficient clearness.[2]

The moral relativism, which in the last analysis is moral nihilism, of Macaulay's political theory may be inferred from the following passages in the same essay:

> Every age and every nation has certain characteristic vices, which prevail almost universally, which scarcely any person scruples to avow, and which even rigid moralists but faintly censure. Succeeding generations change the fashions of their morals, with the fashion of their hats and their coaches; take some other kind of wickedness under their patronage, and wonder at the depravity of their ancestors.[3]
>
> Every man who has seen the world knows that nothing is so

1. Macaulay's method in studying these matters was remarkably like Machiavelli's (see J. W. Allen, *Political Thought in the Sixteenth Century*, part IV, chap. ii, section 7), if allowance is made for the fact that Machiavelli wrote out of experience in the early sixteenth century and Macaulay in the early nineteenth century.

2. *Critical and Historical Essays*, i. 103f.

3. *Ibid.*, i. 86.

> useless as a general maxim. If it be very moral and very true it may serve for a copy for a charity-boy. . . . Few indeed of the many wise apothegms which have been uttered, from the time of the Seven Sages of Greece to that of Poor Richard, have prevented a single foolish action. We give the highest and the most peculiar praise to the precepts of Machiavelli when we say that they may frequently be of real use in regulating conduct, not so much because they are more just or more profound than those which might be culled from other authors, as because they can be more readily applied to the problems of real life.[1]

Views, or insinuations, such as these were abhorrent to Gladstone at every period of his life. Machiavellianism, to which Macaulay was so indulgent, was Gladstone's *bête noire*.[2]

II

The questions raised by these contrasted doctrines of Gladstone and Macaulay are numerous and complicated. We shall consider the following which seem to be of special and permanent importance. First, what is the nature of the State and what are the ends of civil government? Secondly, what concern (if any) has the State with theological truth? Thirdly, what is the nature of the Church, and ought it to regard its relations with the State as a matter of expediency or of principle? Obviously, these questions overlap or intersect. In the present chapter we are chiefly concerned with the first, and in the next chapter we shall be chiefly concerned with the third; in both chapters we are concerned with the second.

We begin then by inquiring whether the State is, as Macaulay supposed, merely a collection of individuals who combine for the pursuit of a temporal end, or whether it is in some sense, as Gladstone held, "a person". The question as to whether there is such a thing as "group personality" has been brought to the fore by some modern political theorists. Gierke in Germany urged that recognition of the fact of "group personality" marks a great

1. *Critical and Historical Essays*, i. 103.

2. See appended note on "Gladstone and Machiavellianism", pp. 159f. *infra*.

advance in sociological understanding;[1] Maitland,[2] and especially Figgis,[3] have given the conception a certain vogue in England;[4]

1. "In any scheme of thought which proceeds on the premiss that the social life of man is the life of super-individual entities, the introduction of the *Volksgeist* into the theory of law will always continue to be regarded as the starting-point of a deeper and profounder theory of society."—Quoted by E. Barker in his introduction to Otto Gierke's *Natural Law and the Theory of Society* (English translation, 1934), p. liv.

2. F. W. Maitland, Introduction to Gierke's *Political Theories of the Middle Ages* (English translation, 1900) and *Collected Papers* (ed. by H. A. L. Fisher, 1911), iii. 304–20, Paper on "Moral Personality and Legal Personality". See also R. H. Murray, *Social and Political Thinkers of the Nineteenth Century* (1929), vol. ii, chap. 9, "Maitland and Pluralism".

3. J. N. Figgis, *Churches in the Modern State*, pp. 41, 59, 87f.; *From Gerson to Grotius*, pp. 204ff. But Figgis modifies Gierke's theory; cp. Barker, *op. cit.*, pp. lxxxiif. Figgis was concerned to establish the group personality of societies in the State over against "the omnicompetent State", and not the personality of the State itself. He maintained that the true idea of the State is that of a *communitas communitatum*, but his own emphasis was on the *communitatum* rather than on the *communitas*.

4. Barker, in his evidence before the Archbishops' Commission on the relations between Church and State, 1935 (*Church and State*, ii. 68f.), said: "I have noticed in the last thirty years (partly under the influence of Dr Figgis) a vogue of certain theories of Gierke (or rather of Maitland, in his introduction to his translation of a chapter of Gierke), and a consequent disposition to advocate what are called the 'inherent rights' of the real 'group-person', whether civil or ecclesiastical".

The subject is discussed by H. J. Laski in a paper on "The Personality of Associations" in *The Foundations of Sovereignty* (1921); by A. J. Toynbee in *A Study of History* [2] (1935), i. 444 and iii. C. (ii); by V. A. Demant in *Christian Polity* (1936), pp. 110ff. L. Susan Stebbing in *Ideals and Illusions* (1941), chap. viii, makes some criticisms of the personification of groups. H. M. Relton, in *Religion and the State* (1937), chap. i, accepts from Gierke and Figgis the doctrine of "corporate personality", but does not criticise it or develop it further. Although published in 1937, his book refers only to Maitland's translation of Gierke, and not to Barker's. The C.O.P.E.C. Commission Report (vol. x) on *Politics and Citizenship* (1924) says: "Clubs and trade unions, universities and academies, religious orders and co-operative societies, have a quasi-personality, which is not merely a legal fiction, but a vital fact, not created by the State, but merely recognised by it" (p. 12).

See also J. S. Huxley, *The Individual in the Animal Kingdom* (1912), p. 143; W. O. Lester Smith, *To Whom do the Schools Belong?* (1942), chap. vi and pp. 174f.; J. C. Smuts, *Holism and Evolution* [2] (1927), p. 348; S. A. Cook, *The Rebirth of Christianity* (1942), pp. 191, n. 2, 193; R. H. Charles, *The Decalogue* (1923), p. 270; Robert Stokes, evidence before the Archbishops' Commission referred to above, *Church and State*, ii. 258ff.; cp. *ibid.*, ii. 15, 84; C. Gore in *Report of the Archbishops' Committee on Church and State* (1916), pp. 247f. Also references to P. T. Forsyth, see p. 65, n. 1, *infra*.

Miss M. P. Follett passionately espoused it in the U.S.A.[1]

Gladstone's advocacy of this conception seems to have been overlooked. It was an essential part of the theory of *The State in its relations with the Church.*[2] There is, he says, "generally in societies a real and substantial personality", but "care must be taken to keep the idea which the term conveys distinct from that of individuality". The latter signifies not only actual unity of life, but that unity "attended with universal indivisibility; whereas moral personality, while it implies unity for certain purposes, is compatible with divisibility in the subjects whose composition goes to form that unity" (*SRC*, i. 65f.). Personality is living, active and moral, and therefore capable of, and subject to, religious responsibility. In this sense the State is a person.

> A State as such is at least as deliberative as an individual: at least as capable, by its nature, of discerning right and wrong, since it may and by its nature ought to command the very best perceptions of right and wrong, which are found among men, to be enlisted in its service; at least as free in the use of its organs to do or not to do, since it owns no human superior (i. 69).

To what extent then are other combinations of men also personalities? Gladstone would say that there are many degrees and variations in the personality of groups.

> The personality may be (*a*) constant and sustained, or it may be intermittent; . . . (*b*) it may be temporary and occasional, or it may be permanent. The power may be (*c*) indefinitely great or indefinitely small. The functions . . . may be (*d*) applicable to few, or many, or most, or all: may be (*e*) grounded in

1. M. P. Follett, *The New State: group organisation the solution of popular Government* (English ed. with introduction by Lord Haldane, 1920).

See also W. E. Hocking, *Man and the State* (1926), pp. 339–362.

2. It is to the credit of the author of *The Ultimate Principle of Religious Liberty* (1860) that he saw the fundamental importance of this question. Thus he writes (p. 121): "The whole syllogistic fabric (*i.e.* of Gladstone's theory) is constructed to support the doctrine of a national conscience and the alleged corporate responsibility of government for the official maintenance of religion.

"If, by fair and intelligible show of reason, we can reduce this idea of a moral personality in the State to the worthlessness of an impalpable or incongruous fiction, the rest will fall to the ground".

natural ordinance, or in human convention and allowance: may be (*f*) narrow, determinate and calculable in amount; or may be overreaching, comprehensive, unlimited, and entirely transcending the range of all foresight and distinct reasoning: may be (*g*) conversant with matters of . . . material interests . . . such as involve no agency of the kind properly termed moral: or may on the other hand be largely and pervasively connected with the moral faculties and habits of the mind, with the passions and the affections; with the deep foundations, and with the entire superstructure of human character (i. 71f.).

As we have already seen (pp. 40f. *supra*), Gladstone maintained that these conditions are met with to the highest degree in the family and in the nation or State. His emphasis on the *moral*[1] personality of these forms of society should be particularly remarked.

But may not this high doctrine of the personality of groups, and of the State in particular, be a tissue of metaphysical or mystical[2] nonsense? No doubt we speak of groups as though they were persons, and no doubt it is convenient for certain juristic purposes to treat them as though they were persons; but, it may be said, the *persona* is *ficta*, artificial or fictitious. If we regard it as anything more than that, we become the victims of the deceptive power of language. Whatever the truth of the matter may be, we may at least agree with Maitland that "something not unworthy of philosophic discussion would seem to lie in this quarter: either some deep-set truth which is always bearing fresh fruit, or else a surprisingly stable product of mankind's propensity to feign".[3]

1. He uses the term "moral" in conjunction with "person" in a positive sense, which must be distinguished from the negative sense that was fashionable in the eighteenth century. Barker, *op. cit.*, pp. lxiii and lxv, calls attention to this distinction, *i.e.* between "moral" used in much the same sense as when we speak of a moral certainty or a moral victory (negative sense) and as denoting the power and capacity of moral action (positive sense). Gladstone means, of course, the latter. See also Maitland, *op. cit.*, p. xxiv.

2. Lord Selborne, in his *Defence of the Church of England* (1886), referring to Gladstone's book, wrote: "I do not, and cannot, take my stand on any mystical view—such, *e.g.*, as that the State is 'a person', with a corporate conscience, 'cognisant of matter of religion' " (p. 72).

3. Introduction to Gierke's *Political Theories of the Middle Age* (1900), p. xii.

The question deserves more extensive discussion than is contemplated here. But we may be able to see what is at issue, and what is the direction in which the truth lies. The most considerable treatment of the subject that is available for English readers is that of Professor Ernest Barker in his long and important introduction to Gierke's *Natural Law and the Theory of Society*, which was published in 1934.[1]

Barker distinguishes three main senses of the term "personality" —psychological, moral, and legal. *Psychological* personality means "the power or capacity of self-consciousness which belongs to a sentient being aware of its own sensations" and also "of self-determination, by considerations of pleasure and pain, which arises from such self-consciousness, and turns it into a higher activity than its primary activity of awareness. Psychological personality, by its nature, is resident in an individual being who is a focus and centre of sentiency". *Moral* personality [2] "signifies the power or capacity of a self-conscious and rational being to determine himself, not by temporary and particular considerations of pleasure and pain, but by permanent and universal considerations of a right way of conducting life which is common to all such beings". While moral personality resides in the individual being, it does so only "in so far as he recognises that he is not unique, but shares with his fellows a common life and common rules of life". *Legal* personality means a power or capacity for legal action, and it presupposes an organised legal association. It is a capacity for rights; and, since rights may belong to groups as well as to individuals, we need not hesitate to assign legal personality to groups (*op. cit.*, pp. lxiiff.).

There are thus organised legal associations which may fitly be called group-persons, but what is the nature of their personality? Barker notes three different answers to this question. First, there is the Fiction theory, according to which "the real fact behind the existence of a legal group is the fact of the many individuals of which it is composed, and the unity of such a group is only

1. There is an earlier and slighter passage on the subject in his *Political Thought from Spencer to To-day* (1915), pp. 175–183, and also in his article on "The Discredited State" in *The Political Quarterly* (February, 1915), pp. 101-121.

2. See n. 1 on the preceding page. Barker also defines "moral personality" in his *Reflections on Government* (1942), p. 16.

a pretence or fiction" (p. lxivf.). This may also be called the Concession theory, according to which the unity of a legal group is due to an act of concession by the authority of the State. Secondly, there is the Collective theory, according to which there is no such real existence as a single group-person and there is no need to introduce even the conception of a *persona ficta*; it is merely a name for a collection of individual persons who make a contract to act together for certain purposes. This has also been called the Bracket theory, which signifies that a group is simply an aggregate of individuals collected together, as it were, in a bracket. Barker also considers that what is called the Representative theory,[1] according to which the unity of a group resides in the individual member or members of it who are chosen to represent it, is no more than a variation of the Collective theory.

Thirdly, there is the theory of the reality of the group-person, as advocated by Gierke and Figgis. According to this, "there really exists, in the nature of things itself, such a thing as a real Group-person, with a real being or essence which is the same in kind as that of the individuals who are its members". On this view, "legal group-personality is the shadow cast by real group-personality: it is the reflection of reality in the mirror of law" (p. lxvif.).

There are historical causes which explain why this last theory was developed in Germany rather than in England, notably the fact that, whereas in England it has been easy for groups to secure legal recognition and scope for activity by means of Trust-deeds, etc., in Germany there were no corresponding facilities, and in Germany therefore there was a motive, whether conscious or unconscious, to the development of a high doctrine of group-personality as a means of securing fuller recognition for the existence and activity of groups.[2] In England, too, it was perhaps the concern of a high-church Anglican like Figgis and a high-church Congregationalist like Forsyth [3] for the independence and authority of the Church that led them in the first place to look with favour on the theory of real group-personality.

1. For a statement of this theory see Hobbes's *Leviathan*, part i, chap. 16.
2. Cp. Barker, pp. lx, lxii, and lxxii.
3. See p. 65 *infra*.

The circumstances which condition the origin or development of a theory do not, however, determine its truth or falsehood, which is the question with which we are here concerned. We need have no hesitation in agreeing with Barker (*a*) that psychological personality, as he defines it, is resident only in individual persons, and that it must not be ascribed to group-persons[1] (this is the point that Gladstone had in mind when he said that care must be taken to keep the idea of personality distinct from that of individuality; see p. 58 *supra*); and (*b*) that legal personality can be assigned to groups. We have therefore to ask whether moral personality can be ascribed to groups and, if so, in what sense?

Barker himself adopts what looks like a mediating view. He will not allow that a group can have moral personality, as he has defined it, but neither is he content to say that a group-person is only a *persona ficta*. He draws a distinction between Society and the State.

> A Society is a *community* of human beings who seek to fulfil the general purposes of human life in all its aspects. A State is an *association* of the same beings, in legal form, for the specific purpose of regulating human life, in the sphere of external action, by rules designed to secure the minimum of friction between its members and the maximum of their development (p. lxx).

This distinction is an important one, in so far as it calls attention to the fact that a nation's life is larger than what is comprised in its organised activities as a State, but it is misleading if it is used to depreciate the significance of its existence as a State. Now, Barker, having drawn this distinction, centres his discussion on the meaning of group-personality in the case of groups within the State,[2] and he hardly faces the question whether and in what sense the State, or a national community, or again the

1. Nor is what Gierke means by "group-personality" to be confused with the "group-mind" of the social psychologists, see Barker, p. xxxi.

2. "Was it possible to find a theoretical basis for liberty of association, without recourse to a doctrine of the real personality of groups"? (Barker, p. lxf.). "The problem of liberty of associations thus carries us forward . . . into the problem of the real personality of associations" (p. lxii).

Church,[1] is a group-person. This seems to be because he is primarily and properly concerned with the legal aspect of the subject, and with the nature of subordinate groups within the State. But when Gladstone ascribed moral personality to the State, he certainly meant more than the State in its legal form. He would have said that a national community or society as a whole was a moral person which however was chiefly (though not exclusively) operative in the (legal) State and that for this reason it was commonly spoken of as the State.[2] Further, he was more concerned with the ethical, metaphysical and theological aspects of the subject. Barker writes: "The State, we may say, is a national society which has turned itself into a legal association, or a juridical organisation" (p. xxiii; but in becoming a legal association it has not ceased to be a national society). He admits that "the legal approach to political science" tends "to convert the State into a legal institution, rather than 'a fellowship in the good life' " (p. xx). It may be that his own discussion illustrates this tendency.

As regards legal associations within the State, Barker asks "whether the State is free to choose, at its own discretion, the objects to which it concedes (legal) personality; or whether it is not rather bound, by its own very nature, to concede such personality to certain objects, in virtue of their nature" (p. lxxii). In accepting the latter alternative, he defines the criterion by which the State should be guided as follows:

> (The State) will award legal personality to every organising idea, every common purpose, which permanently unites a number of individuals as the common content of their minds and the common intention of their wills, provided that such idea and purpose are compatible, or to the extent that they are compatible, with the free action and development of all members of the State (p. lxxiii).

1. *The Tablet* (August 8, 1942) says that Barker, in his *Reflections on Government* (1942), envisages "the Church" as the Nonconformist sect, claiming its liberty. This remark might also be applied to the essay at present under consideration. On the other hand, reference should be made to his essay in *Church and Community* (1938), which comes much nearer to recognising the peculiar character of the Church, and to his evidence before the Archbishops' Commission on the relations between Church and State, 1935, see *Church and State*, ii. 64–78.

2. See p. 40, n. 2 *supra*. As Barker has said elsewhere: "The nation finds itself, or expresses itself, in a State."—*Church and State*, ii. 70.

He speaks of the State as "awarding", "assigning" or "conceding" personality to groups and as "creating" it. But the crucial question from our point of view is whether the State is morally bound to *recognise* such personality, and not merely whether it is legally justified in awarding it. Does the personality of groups really exist prior to its being conceded, or is it created by, and so subject to, the State?[1] Further, would not the qualifications, introduced by Gladstone between the many degrees and variations in group-personality,[2] have illuminated Barker's argument? He does indeed note that "each society is a plurality. It is a rich web of contained groups—religious and educational; professional or occupational; some for pleasure and some for profit; some based on neighbourhood and some on some other affinity" (p. xxiii); but, when he comes to consider group-personality he does not sufficiently reckon with the distinctions, noted by Gladstone, between groups that are permanent and those that are temporary; between those that are grounded in natural ordinance and those that are grounded in human allowance; and between those that are concerned with material interests and those that are concerned with moral habits and the deepest foundations of human character. But we have no right to complain of the limitations of Barker's valuable discussion. "Reality", he says, "is a term of high metaphysics; and it lies beyond our scope" (p. lxii). Though it is not clear that he intended altogether to exclude metaphysical considerations, it is clear, as has been said, that he is primarily occupied with the legal aspects of the subject.[3] We may there-

1. E. B. Greene, in *Religion and the State* (1941), asks: "Assuming that the church, or churches, on the one side and the state on the other have their appropriate spheres of action, are they mutually independent within those spheres? Does the church, for instance, possess inherent rights, independently derived and therefore not to be controlled or abridged by the state? Or is the corporate action of the church, in external matters at least, subject like that of other nonpolitical associations to the control of the sovereign state"? (p. 103).

2. See pp. 58f. *supra*.

3. In connexion with this limitation we may recall Maitland's account of an incident in the House of Commons in April, 1904. When Mr Balfour spoke of the Trade Unions as corporations, an opposition member, who was a distinguished lawyer, interjected: "The trade unions are not corporations". To which Mr Balfour replied: "I know, I am talking English, not law". Maitland comments: "A long story was packed into that admirable reply".—F. W. Maitland, *Collected Papers* (1911), iii. 305.

fore turn for further light to a theologian, who maintained the real personality of groups.

III

P. T. Forsyth in his book, *Theology in Church and State*, which was published in 1915, has a chapter on "Corporate Personality and its Rights". He is chiefly interested in the corporate personality of the Church, and minimises, if he does not deny, the corporate personality of other groups except the State, whose real personality he takes for granted,[1] and the family.[2] Though he has little to say about personality in the State except by way of implication, yet what he says about personality in the Church is so relevant to the subject of group-personality in general that, even if it belongs properly to a later stage in our discussion, I must call attention to it now.

Forsyth brings out the distinction between the recognition of rights and the conferring or concession of rights. In the case of the Church at all events, what the State has to do with is the intrinsic rights of a creative society, which are analogous to those of a living person. These rights exist inherently in the society. ("The mind of a crowd is lower than the minds of its units, but the mind of a society is higher." [3]) That this is so, he maintains, is borne out by what we may observe in history.

> The notion of such a society, corporately personal, as we find in the Church does not rest upon theological theories simply, however true, but upon history, on the behaviour and experience of such bodies in history, on their growing moral power and their tough resistance to extinction. They have a native recalcitrance to any such denial of their rights by man as would reduce these to a gift *ab extra* instead of a recognition *ad intra*. Right is proportional to personality.[4]

1. *Op. cit.*, pp. 157, 162, 166, 169, 182. See also his *The Christian Ethic of War* (1916), pp. 96, 162, 189. At the same time, in *The Justification of God* (1916), p. 21, he writes: "No nation is an end in itself as a soul is. The idea of a group personality is a great and fertile one, but it can hardly be allowed to go as far as that".

2. *Theology in Church and State*, pp. 162, 179.

3. *Op. cit.*, p. 156.

4. *Op. cit.*, pp. 159f. He continues: "If the Church has not a corporate personality then its rights within the State are conferred instead of recognised. They are *conferred* by the State, and are a fiction for legal purposes instead of being *recognised* by the State as gift and moral prerogative from God. And

There are two cognate assertions here which bear on the nature of group personality in general. First, the view that a society may have intrinsic rights to existence and to liberty of growth,[1] independently of or prior to its recognition by the State, corresponds to the assertion that "legal personality is the shadow cast by real personality".[2] If we acknowledge the existence of such intrinsic rights, is not a doctrine of *real* group-personality the best way of expressing and safeguarding the truth? Secondly, "real rights", says Forsyth, "reside only in some form of personality".[3] "Right is proportional to personality"; and, we may add, not only right, but duty and moral obligation also. Instead of the category of personality Barker wishes us to use the category of purpose. "The essence of the unity of a group is its expressed purpose." [4]

that vassalage is a situation which no Church could accept and remain a Church of grace, of the Holy Ghost and the new creation" (italics his).

Forsyth would not have accepted Barker's statement that "if we once accept the theory of the real personality of groups, we are bound to see behind the State the figure of the greatest and the most real of all groups—the figure of the nation and Folk itself" (Barker, p. lxxxiv). For Forsyth would say that the Church, not the nation, is the greatest and most real of all groups.

1. Barker, on the other hand, appears to hold that "individual personality is the one intrinsic value of human life" (p. xlix).

2. See p. 61 *supra*.

3. *Op. cit.*, p. 162.

4. *Op. cit.*, p. lxxvi. Readers who are familiar with Martin Buber's *I and Thou* (English translation, 1937) may be asked to consider the matter in this way. Does the State as such belong to the world of *It*? Admittedly, in so far as it is a legal institution or a juridical organisation, it does so; but if the community or national society is a group-person, which expresses itself in, and operates through, the institution and organisation of the State, does it not belong also to the world of *Thou*? "The communal life of man can no more than man himself dispense with the world of *It*, over which the presence of the *Thou* moves like the spirit on the face of the waters" (Buber, p. 48). The question is whether a *Thou* is not present in the group personality; whether what Buber calls "meeting" occurs not only between individual persons and group-persons, but also between one group-person and another, and in particular between the State and the Church. If so, the essence of the unity of the group is most adequately described as a person rather than as a purpose. The State is not merely a thing or object for us to use; through it a group personality addresses us. But the State is also addressed by the eternal *Thou* through the Church which bears witness to the Word of God. A doctrine of the State which confines it to the world of *It* I call a low doctrine; a doctrine which also recognises in it the world of *Thou* I call a high doctrine.

> The recipient of legal personality . . . is a common and continuing purpose, continuously entertained by a continuing body of persons, which owns the capacity and constitutes the legal person. The "person" which owns the property of an Oxford or Cambridge college is neither the founder, now gone, nor the body of his living successors. It is the purpose which animated the founder and which continues . . . to animate his successors.[1]

But is it not the founder and all his successors, whether living, dead, or yet to be born? It is apposite to recall Burke's glowing, and often quoted, definition of Society.

> (Society) is not a partnership in things subservient only to the gross animal existence of a temporary and perishable nature. It is a partnership in all science; a partnership in all art; a partnership in every virtue, and in all perfection. As the ends of such a society cannot be obtained in many generations, it becomes a partnership not only between those who are living, but between those who are living, those who are dead, and those who are to be born.[2]

What has been said shows the need for a doctrine and a term that will do justice to the moral nature of the State, but must such a doctrine involve acceptance of the reality of group personality?[3] If we use the term, our interest is in asserting the moral responsibility of the State; we may not assert that group personality, however long it may endure in time, is immortal or a metaphysical essence like individual personality, though F. D. Maurice, preaching on Rev. vii. 9f., vigorously denied that orthodox Christians must hold that after death all family and national relationships cease.[4] Opinions will differ as to the desirability of using the term. If another term were available which expressed capacity for moral responsibility, but did not suggest that the State or other

1. *Op. cit.*, pp. lxxiiif.

2. *Reflections on the Revolution in France* in vol. v of the 1826 ed. of his *Works*, p. 184. Cp. Disraeli's description of a nation in "The Letters of Runnymede"—W. Hutcheon, *Whigs and Whiggism* (1913), p. 251.

3. What we have said does not carry us much farther than the cautious observation of Professor Geldart that "there seems to be at least a *prima facie* case for holding that our legal theory ought to admit the reality of a personality in permanent associated bodies, or at least of something so like personality that we may provisionally call it by that name for want of a better".—Quoted by E. Barker, *The Political Quarterly* (February, 1915), p. 111.

4. *Lincoln's Inn Sermons* (1891 ed.), ii. 278f.

natural communities are metaphysical essences, it should be preferred.

At the same time, Christians must acknowledge that there is such a thing as real group personality in the case of the Church. Holy Scripture appears to attribute it to a family, the seed of Abraham, and to a nation, Israel, and unquestionably the Church, the new Israel, is so regarded when it is described as the body of Christ or as the Bride of Christ.[1] Here we certainly have to do with a real corporate personality, whose personality resides not only in the common purpose by which it is animated (which is all that Barker's theory would allow), nor only in the individual human persons who are members of it (which is all that the atomistic theory of society would allow), but in the divine-human person of Christ Himself. But it resides in Him, not in such a way as to absorb or eviscerate the human person-members (whether individual—or group-persons), but rather in such a way as to give them their true independence and their mutual interdependence which are to be found only in their dependence on Him.[2]

This consummating group personality, which is the Christ as Head of the human race redeemed by His death on the cross, recreated by His resurrection, and exalted to the heavenly places by His ascension, we apprehend here by faith and not by sight.

1. On the conception of the body of Christ, see E. Mersch, *Le Corps Mystique du Christ* (1933). On the conception of the Bride of Christ, see C. Chavasse, *The Bride of Christ* (1940). For the biblical conception of corporate personality, see H. W. Robinson, *The Cross of the Servant* (1936); also in *Record and Revelation* (1938), pp. 332f.; A. R. Johnson, *The One and the Many in the Israelite Conception of God* (1942); Vincent Taylor, *Jesus and His Sacrifice* (1937), pp. 284f.; George Johnston, *The Doctrine of the Church in the New Testament* (1943), pp. 92f.; H. H. Rowley, *The Relevance of Apocalyptic* (1944), pp. 150f.; H. F. Lovell Cocks, *By Faith Alone* (1943), p. 159.

2. Cp. Coventry Patmore, *The Rod, the Root, and the Flower*[2] (1923), p. 194: "Theologians teach that our ultimate felicity will consist in the development of a single divine humanity made up of innumerable unique and sympathetic individualities or 'members', each one shining with its proper and peculiar lustre, which shall be as unlike any other lustre as that of a sapphire is from that of a ruby or an emerald; and they further teach that the end of this life is the awakening and growth of such individualities through a faithful following of the peculiar good which is each individual's 'ruling love'; since each has his ruling love, if he knew it, that is, his peculiar and partial way of discerning and desiring the absolute good, which no created being is capable of discerning and desiring in its fullness and universality".

There the kingdom of God already is; on earth it is in process of becoming. Thus it has been said that the Church is the kingdom of God in the making. It witnesses to the already existing kingdom of God by its preaching, its sacraments, and its common life. The Church on earth is, however, imperfect, limited by finitude and marred by sin; it is *in via*, and not yet fulfilled in the perfect realisation of its end. The members of the Church know themselves by faith in Christ to be members of a real group personality, the new Israel, which is the mystical body of Christ; but they do not yet see Him as He is, nor themselves as they will be. The Church on earth is, as it were, a broken arc of the perfect circle which is in the heavenly places, and which is the perfect group personality.

If this be so in the case of the Church, which is a supernatural community, it is not surprising that the personality of natural communities, like families and nations, is much more partial and incomplete.[1] It may indeed be said that natural communities witness by their need of completion and fulfilment to that which lies beyond themselves,[2] namely the only real corporate personality which is Christ together with His mystical body. On this view, the difficulty of arriving at a satisfying definition of group personalities, considered as natural phenomena, is due to the fact that their personality is partial and not complete. It will become real and complete only when all persons and all natural

1. And, we might add, individual personalities are incomplete too, as we know them in this world. There is a sense in which we do not start life ready-made as persons, but throughout life have the opportunity of becoming persons. (Cp. Smuts, *Holism and Evolution*,[2] pp. 303, 306f., 318.)

Individual persons may also, as we say, become impersonal, or they may become divided personalities. If then there are degrees in which individual or psychological personality is realised, it will not appear strange that the personality, which analogously we ascribe to groups, is also realised in many different degrees. See also W. R. Inge, *Christian Mysticism* (1899), pp. 30f.

2. In *The New State* (pp. 37f.) Miss Follett writes: "The like-mindedness which is now to be demanded of us is the like-mindedness which is brought about by the enlargement of each by the inflowing of every other one. Then I go forth a new creature. But to what do I go forth? Always to a new group, a new 'society'. There is no end to this process." But, according to Christian teaching, there is an end. As St Augustine said: "Ipsa est consummatio omnium operum nostrorum, dilectio. Ibi est finis: propter hoc currimus; ad ipsum currimus: cum venerimus ad eam requiescemus." *In Epistolam Joannis*, x. 4. Miss Follett, however, is a pragmatist.

communities are taken up into Christ at the consummation of the kingdom of God—when "the kingdom of the world is become the kingdom of our Lord, and of his Christ".[1] Because they have now in varying degrees this partial or provisional personality, and the promise of being taken up into the real and complete corporate personality of Christ, we cannot be content either with an atomistic theory of the nature of societies or with a merely fictitious or legal theory of group personality. By the design of God, by His redeeming acts in Christ, and by the outpouring of the Holy Spirit, men on earth and natural communities[2] are already bound to one another more intimately than such theories acknowledge, and in the end they will be one even as the Father and the Son are one.

IV

As soon however as we have said so much on the side not only of the reality of group personality but of a high doctrine of the State, we must at once go on to make some further qualifications. Such a doctrine can be safely entertained by sinful men with their proneness to abuse all power and to distort all truth, only if it is being constantly checked and kept in its place by complementary doctrines, only if it is a doctrine of *moral* personality, and in particular only if a high doctrine of the State is balanced by and held together with a high doctrine of the family and of the Church.

At present the British people are liable to be more sensible of the dangers than of the truth in a high doctrine of the State. Because we see to what results the development of an amoral form of the doctrine has led in Germany and in other totalitarian States, it is tempting to deny it flatly and without discrimination. In the case of Germany, however, we must remark that the doctrine of

1. Rev. xi. 15. For the sense in which Christ is the Head of all men, see St Thomas Aquinas, *Summa Theol. III.* viii. 3. Cp. E. Brunner, *The Divine Imperative* (English translation, 1937), p. 300: "The 'Church' is . . . rather the Divine created order of community restored by Jesus Christ in His Atonement, and it is the community of the Redeemed, directed towards the perfecting of Creation. The *communio sanctorum*, the ἐκκλησία of the κλητοί is *the only true community*."

2. Cp. K. Hartenstein on "The Biblical View of Religion" in *The Tambaram Madras Series* (1939), i. 136.

real personality in the State came in practice to be applied exclusively to the State (which was never the intention of Gierke), and that its working out there might have been very different (*a*) if it had been moralised in Gladstone's sense, (*b*) if it had been applied to groups within the State as well as to the State itself, and above all (*c*) if the Church in Germany[1] had in the modern period been aware of, and had borne effective witness to, the significance of the doctrine both for its own life and for all forms of human association.

As it is, we may well see in Nazi Germany a horrible manifestation of the exclusive application of a debased form of the doctrine to the State or Race or *Volk*. We see, then, how, when the group personality of the State is made exclusive, absolute and amoral (or supermoral),[2] it issues in an idolatry which absorbs into itself the personality of both individuals and of all groups within the State (and outside it as well, if it can).[3] A particular consequence

1. We may not flatter ourselves that the Church of England in similar circumstances would be sure to bear a more definite witness. "How often", said the late Bishop of Norwich (Dr Pollock) with complacency, "in political and public life does a defeated party work good-humouredly to make the best of a situation created by legislation that it opposed! So might it well be with the Church. It is un-English to refuse to go on trying after a disappointing surprise."—Evidence before the Archbishops' Commission on the relations between Church and State, 1935: *Church and State*, ii. 167.

2. In *SRC*, ii. 358 Gladstone asked "whether, by taking out of public institutions their sanctifying principle, you do not give them over to become the depositories and manifestations in a collective and, as it were, authoritative and ultimate form, of that selfishness and self-worship, wherein consists our apostacy from God, and in the completion of which is accordingly contained the consummation of that apostacy".

"Nothing tends more", writes E. Brunner, "to conceal God from man than the State, for it is always able to invest itself with a peculiar glory, almost numinous in character. That is: the State transforms its undoubted relative right—as an order given by God, and as a particular form of human life willed by God—into an absolute."—*The Divine Imperative*, p. 617. "Material power makes the State terrible; religious power makes it horrible. . . . It is therefore no accident that in the New Testament the State is described quite as often under the figure of the Dragon (Satan), as by the title of an authority, ordained by God." *Ibid.*, p. 448. The last statement is, however, misleading.

3. One instance will suffice, viz. the oath taken by all German teachers under the Nazi régime: "Adolf Hitler. We swear that we will so train the youth of Germany that they grow up in your ideology, for your aims and purposes, in the direction set by your will. This is pledged to you by the whole German system of education, from the primary school through to the university."—*Sunday Times*, February 23, 1941.

is that moral responsibility then comes to be transferred from individuals to the State as a transcendent being,[1] and, where there is no consciousness or reminder of the State's being subject to an objective moral law above itself—namely, the commandments of God—the sense of moral responsibility, not only in individuals and groups within the State, but in the State itself, is dulled or evaporates altogether.

Nevertheless, this in no way justifies us in reacting to this idolatry by a complacent reaffirmation of that atomistic individualism which has been the fashionable or latent assumption of our own politics. It is quite true that individual persons have direct, intrinsic and inalienable rights and duties in virtue of their creation by God and of their redemption by Christ, and also that on occasion the individual person may have to assert his rights of conscience against any and every earthly society—the Church as well as the State. But we must never forget that societies, especially the family and the State, have been ordained by God for the being and well-being of men, and that individual persons cannot even exist except in society and can fulfil their destiny only in society.

Societies in this world, because they are always societies of sinful men, are always prone to be corrupted and to turn into their opposite, *i.e.* into a depersonalised mass; it is then that the individual person has to set himself against society, or, when it is the case of one form of society, *e.g.* the State, threatening to deprive all other forms as well as individuals of their rights to existence and to growth, these other forms are entitled, and indeed bound, to assert themselves by every possible means. For this reason we need to have a clear doctrine of the respective functions and obligations of the various types of human society according to God's order, and we see why they ought all, so far as is possible, to be humbled and consecrated by religion, as Gladstone taught. This is especially important in the case of the State, since by definition it is in the temporal order superior over all other societies and

1. Cp. Barker, p. lxxv; but when he says (p. lxxxv): "If we make groups real persons, we shall make the national State a real person. If we make the State a real person, with a real will, we make it indeed a Leviathan. . . . When its will collides with other wills, it may claim that, being the greatest, it must and shall carry the day, etc.", he leaves out of account the belief that the Church as a group-person, and the greatest of group-persons, stands over against the State to check its monistic pretensions. See p. 65, n. 4 *supra*.

wields the weapons of life and death, and is for that very reason most tempted to turn itself into an idol. It is regrettable that writers such as Figgis and Forsyth, who had a more realistic understanding of the things which were coming to pass on the earth than most British Christians in their time, were too exclusively interested in the corporate personality of the Church and so failed to develop a corresponding doctrine of the State.

Gladstone, on the other hand, who also had, as we shall see in the next chapter, a definite doctrine of the Church, meets this deficiency with his carefully worked-out doctrine of the moral personality of the State. Was he not right in saying that the State is by its nature and by the ordinance of God most truly regarded as a moral person which has, in addition to the function of preserving the being or bodily goods of a nation, the moral and spiritual function of preserving and fostering its *well*-being?

After all, the question here is what analogous concept throws most light on the real nature of the State, since the State, as a people contemplated "wholly and singly in respect of their partnership in the national life and order, not as individuals", is, like the family too, a form of human association that is *sui generis*. If by "real nature" we mean the true idea of the State according to the purpose of God, as distinguished from the actual character of any particular existing State, Gladstone's answer that the State is most truly regarded as a moral person is justified, provided we bear in mind that the concept of personality is in this case analogous to, and not univocal with, that of individual personality. In particular, personality in the State is analogous to personality in the individual human being, if both are subject to moral obligation, including the obligation to acknowledge truth.

V

If then we speak of the State as a moral person, we shall do so only with the qualifications and hesitations that have been indicated. The obligation of the State to concern itself with the moral and spiritual welfare of the whole people, and therefore with theological truth, is the corollary of its function to serve the well-being of the nation. But according to the *laissez-faire* theory of the State, it is subject to no such obligation. Its task is more like that of a policeman, than of a father or schoolmaster.

In moral and spiritual affairs, it fulfils its function if it secures the most extensive liberty that is compatible with the maintenance of its own existence and coherence.[1] On this view, the State has no direct concern with the ultimate truth of ethical or theological doctrines; its only concern is with their civic usefulness or danger, if any. Apart from that, the people should be left to believe what they like, without guidance or direction, and no problem arises from the toleration and even support by the State of any number of different and inconsistent religious institutions which maintain contradictory doctrines. Political unity in no way depends on religious unity. "During the nineteenth century", writes Mr Christopher Dawson, "in the heyday of economic expansion and bourgeois prosperity, it seemed as though the world could get along very well if everybody looked after their own interests and agreed to differ on everything else."[2]

1. *E.g.* John Stuart Mill, *On Liberty* (1859):

"The only freedom which deserves the name, is that of pursuing our own good in our own way, so long as we do not attempt to deprive others of theirs, or impede their efforts to obtain it. Each is the proper guardian of his own health, whether bodily, or mental, or spiritual. Mankind are greater gainers by suffering each other to live as seems good to themselves, than by compelling each to live as seems good to the rest" (p. 27).

"I believe that other ethics than any which can be evolved from exclusively Christian sources, must exist side by side with Christian ethics to produce the moral regeneration of mankind; and that the Christian system is no exception to the rule, that in an imperfect state of the human mind, the interests of truth require a diversity of opinions" (p. 92).

"The liberty of the individual must be thus far limited; he must not make himself a nuisance to other people" (p. 101).

Cp. p. 88, n. 2 *infra*. At a time, however, when there is a growing tendency to depreciate everything that goes under the name of "liberalism", the many just observations in Mill's book call for acknowledgement, and deserve attention. He saw in some respects the trend to totalitarianism and its dangers. Moreover, he was at least more consistent than his descendants in that he objected to a State system of education, as distinguished from the enforcement of education by the State, *i.e.* in independently controlled schools. "The objections which are urged with reason against State education, do not apply to the enforcement of education by the State, but to the State's taking upon itself to direct that education; which is a totally different thing. That the whole or any large part of the education of the people should be in State hands, I go as far as any one in deprecating" (*ibid.*, p. 190).

"All attempts by the State to bias the conclusions of its citizens on disputed subjects, are evil; but it may very properly offer to ascertain and certify that a person possesses the knowledge, requisite to make his conclusions, on any given subject, worth attending to" (p. 193).

2. *Dublin Review* (April, 1942), p. 113.

The practical implications of this did not become clear in this country for a long time, because there was—indeed there still is—a protracted hang-over from the past of a diffused and diluted Christianity in the State, so that a condition of moral and spiritual chaos did not immediately appear. Is it not beginning to appear now? It may be that, as has been said, the English have an unrivalled capacity for diluting their Christianity; but there is a term to this process.

Thus, in the peculiar circumstances of the age of liberalism, the idea gained ground that it is not needful for political health, still less is it ordained by God, that members of a national society should share a common religious faith and be members of one Church. We find, for example, Dr William Temple writing in 1928:

> For a long time it was supposed that religious diversity must be incompatible with political unity. It has long ago become clear that, if this was ever true, it is true no longer. The State is, no doubt, perfectly at liberty to say to a Church what are the conditions on which the relations of Church and State called Establishment may exist or continue; but it exceeds its proper province if it uses the machinery of establishment to impose or to prohibit any forms of worship.[1]

1. *Christianity and the State*, p. 125. In the same book Dr Temple wrote: "It is only in the writings of some philosophers and the semi-conscious theories of ordinary citizens that the State has preserved its universal sovereignty. . . . This theory of omni-competence has so far outlived any correspondence with the actual facts that it is become partly ludicrous and partly perilous": p. 118, cp. p. 171. It would be rash to infer from Dr Temple's subsequent writings and pronouncements that he substantially modified his political liberalism. The confidence with which he declared his opinions in 1928 did, however, later show signs of disturbance; *e.g.* see *Citizen and Churchman* (1941), chap. ii. A statement of his that "the Church as such ought not to be interested in the question of establishment one way or the other" has been criticised by Canon Charles Smyth in *Religion and Politics* (1943), pp. 12, 16f.

For earlier statements about the alleged change in the relation between political and religious unity, see Mandell Creighton, *The Church and the Nation* (1901), p. 33: "There was a time in England when the State decided that national unity was only possible on the basis of religious uniformity. The State failed to secure uniformity, but discovered that outward uniformity was no longer necessary for political security, and consequently withdrew from the

With this we should contrast what Gladstone wrote in *The State in its relations with the Church*, before he himself came to terms with the liberal assumption:

> According to the principles which have been laid down in this volume, it is evident that unity of religion is a condition of the highest practicable well-being of the State; that it is an object which the State should endeavour to realise; that when its absolute form can no longer be retained, the nearest approximations to it should be embraced; that in the ordinary course of things, so long as the principle of civil support to religion is recognised, both the State will be coloured by the religion of the people, and the people will tend to conform to the religion of the State (i. 277f.).
>
> The last and greatest maxim of practical conduct, which the theory of connection between Church and State inculcates upon the individual, is, the personal avoidance of all that leads to religious divisions. We cannot but see how they tend to every social evil, and how they are faithful to the source from which they arise; what dilemmas defying solution they are intrinsically calculated to produce; how they draw law into disrepute and dishonour, and either at once shake social order to its centre and its base, or, by robbing the State successively of all the conditions of a true national life, carry political organisation and the nature of a State out of the place which God appointed them into one for which He appointed them not (i. 341f.).

What, according to Dr Temple in 1928, had long ago become clear, is not so clear to-day. For States, which had acted upon the *laissez-faire* assumption, declined to concern themselves with theological truth, and disregarded its importance, have swung round and have begun to use all their resources for the inculcation of what Christians must regard as theological falsehood. Even in such a stronghold of political liberalism as Britain the demand for

attempt to secure it." But in what follows Creighton does not go so far as Temple.

Also, J. N. Figgis, *From Gerson to Grotius* (1907), p. 19: "The notion that uniformity in religion is necessary to political stability was disproved by facts, and then became discredited in theory." On p. 116 Figgis describes the attitude of the *Politiques*: "Religious uniformity is a blessing; it is of the *bene esse* of a State. But it is not of the *esse* and, in case of need, we can live without it."

What is in question, however, is not "uniformity" but "unity".

a positive national faith begins to be voiced, and the change of attitude is reflected in the agitation for a religious education in the State schools. The *laissez-faire* assumption that the State may accommodate all doctrines and need not itself make profession of any is inevitably being called in question. Was it too readily embraced, or acquiesced in, by Christians? Is political well-being, and political unity, compatible in the long run with every degree of religious diversity? Is this in the end only a polite name for religious chaos, moral relativism and even nihilism, and the disintegration of community?

History does not allow this question to be answered with a simple affirmative or negative. There is more than one kind of religion, as well as more than one kind of State. There are, on the one hand, religions of special revelation which make an exclusive, universal and total claim upon the allegiance of all men, and which therefore cannot contentedly cohabit with a State which acknowledges or treats the rival claims of other religions as equally valid. A religion of special revelation is always likely to be a source of disturbance in a State where its claim to truth and authority is not recognised. Its aim will always be not necessarily identification with, or complete control of, but at least a monogamous union[1] with, the State.

On the other hand, there are religions of discovery, of temperament and of taste, which are capable of syncretism and have no objection of principle to polygamous relations with one another and with States. The claims of religions of this kind are departmental and can easily be compounded with other claims. They cater for the emotions or the speculative intellect, and do not impose a sovereign and total demand upon the will either of the individual or of the society. Apart from the actual rites or mysteries or phantasies which they provide, and the social customs connected with them, they leave their votaries free to do more or less what they like. They will not necessarily be a source of disturbance in one State. Indeed, a State may tolerate and even welcome many religions of this kind, witness the Roman Empire. But it should also be remarked that, in addition to the countenance it gave to manifold religions of this kind, Rome found it needful for the preservation of political unity and the stability of the

1. On this matrimonial analogy, see p. 94, n.2 *infra*.

Empire to have an official cult of its own which everyone was bound to observe. Difficulties arose only with religions of special revelation—Judaism and Christianity, which refused to fit into the general scheme, and especially with the latter because of its manifest universalism.

How then did it come about that in the age of liberalism different Christian Churches, each of which purported to be the bearer of divine revelation, and which in theory regarded one another as heretical or at least as in sufficiently grievous error to require their separation from one another, not only became apparently content to exist permanently side by side in the same State, but were also content that non-Christian religions should be equally countenanced? Even the Church of Rome, which was most intransigent in this respect,[1] eventually came to accept the Liberal State as a legitimate hypothesis,[2] *i.e.* Roman

1. Among the "principal errors of our time" condemned by Pius IX in 1864 were the following: "55. Ecclesia a statu statusque ab Ecclesia seiungendus est . . . 77. Aetate hac nostra non amplius expedit, religionem catholicam haberi tanquam unicam status religionem, ceteris quibuscunque cultibus exclusis. 78. Hinc laudabiliter in quibusdam catholici nominis regionibus lege cautum est, ut hominibus illuc immigrantibus liceat publicum proprii cuiusque cultus exercitium habere. 79. Enimvero falsum est, civilem cuiusque cultus libertatem itemque plenam potestatem omnibus attributam quaslibet opiniones cogitationesque palam publiceque manifestandi conducere ad populorum mores animosque facilius corrumpendos ac indifferentismi pestem propagandam. 80. Romanus Pontifex potest ac debet cum progressu, cum liberalismo et cum recenti civilitate sese reconciliare et componere."—H. Denzinger, *Enchiridion Symbolorum* [11] (1911), pp. 470–3.

2. Leo XIII, in his Encyclical *Immortale Dei* (November 1, 1885), said: "Insuper neque caussa iusta nascitur, cur Ecclesiam quisquam criminetur, aut esse in lentitate facilitateque plus aequo restrictam, aut ei, quae germana et legitima sit, libertati inimicam. Revera si divini cultus varia genera eodem iure esse, quo veram religionem, Ecclesia iudicat non licere, non ideo tamen eos damnat rerum publicarum moderatores, qui, magni alicuius aut adipscendi boni, aut prohibendi caussa mali, moribus atque usu patienter ferunt, ut ea habeant singula in civitatem locum. Atque illud quoque magnopere cavere Ecclesia solet ut ad amplexandam fidem catholicam nemo invitus cogatur, quia, quod sapienter Augustinus monet, *credere non potest homo nisi volens*."—*Leonis Papae XIII Allocutiones, etc.* (1887), ii. 162. (The quotation from St Augustine is somewhat disingenuous in view of his final and singularly influential teaching about persecution!)

See also F. R. Hoare, *The Papacy and the Modern State* (1940), pp. 205, 220, 268; and R. W. Church, in *The Christian Remembrancer* (April, 1850), pp. 511ff.

Catholics were permitted to work it, while formally reserving their adherence to the thesis that the State ought to be Catholic.[1]

It may be suggested that the acceptance of this state of affairs by the Christian Churches was due to the following causes: (1) to reaction against the obvious failure in the seventeenth and eighteenth centuries to secure religious unity by persecution and the penalisation of dissenters (cp. p. 14 *supra*), and to a recognition that, whatever may be right, that must be wrong; (2) to the intoxicating effects of the great Liberal experiment which, whether in its French, British or American form, the Christians supposed had come to stay; (3) to the lowering effects of a secularised civilisation upon the spiritual vitality of the Churches; and (4) to the facts that some of the "Churches" had never been conscious of an obligation to become more than a sect ("a gathered church") within the State, and that in all of them the consciousness of bearing an ultimate and universally authoritative revelation had been gravely impaired by the difficulty of coming to terms with fresh knowledge and by accommodation to evolutionary and relativistic ideas. They had all become since the Renaissance, the Reformation and the Counter-Reformation increasingly departmentalised or sectarianised, so that, provided their members were free to engage in specifically religious activities, such as association for public worship, they had no urgent interest in, or influence upon,

1. *E.g.* see Theodore Maynard, *Apostle of Charity: the life of St Vincent de Paul* (1940), p. 231: "The cooperation of the civil and ecclesiastical functions, and the establishment of the Church, is still—at least officially—the Catholic ideal. But it must be admitted to be one which is perhaps impossible of attainment except under exceptional conditions and (such is the tendency of all things human to corruption) only for short periods of time."

See also A. J. Toynbee, *A Study of History* (1939), iv. 219; and *The Tablet* (September 30, 1944), p. 158.

Gladstone in *CP* (pp. 367–370) calls attention to some striking inconsistencies in the Roman Catholic attitude to this question.

H. E. Manning, in *The Vatican Decrees in their bearing on Civil Allegiance* (1875), wrote: "It is a silver age in which we can peacefully accept what we cannot either justify as the will of God, or extol as the normal state of the Christian world. In our shattered state of religious belief and worship there is no way of solid civil peace, but in leaving all men free in their amplest liberty of faith" (p. 136).

Cp. article on "Toleration, Religious" in the *Catholic Encyclopædia*, xiv. 763–773.

the conditions or conduct of society as a whole—and the State loved to have it so.[1]

The Liberal State, when it turns into an authoritarian State, has been comparatively little inhibited by the Churches, since they had lost or surrendered their spiritual power by restricting the range of their interests and limiting their witness. Only a religion of revelation and a Church that knows itself to be an agency of universal truth and ultimate authority can be a match for the powerful State which is sovereign in its own sphere. Only a Church, which is conscious of bearing an intrinsic and transcendent authority from God, is fitted to confront the temporal sovereignty of the State. Such a Church would teach a high doctrine of the State as well as of the Church and would bear a constant witness to the tasks assigned by God to Church and State respectively.[2]

1. "The axiom of all modern statesmanship, more and more plainly avowed, is this, that nations, as nations, have nothing to do with God: that religion is the affair of the individual solely and exclusively, and one in which the State, has, or ought to have, no concern whatever; that the Church—like any other voluntary association of individuals—is to be protected so long as it is peaceable, and sternly repressed whenever it grows in any way troublesome. But the idea that Church and Nation are each a divine institution—powers, both of them, 'ordained by God', having each their ground in real relations to God and to each other, having therefore duties to each other, which they may not neglect without peril and without sin,—this is scouted as the merest folly . . .

"Statesmen are questioning whether the State, as they think it ought to be, can continue its union with the Church as it is. Churchmen are questioning how long the Church, as they think it ought to be, can continue its union with the State, as it is likely to be; how long the unbelieving husband may be sanctified by the believing wife, and at what point the infidelity or the cruelty of the husband may compel the wife to accept, nay even to seek, her putting away . . ."—W. C. Magee, Sermon on "The Breaking Net", preached before the Dublin Church Congress, 1868, and published in *The Gospel and the Age* (1884), pp. 195ff. But this has not been the usual language of the Church, except when its traditional privileges were menaced, as they were in 1868.

"The business of the State has been *secularised*, together with the arts and sciences. To religion has been assigned the province of subjective motivation, purity of soul, and the destiny beyond. The State 'tolerates' religions of all sorts on condition that religion lets politics severely alone.

"In our country (U.S.A.) we have been especially enamoured of this view; yet it is a view which everywhere to-day shows its untenableness."—W. E. Hocking, *Man and the State* (1926), p. 422.

2. "We should be 'high-State' as well as 'high-Church'. The State is God's as well as the Church—though the latter is the more sacred, as having been purchased by the sacrifice of Christ—and the rights of the State are to be

It is not good for man to be in a position where he imagines he can exercise unrestricted lordship. The position of rulers in the social structure should be such as to curb this imagination. Civil rulers need to be made aware that, however powerful in their own sphere, they are men under spiritual authority, and this is expressed by the subordinate place they occupy in the Church and by the fact that they are subject to spiritual censure and to the penalty of excommunication. Likewise, ecclesiastical rulers need to recognise that, however august the authority they represent, they are subject to the civil power like any other citizen. Only a high doctrine of both Church and State will secure conditions in which those who wield authority in one sphere have to acknowledge their submission to it in another; the social structure should express the truth that all men, especially great men, are men under authority, and authority which is under the ordinance of God.

If then we recover a high doctrine of the State, we shall also need to recover a high doctrine of the Church. The question, however, is not only one of need, but, as Gladstone saw, of truth. We must now, therefore, as he did, turn to consider the nature of the Church. Then we shall be in a position to see that the Christian faith not only implies a high doctrine of the State, assigning to it a noble function in God's purpose, but also checks the State's propensity to proud pretensions by knitting it to another society which is charged with the declaration of God's Word and with a moral authority which transcends that of the State, though it is denied the State's use of coercive power. We may have to abandon the Liberal formula "A free Church in a free State" as specifying the ideal or norm for the relations of Church and State, and, if a formula is to meet the case at all, substitute for it Forsyth's pregnant phrase "A free State in a free Church."[1]

respected in any claim by the Church."—P. Carnegie Simpson, Evidence before the Archbishops' Commission on the relations between Church and State, 1935, *Church and State*, ii. 190.

1. *Theology in Church and State* (1915), pp. viii, 177; contrast what Forsyth had written sixteen years earlier in *Rome, Reform and Reaction* (1899), pp. 24, 31.

Mr B. L. Manning, in his evidence before the Archbishops' Commission, to which reference is made in the preceding note, said: "Free Churchmen to-day (whatever they may or may not have done in the past) do not imagine that the problem of establishment is a perfectly simple one, to be settled by some phrase like 'a Free Church in a Free State'."—*Church and State* (1935), ii. 80.

CHAPTER FIVE

THE VISIBLE CHURCH

A normative theory of the relations between the State and the Church depends on what are held to be the nature of the State and the nature of the Church respectively. Gladstone was quite aware of this, and he followed up his book on *The State in its relations with the Church*, in which he had been primarily concerned with the nature of the State, with a book on the doctrine of the Church and on the specific claims and present circumstances of the Church of England.

I

Church Principles considered in their results was published in 1840, *i.e.* two years after the first edition of its predecessor. It is a volume of 562 pages. Morley says that "it was stillborn".[1] Macaulay did not review it, although he considered the question of doing so. On October 14, 1840, he wrote to Napier:

> Gladstone advertises another book about the Church. That subject belongs to me, if I think it worth treating, particularly as he will probably say something concerning my former article.[2]

But on November 13 he wrote again :

> Yesterday evening I received Gladstone's book, and read it. I do not think it would be wise to review it. I observed in it very little that had any reference to politics, and very little indeed that might not be consistently said by a supporter of the Voluntary system. It is, in truth, a theological treatise; and I have no mind to engage in a controversy about the nature of

1. Morley, i. 181. We might compare the reception that was accorded to W. Palmer's *A Treatise on the Church of Christ*, a more comprehensive book than Gladstone's, and one that he valued very highly (cp. p. 27, n. 1 *supra*). See what R. W. Church says about the coldness of its reception in *The Oxford Movement*,[3] pp. 215f. Palmer's book, however, went into three editions within four years.

H. L. Goudge, in *The Church of England and Reunion* (1938), sai d: "Gladstone' *Church Principles* . . . is an old book, and written in an idiom different from our own; but it is a book of abiding value, which ought not to be so much forgotten" (p. 197).

2. *Correspondence of Macvey Napier*, p. 330.

the sacraments, the operation of holy orders, the visibility of the Church, and such points of learning; except when they are connected, as in his former work they were connected, with questions of government. I have no disposition to split hairs about the spiritual reception of the body and blood of Christ, or about baptismal regeneration.[1]

Macaulay was not wrong in describing the book as a theological treatise, although the author modestly professed not to be writing as a theologian,[2] and only by implication is it connected with questions of government. Morley accounts for its failure to attract interest by saying that "the public are never very willing to listen to a political layman discussing the arcana of theology".

1. Trevelyan, *op. cit.*, ii. 79. Macaulay's remarks again have a characteristically Whig, not to say English, ring; cp. pp. 49ff. *supra.* Gladstone, in his copy of Trevelyan's book (*SDL*), put a mark against the sentence about the Voluntary system, as though in retrospect it seemed to him a just observation, or at least a significant one. Although, however, when he became a Liberal statesman Gladstone was prepared to deal with the Anglican, as with other, Churches as though they were voluntary societies, yet as a churchman he never adopted the "voluntary" view of the Church (cp. p. 93 *infra*). In his *Remarks on the Royal Supremacy* (1850) he defined the two positions, leaving no doubt which was his own:

> They who view the Church as a voluntary association of men for the purposes of what they think to be the Christian religion, may well, for the sake of peace, be minded, under supposable circumstances, to quit it, and to form another such voluntary association, as they would take a new house, or choose a new coat when they might think fit so to do.
>
> But they who regard a given body, called the Establishment, as being likewise the Church, and as therefore charged with the care and nurture of their souls, cannot go out of her, until she denies the Faith, and ceases to be the Church, so that they must seek the Church elsewhere (p. 78).

Cp. *Vaticanism* (1875):

> Attached to my own religious communion, the Church of my birth and my country, I have never loved it with a merely sectional or insular attachment, but have thankfully regarded it as that portion of the great redeemed Christian family in which my lot had been cast—not by, but for me (p. 113).

On the abuse of the term "Voluntaryism", see *SRC*, i. 210f.

2. He was not, that is, writing as a professional expositor of Scriptural or Catholic dogma. He intended, as a layman, to examine the specific and particular bearings of (Church) principles "upon the religious interests and feelings of the day in our own country"; see *CP*, pp. 30ff. *CP* was not a theological treatise in the same sense as Palmer's *Treatise on the Church of Christ*, which, as its title-page says, was "designed chiefly for the use of students in theology".

For Döllinger's opinion of Gladstone as in the front rank of English theologians, see M. MacColl in *op. cit.*, p. 245.

They were, however, willing enough fifty years or so later to read A. J. Balfour's *The Foundations of Belief.*[1] Admittedly, the style of Balfour's book was more engaging, but this alone does not account for the difference in its reception. Balfour was manifestly discussing what the reading public of the time recognised as the foundations of belief; it was the noon-day of naturalism, and here was a brilliant attack upon the creed that was most fashionable in "advanced" circles and also that was most formidable to Christian believers.

Gladstone's book too had to do with the foundations of belief, and its subject-matter was closely connected with the Tractarian controversy that was raging at the time of its publication. But the public was interested more in the superficial than in the fundamental aspects of that controversy. Gladstone was concerned with the latter. He did not identify himself with the Tractarian party, although he was friendly and sympathetic with the Tractarians. His theological approach was independent,[2] so that his book made no strong appeal to the partisans on the one side or the other.[3]

His relation to the controversies of the period somewhat resembles that of F. D. Maurice,[4] and his theological teaching

1. For an account of the reception accorded to this book, see a revised review of it by H. C. L. Heywood in *Theology* (February, 1941), p. 107.

2. See, *e.g.*, *CP*, pp. 320f., 514; *CCR*, i. 263ff., ii. 293f.; Morley, i. 161f. On February 9, 1842, Newman wrote to J. R. Hope with reference to Gladstone's attitude to the Jerusalem Bishopric: "Everyone must admire a man like Gladstone, in spite of his Tylerizing."—*Correspondence of J. H. Newman with J. Keble and Others*, 1839–1845, p. 185. For the meaning of "Tylerize", see *N.E.D. ad loc.* It means at least that Gladstone was not a good party man.

3. Newman said of it in a letter to J. W. Boden: "Gladstone's book is not open to the objections I feared; it is doctrinaire, and (*I* think) somewhat self-confident; but it will do good."—Anne Mozley, *Letters and Correspondence of John Henry Newman* (1891), ii. 321f.

D. C. Lathbury apparently thought the book of no importance, for he does not refer to it in *CCR*.

4. On Gladstone and Maurice, see p. 31, n. 1 *supra*. Maurice's opinion of *CP* is given in a letter to Archdeacon Hare (December 28, 1840): "I agree with you as to the ponderousness of Gladstone's style. But is it not very much improved since his last volume? It struck me that it had become really grave and laden with earnest thoughts; not as before, oppressed with the phrases and notions of the House of Commons and the Debating Society. His Aristotelianism is, however, it strikes me, more deeply fixed in him than before . . ."—

may be more readily appreciated at its real value now than it was a century ago. But whereas Maurice's teaching has already been to some extent unearthed and advertised,[1] Gladstone's has yet to be.

As in the former case, I do not intend to give here a complete account of Gladstone's argument in *Church Principles*, though it seldom dates in the way that a considerable part of *The State in its relations with the Church* does. My purpose is to dwell on three points that are specially relevant to the present study: (1) the relation between revelation and reason; (2) the doctrine of the nature of the Church; and (3) the predicament that arises from Christian disunity.

Life of Maurice,[2] i. 302. (Keble also remarked on Gladstone's Aristotelianism in his review of *SRC*; see reprint (1869) with preface by Liddon, p. 11.)

Gladstone's analytical, logical cast of mind was naturally unattractive and uncongenial to Maurice, and *vice versa*. On April 11, 1884, after reading the *Life of Maurice*,[1] Gladstone wrote to Mr Macmillan: "The picture of him as a Christian soul is one of the most touching, searching, and complete that I have ever seen in print. He is indeed a spiritual splendour, to borrow the phrase of Dante about St Dominic.

"His intellectual constitution had long been, and still is, to me a good deal of an enigma. When I remember what is said and thought of him, and by whom, I feel this must be greatly my own fault".—See *Life of Maurice*,[2] ii. 207f. Mary Gladstone's entry in her diary for April 1, 1884, may also be noted: "The P.M. in such form at dinner . . . talking of Maurice, whom spiritually he still intensely admires but intellectually almost despises."—*Diaries and Letters* (1930), p. 311.

The differences in their mental make-up or ways of thinking maybe prevented them both from realising how near they were to one another theologically and ecclesiastically. For their relations, see also *Life of Maurice*,[2] i. 108f., 436–43. For Gladstone on Maurice's criticisms of Bishop Butler, see his *Studies subsidiary to the Works of Bishop Butler* (1896), pp. 73f.

1. See W. E. Collins on "Frederick Denison Maurice" in *Typical English Churchmen from Parker to Maurice* (1902), pp. 327–360; H. G. Mulliner on "John Frederick Denison Maurice" in *The Modern Churchman* (October, 1927), pp. 474–80; C. E. Raven on "A Fore-runner" in *The Modern Churchman* (January, 1929), pp. 582–6; Charles Gardner on "Frederick Denison Maurice, 1805–1872" in *The Hibbert Journal* (January, 1930), pp. 311–19; W. Moore Ede on "What we Owe to Frederick Denison Maurice and his Disciples" in *The Modern Churchman* (December, 1933), pp. 527–34; H. Hodkin on "The Theological Teaching of F. D. Maurice" in *Theology* (February, 1937), pp. 97–107; C. Jenkins, *Frederick Denison Maurice and the New Reformation* (1938); A. M. Ramsey, *The Gospel and the Catholic Church* (1936), pp. 210–16; W. L. Knox and A. R. Vidler, *The Development of Modern Catholicism* (1933), pp. 47–56. Also the histories of the Christian Socialist movement.

II

Christianity, according to Gladstone, is a religion of revelation, in the sense that it

> is, in its first, highest, and most essential character, *a religion of influences which transcend, though they do not oppose, the understanding* (*CP*, p. 36; italics his).

On the other hand,

> rationalism is commonly, at least in this country, taken to be the reduction of Christian *doctrine* to the standard and measure of the human understanding (p. 37).

Natural reason, or the human understanding in its natural or unregenerate state, is not competent to determine what is revealed truth.

> The understanding . . . was appointed by God to conduct a sound machine, but not to reconstitute a deranged one. It is the very substance and brunt of the charge against the actual human nature, that truth has lost its power over the understanding in a practical and moral sense; that is, its absolute and plenary, above all its *impelling* power (p. 42).

This is to say that man is a fallen being, and that as a result of the Fall he is not only *spoliatus gratuitis* but also *vulneratus in naturalibus*. Owing to original sin man's natural powers, including his reasoning faculty, are deranged.

> This faculty is now subject to a distracting bias, which counteracts by an opposite force the force of truth, and blindfolds the understanding by the fumes which passion can, and habitually does, emit (p. 43).[1]

In order that man shall be able to reason and conclude aright upon the divine revelation given in the Gospel, it is necessary for his whole nature to be restored by grace, and in particular

> spiritual influence upon the heart is necessary to furnish the understanding with those primary perceptions by which we become adequately cognisant of spiritual objects, and capable of exercising that faculty with profit upon the Christian doctrines at large (p. 73).

It is not enough then to teach men religion in the abstract; the Gospel must also be presented to their affections and imaginations

1. Cp. *SRC*, ii. 138.

with winning power, which can come only through its concrete embodiment.[1]

By making these affirmations at the outset of an argument concerning the Church, Gladstone shows that he was aware how controversies about the nature of the Church and its relation to the world reach back to questions concerning the nature of man and God's scheme of salvation, and that these ulterior questions must be laid bare and answered before Church principles can be usefully discussed.

We observe too that the particular affirmations which Gladstone makes are such as had been obscured, if not denied, not only in post-Reformation scholasticism, but in latitudinarian, rationalistic or (as it came later and more loosely to be called) liberal theology.[2] Indeed, he may be said to have anticipated the renewed emphasis on the dependence of nature on grace and of reason on revelation, which in various forms and fields is becoming characteristic of theology, both Catholic and Protestant, in the twentieth century. He saw that divine revelation is not merely another name for the human discovery of religious truths, but is the total act of God in Christ, whereby the race has been redeemed and recreated. This act of God, mediated to every age by the operation of the Holy Ghost through the Scriptures and the Church, confronts man with the truth and enables him to apprehend and appropriate it. This act of God challenges man with

1. In *SRC* (ii. 367) Gladstone said: "Revealed religion derives its strength from its entireness; from the fact that it not merely presents to us a body of abstract truths, but carries with it the executory powers necessary to procure their acceptance, the vital influences without which we cannot receive, digest, and assimilate those truths." Cp. his *Remarks on the Royal Supremacy* (1850): "Truth itself, when not held as truth, but as a mere prize in the lottery of opinions, loses its virtue; that, namely, of uniting us to its fountain; since it is not by any mere abstractions, whether false or true, that we are to be healed, but by being placed in vital union, through the joint medium of His truth and His grace, with the Source of healing" (p. 82).

Canon Leonard Hodgson, in *The Doctrine of the Trinity* (1943), writes: "Preaching of the gospel addressed to the intellect has to be prepared for by influences affecting underlying levels of the self"; p. 210f.; cp. pp. 130, 138. (The "Gladstone" referred to on p. 125 of Hodgson's book in a quotation from E. S. Talbot was no doubt Herbert Gladstone. Hodgson has omitted the words "my friend" before "Gladstone" which Talbot used in the passage quoted.)

2. Cp. E. L. Mascall on "The Nature and Task of Theology" in *Theology* (February and March, 1941), pp. 71–80, 133–43.

the duty of decision and of self-commitment to an authority outside himself, which not only informs the mind, but grips the affections and heals the will.

This has important consequences not only, as we shall see in a moment, for the doctrine of the Church, but also for the Church's relation to the world. By the world is here meant human life organised without direct dependence on the grace of God.[1] In this sense the State, until it has been penetrated by the Church, is an expression or embodiment of the world. If the world were capable of saving itself by its own rational powers, religion would be a function of the State, and the Church a department of the State. But since that is not so, the State needs to be confronted by, and brought into relations with, the Church. Not only the individual man, but the State, as an organised society, needs to be met by the Church, which is the bearer of an authority outside itself, and brings into effective operation the witness of the Holy Spirit to God's judgment and mercy, and to the fact that the world has been regenerated in Christ—in other words, that the orb is under the cross, whether it knows it or not.

It was the assumption of the *laissez-faire* State that human society, left to its own resources, would work satisfactorily, if not perfectly. In particular, in regard to matters of religion, men should be left as free as possible to form their own opinions,[2] without public guidance or direction. The better educated they were, *i.e.* the more their capacity for reasoning was developed, the

1. Cp. F. D. Maurice's *Theological Essays* [3] (1871), p. 403: "The world contains the elements of which the Church is composed. In the Church, these elements are penetrated by a uniting, reconciling power. The Church is, therefore, human society in its normal state; the World, that same society irregular and abnormal. The world is the Church without God; the Church is the world restored to its relation with God, taken back by Him into the state for which He created it." Cp. Cocks, *By Faith Alone*, p. 179.

2. See, *e.g.*, *The Ultimate Principle of Religious Liberty* (1860), p. 24: "To do anything whatever, beyond such employment of civil power as may be necessary for insuring (and *this* by main force, if need be) to each member of the community such liberty and privilege in the exercise of his religious convictions and performance of his religious duties, as may be consistent with the enjoyment of the same privilege and protection by every other subject of the government, is an unjust use of governmental power."

Cp. Morley, *On Compromise* (1874), p. 156: "The great object is to keep the minds of the young as open as possible in the matter of religion."

See also p. 74, n. 1 *supra*.

more satisfactory the results would be. The State, therefore, ought not to lend its weight to any religious dogma or Church (except perhaps where or as long as this remained expedient in the interests of its own safety). Its object should be to secure for those of its members who may wish to hold or propagate any dogma that commends itself to them, such liberty of expression and association as is not subversive of political order and stability.[1]

Christian Liberals were, to say the least, inclined to accept this view. They supposed that Christian teaching had only to be submitted to reasonable men in a reasonable way and it would win their assent. If the evidence that this happened in fact was not yet conspicuous, the failure should not be ascribed to any fundamental defect in the supposition, but to the inadequate way in which it was so far being acted upon. Before many years passed, Gladstone himself was to go a considerable way, if not to countenance, at any rate to meet this position. In his *Letter on the Functions of Laymen in the Church* (1852), he wrote as follows:

> When I speak of a lover of religious freedom, I mean one who, desiring the full enjoyment of it for his own communion, is not willing only, but anxious, as he prizes the sacred principle of justice, to accord to all other religious bodies precisely the same measure, and to guard against all secular interference in their concerns, so long as they do not trespass upon the sphere of secular affairs. In this sense of religious freedom . . . its future progress is absolutely certain. . . . As with property, so with religious freedom: the rights of each man are the rights of his neighbour; he that defends one is the defender of all; and he that trespasses on one assails all.[2]

And a time was to come when Gladstone as a Liberal statesman, called upon to justify a Liberal measure (the disestablishment of the Church of Ireland), would use this argument with regard to the future of Ireland:

> Creeds will compete upon the level, and will thrive according to their merits . . . each man who has faith in freedom, faith in justice, faith in truth, anticipates a harvest of benefit for his own.[3]

1. Cp. J. J. Rousseau, *The Social Contract* (English translation, H. J. Tozer, 1895, p. 229): "Now that there is, and can be, no longer any exclusive national religion, we should tolerate all those which tolerate others, so far as their dogmas have nothing contrary to the duties of a citizen."
2. *Op. cit.*, pp. 13f.; reprinted in *Gleanings*, vol. vi.
3. *Gleanings*, vii. 125.

But at the time of *Church Principles* he would have detected in this position the error of rationalism. The question is open again [1] whether the earlier or later Gladstone, the Conservative theologian or the Liberal statesman, was right, or at least whether the enthusiasm of the latter did not too easily gloss over the insights of the former, and whether the truth does not lie somewhere between them. Liberalism asked for liberty for men to worship, to believe and practice, according to their own disposition, and not for recognition by the State of man's obligation to worship God according to His revelation. Such recognition, Gladstone had maintained, required recognition of the historic Church. (We shall have to inquire later whether he could have continued to maintain this, and at the same time have done justice to the case for "religious liberty": see the next chapter.) In *The State and its relations with the Church* he wrote:

> Revealed religion derives its strength from its entireness; from the fact that it not merely presents to us a body of abstract truths, but carries with it the executory powers to procure their acceptance, the vital influences without which we cannot receive, digest, and assimilate those truths. But when we reject the belief in those powers, when we bring down the Christian Church from "what is transcendental in her pretensions", when we analyse and dissect the body which God has given, and when, impiously dividing it into parts to be rejected or retained at pleasure, we further ridiculously suppose that each of those parts is to retain the vitality which belonged only to the aggregate, we are the victims of a wretched delusion, and the portion of truth, which we have torn from the quivering trunk, will but as a severed limb putrefy within our grasp (*SRC*, ii. 367f.).

III

As regards the nature of the Church, Gladstone postulates that the Redeemer of the world came to redeem the whole man in the

1. "The Liberal notion that religion was a matter of private belief and of conduct in private life, and that there is no reason why Christians should not be able to accommodate themselves to any world which treats them good-naturedly is becoming less and less tenable. This notion would seem to have become accepted gradually, as a false inference from the subdivision of English Christianity into sects, and the happy results of universal toleration. . . . In the modern world, it may turn out that the most intolerable thing for Christians is to be tolerated."—T. S. Eliot, *The Idea of a Christian Society* (1939), pp. 21ff.

full extent of his need—body as well as spirit, affections as well as understanding, man in society as well as the individual. The new principle of life which the Redeemer brought needed, therefore, to be externally and socially embodied.

> Religion contemplates and ordains the co-operation of individuals for a common end: not their unconscious, but their designed and deliberate co-operation in the government and extension of the kingdom of Christ, and the maintenance of His truth, a perpetual system of joint and organised action. But there can be no such co-operation on a permanent footing, and on an effective scale, except through the medium of some institution whereinto individuals are introduced by some known and palpable method, which, in order to be known and palpable, must have outward form: and wherein also they remain under common laws, which laws must have application to other than merely inward and mental acts: otherwise the reality of the bond of union could not be ascertained, nor any substantive result secured (*CP*, pp. 89f.).

Thus a scrutiny of the conditions of our nature as well as the range of the Christian revelation prepares us to recognise a visible Church as divinely founded. The Church is quite different from a sort of religious club or voluntary combination (p. 99). And "the very phrase 'invisible Church', when it is applied to the Church militant here on earth, presents a contradiction in terms" (p. 112). The Church is in truth, as Holy Scripture teaches, the body of Christ, the organ of His redeeming action in the world; it is one and it is visible.[1] Scripture, he says, has met in advance the objection that a Church composed of faithful and unfaithful members cannot be entitled to the prerogatives of the body of Christ. Evidently, there is a paradox here, but it is no less striking in the case of the individual Christian than in the case of the Church.

> If the contrast be wide between the high privileges and destinies of the Church on the one hand, and that inward state where evil continually contends for and at times seems well nigh

1. Cp. what Gladstone's friend, Samuel Wilberforce, wrote about this time (September 9, 1841) in a letter: "The *visible* has been far too much given up by us, as if the Church was not in her very constitution essentially visible, and must be so if we are to see her ruling over the hearts of the remarkable compound called *man*."—Ashwell, *Life of S. Wilberforce*, i. 197.

to obtain the mastery: is there not in miniature precisely the same conflict, and a discrepancy as horrible and appalling, between the state of grace into which the individual is adopted, the hopes of which he is made heir, nay and the gifts of which he is put actually in possession, and that subtle and deep enemy of his fallen nature, which still abides in him, and lives and struggles in a thousand forms and with desperate tenacity? (p. 115).

The Scriptures . . . hold out to our view the actual, historical Church as the great object of the love and regard of Christ, as the medium whereby was conferred that title under which His favour is conveyed to His individual members: and as intended to have unity in the body and the spirit, with universality, authority, visibility, permanency, sympathy . . . as destined to a present warfare, and a final glorification. Why have we lapsed from this magnificent conception of a power incorporated upon earth, capable of resistance to all the enemies of Divine truth . . . this conception which comprehends alike all space and all time, concentrating to tenfold efficacy the power of every noble motive, and realising and bringing home to our gross and feeble minds the sublime doctrine of supernatural grace? (p. 116).

Gladstone attributes this lapse from the Scriptural conception of the Church partly to the policy of the Roman Church which, instead of leading her members near to their Head through the grand idea of incorporation, interposed herself between them and the Redeemer and took into her own hands the powers that belong to Deity alone.[1] Then, "the Reformation generally took vengeance upon this excess by establishing its opposite" (p. 117).

Free assent came to be considered not only as the condition of adequate religion in a rational being, but as the arbiter and criterion of truth: and thus the throne of authority being set up within each individual breast, we have deprived the Church of her prerogative, and therein ourselves of some of our substantial advantages (p. 118; cp. p. 395).

But the loss of the true idea of the Church is also due to proud and self-centred individualism.

If I individualise my religion, if in modern language I place the account only between God and my conscience, free from all inspection and controul, I manifestly rid myself of a host of troublesome remembrancers. . . . There surely can be no

1. Cp. F. D. Maurice, *Theological Essays*,[3] pp. 241ff.

> doubt that a view of the Church not as a voluntary combination but as one preordered for us, and entailing obligations and even having parental claims upon us, should naturally tend to disturb the fatal ease of a deluded conscience fortified within its own fancied independence, and should bring near and obtrude upon us the idea that there is a God in the world whose will asserts audibly in the Church its title to be preferred to our own (pp. 118f.).

A number of objections, which may be brought against this high Scriptural doctrine of the Church, are then considered and answered, and the thesis is developed that the Church with its ministry and sacraments embodies the truth that the entire Gospel is adapted to the entire nature of man. Here too Gladstone was saying things, which are not indeed now commonplaces, but which are being rediscovered and reaffirmed from various points of view in contemporary theology, both Catholic and Protestant. Gladstone may thus be regarded as one of those who heralded this renewal in the Church of the sense of its being a community *sui generis*, both natural and supernatural, the new Israel of God, and the body of Christ.

We may turn again at this point to the teaching of another and a later herald of this renewal who, as we have seen before (see p. 65 *supra*), a generation ago was delivering a message that had a remarkable consonance with that of Gladstone, although he was a Congregationalist. In his *Theology in Church and State*, published in 1915, P. T. Forsyth wrote:

> The development or the recovery by the Church of this faith in its spiritual and collective personality is the first condition and the only plea for demanding from such a moral personality as the State that respect which is its due recognition of the Church's unique life and liberty (p. 185).
>
> Certainly individualism provides no ground for (the Church's) freedom and autonomy. A purely individualist view of the Church as a covenanting group that meets to protect and fortify each member in the enjoyment of his own peculiarity within a State which has nothing to do with religion—such a view is no ground whatever for the Church's autonomy in the State. Such a Church offers nothing intrinsic to itself, no power or right that the State can be asked to recognise and even

greet; but it only seeks something, some freedom of association or tenure, which the State can confer as a franchise (p. 161).[1]

The bearing of this on our main theme is as follows. If the Church be what Gladstone and Forsyth, interpreting Scripture and the Church's own traditional witness, affirm, then it is bound by its own intrinsic nature to demand that the State should recognise its right to fulfil its God-given task. It may never be satisfied with mere toleration by the State or with the *concession* of rights (cp. *CP*, pp. 282f.). It must seek to be *recognised* on grounds of truth and not of civil expediency alone, so that it is provided as a partner of the State with scope to do its distinct and divinely-appointed work in every sphere of the national life, which will include witnessing to man's adoption in Christ into a community that transcends all national boundaries. "The normal relation of State and Church is not divorce but true marriage," said Forsyth,[2]—who was a "Free Churchman", though his interpreta-

1. A recent Roman Catholic writer makes a point which Gladstone would have appreciated: "It is by preserving her visibility that the Church has been enabled to preserve her separateness from natural societies and her primacy among them as the representative of the spiritual order."—F. R. Hoare, *The Papacy and the Modern State* (1940), p. 31.

2. *Theology in Church and State*, p. 241. Gladstone, in *SRC* (ii. 213), used the term "public marriage" of Hooker's Church-State doctrine. For the sense in which he would himself accept the analogy, see *ibid.*, i. 117: "These powers are co-ordinate; and each is ordained to ends included within the purview of the other; but the specific function of the one is the less proximate though still morally essential function of the other. Thus a father and a mother are jointly ordained for the same end, as to the nurture of children: thus parent and tutor are jointly, and with distinction of rank, charged with their education."

For other allusions to this idea of a marriage of Church and State, see *CCR*, ii. 376; W. C. Magee, quoted on p. 80, n. 1 *supra*; J. C. Macdonnell, *The Life of Archbishop Magee* (1896), i. 157; J. N. Figgis, *From Gerson to Grotius*, p. 70, who refers to Bluntschli's much canvassed statement that the State is male and the Church female.

A writer in the *Catholic Encyclopædia*, xiv. 771: "As it is unnatural for a married couple to live separated, although separation may be defended in particular instances as the better or less harmful arrangement in view of quarrels which have arisen, so also the ideal relation between Church and State is to be found, not in the separation of the two, but in their harmonious co-operation." The same writer speaks of the "mystical marriage of Church and State" in the Middle Ages.

A writer in *The Quarterly Review* (1839), lxiii. 561: "The Church is not united to the State as Israel to Egypt; it is united as a believing wife to a husband who threatens to apostatise; and as a Christian wife so placed would act

tion of that designation differed considerably from the popular one. He also said: "It is as Churchmen that we define the place of the State; it is not as statesmen that we define the place of the Church".[1]

The Church will then demand a full opportunity for the preaching of its entire Gospel, which includes the practical offer of incorporation in the Church itself. The Church must also declare the true relation of the State to the Church and the respective tasks of each. Church and State are both ordained of God, and they have complementary tasks. The following words of Forsyth are like a precise echo of words of Gladstone which have been quoted above (see p. 45):

> Both (Church and State) are divine agents for human perfection. But the one by way of law and its evolution, the other by way of conscience and its redemption. The State does not exist to make men good, the Church does. The State exists to secure the conditions of goodness, the Church to create the thing itself. . . . The State is an agent of the Kingdom of God, the Church is the Kingdom of God in the making.[2]

—with patience, and love, and tears, and zealous entreaties, and prayers, hoping even against hope, and clinging to the connexion until a law from God dissevered it—so the Church must struggle even now, to save—not herself, but the State—from the crime of a divorce." J. Keble, referring to this statement in his review of *SRC* in *The British Critic* (October, 1839), said: "We had thought that the Spouse of the Church was a very different Person from any or all States, and her relation to the State, through Him, very unlike that whose duties are summed up in 'love, service, cherishing, and obedience'. And since the one is exclusively of this world, the other essentially of the eternal world, such an alliance as the above sentence describes, would have seemed to us not only fatal but monstrous."—1869 Reprint of the review, p. 6. (Newman alluded with warm approval to this passage in Keble's review in his *Letter addressed to His Grace the Duke of Norfolk*, 1875, p. 20.)

What Keble says shows that the idea of a marriage between Church and State, if it is a tolerable idea, must always be qualified by recognition of the Church's fundamental character as the Bride of Christ, but it does not follow that this Scriptural analogy excludes the propriety of the other. The point of the analogy differs in the two cases, and in the case of the relation between Church and State is fatal and monstrous only if pressed beyond its point.

Coventry Patmore, in *The Rod, the Root, and the Flower* [2] (1923), p. 215, asks: "The Holy Spouse of Christ, can she become the poor strumpet of the State?" See also Charles Wordsworth, *National Christianity an Article of the Christian Faith* (1851), p. 14.

1. *Theology in Church and State*, p. 255.
2. *Ibid.*, p. 209; cp. F. D. Maurice, *Social Morality* [2], p. 317.

Forsyth spoke of a true marriage as the *normal* relation between Church and State. Both he and Gladstone (though they would have differed as to the precise form in which this relation should be expressed) were concerned with the fundamental question of the norm which Christians ought always to be seeking to realise, and which must be realised in principle if a State is to be entitled to be called a Christian State in a strict sense. Gladstone noted in a speech in Parliament in 1847 various possibilities short of this.

> There are several senses in which a legislature may be called Christian. For example: either because all its members profess a known and definite body of truth constituting the Christian faith; or because they all adopt the designation of Christians; or because from the great preponderance of Christians in its personal composition . . . a Christian spirit pervades their legislation.[1]

No norm is ever perfectly realised in history,[2] but a norm affords a criterion by which to judge any existing state of affairs, and a standard which determines the eventual aim or aspiration of Christian politics. We say "eventual" advisedly, for historical conditions at a given time and in a given place may prohibit a realisation of the norm in the present and also the hope of its

1. Speech on the Jewish Disabilities Bill (December 16, 1847). He continued: "Our legislature was once Christian in the first of these senses. It is now Christian in the second. If the Jews shall be allowed to enter it, it will, I fervently hope and firmly believe, remain, much as it now is, Christian in the third. . . .

"It appears to me, that the interval between the first and second of the three states of national or legislative Christianity . . . is a wide one; and the interval between the second and the third, a narrow one."

On January 21, 1845, at the time of his resignation over the Maynooth Grant question, Gladstone had written to Sir Robert Peel: "I have given in print a deliberate and detailed exposition of the principles upon which, as it appears to me, it is best that national religion should be professed in Christian States (*sc.* in *SRC*); and have treated every departure from them as a sign of declension in the tone of society, a descent from a higher condition of public sentiment to a lower one. Nor can changes in this department be regarded as of anything less than the first order of importance; they are, as I believe, the notes of the ebb and flow of national life."—C. S. Parker, *Sir Robert Peel* (1899) iii. 166.

2. Even in 1839 Gladstone wrote to Macaulay: "There are some of these deflections from abstract theory which appear to me allowable; and that of the admission of persons not holding the national creed into civil office is one which, in my view, must be determined by times and circumstances."—See *A Chapter of Autobiography*, pp. 16f.

being realised in the proximate future. At the time when Gladstone wrote the two books, which have been under consideration, conditions had already gone far towards making inevitable a dissolution—or at least a substantial modification—of the existing marriage between Church and State in England, although many of the appearances were kept up, as they are to this day.[1] Perhaps, it is only the English and Anglican genius for compromise—or the national security and stability which, during the last century or two, have been favourable to the exercise of such a genius—that has prevented the formal dissolution of the marriage, or a general acknowledgement that it has ceased to be a true marriage and is no longer what it was or ought to be.

Gladstone's subsequent "conversion" to liberalism implied not his rejection in principle of the norm for which he had argued in his books,[2] but his acceptance in practice of the fact that its realisation was no longer possible and that Christian statesmen must act upon some other theory. Whether or not he expected that the norm would ever again be realisable in this country is uncertain. What is certain is that he accepted the fact that in the nineteenth century the actual drift was altogether away from that possibility, and that a reversal of the drift was not worth taking into account in practical politics. His decision to work the liberal or *laissez-faire* system and his opportunity to take a leading part in its application, together with its apparent success at the time,[3] had the effect of bringing him to regard what had become historically inevitable in nineteenth-century Britain[4] as not only

1. "Whilst the reality and meaning of the medieval system has vanished, its shell still survives."—Evidence of the Church Self-government League before the Archbishops' Commission on the relations between Church and State, 1935, *Church and State*, ii. 27f.

2. Cp. *A Chapter of Autobiography*, pp. 60, 62, where, in 1868, he still speaks of it as "a standard theoretically higher." See also pp. 143f. *infra*.

3. In November, 1868, Gladstone said in the House of Commons: "I make an appeal to the history of the last thirty years. During these years, what may be called the dogmatic allegiance of the State to religion has been greatly relaxed; but its consciousness of moral duty has been not less notably quickened. I do not say this in depreciation of dogma." See R. Ingham, *Church Establishments Considered*, p. 449.

4. In a speech on the Ecclesiastical Titles Bill, 1851, Gladstone said: "We cannot change the profound and resistless tendencies of the age towards religious liberty. It is our business to guide and control their application. Do this as you may. But to endeavour to turn them backwards is the sport of children."—Reproduced in *Gleanings*, vii. 127.

tolerable but also desirable, and of causing him to entertain sanguine hopes of its success in the future. Nevertheless, to the end of his life, his political optimism was accompanied by a recurring undertone of anxiety concerning the future of Christianity.[1]

There was, however, a further reason (*i.e.* in addition to the logic of the liberal experiment and the resistless tendency towards "religious liberty") why it was impossible to maintain the existing marriage of Church and State. The condition of the Church itself prohibited the maintenance of such a marriage. As Gladstone wrote, in 1868, in *A Chapter of Autobiography*:

> There are two causes, the combined operation of which, upon reaching a certain point of development, relaxes or dissolves (the) union of (Church and State) by a process as normal (if it be less beneficial) as that, by which the union was originally brought about. One of these is the establishment of the principle of popular self-government as the basis of political constitutions. The other is the disintegration of Christendom from one into many communions (pp. 59f.).

The C.O.P.E.C. Commission Report on *Politics and Citizenship* rightly said that

> In seeking to realise a Christian theory (*sc.* of the relations of Church and State) we have to face the fact that there is to-day no united Church, and that in society the Christian faith is not, as in the mediæval world, in possession, nor yet, as in the early Church, a new challenge.[2]

We must now consider how Gladstone faced this fact, and what is its bearing to-day on a theory of the relations of Church and State.

IV

Gladstone's high doctrine of both Church and State forced upon him the predicament of Christian disunity, and so embarrassed his theory of their normal relations that a large part of

1. *E.g.* "The religion of Christ as a whole, nay, even the pallid scheme of Theism, is assailed with a sweep and vehemence of hostility greater probably than at any former time."—Article on "Is the Church of England worth preserving"? in *The Contemporary Review* (July, 1875), p. 205.
See also *CCR*, i. 142, 381; ii. chap. 3.

2. Vol. x, p. 19.

both the books under review here had to be devoted to its consequences. He believed, as he said in *Church Principles*, that "the Church of the Scriptures is a visible and authoritative body, perpetuated through the medium of sacraments and a commissioned ministry" (p. 403); the Church, that is to say, is organically one. He believed that the Church of England was the part of this Church of the Scriptures in England. But how was he to reconcile this belief that the Church of the Scriptures was visible and one, and that the Church of England was the national incorporation of this Church, with the existence alongside it of other Christian bodies—Roman Catholic and Protestant—which not only made a similar or identical claim, but also brought forth fruits to substantiate the claim.

According to Gladstone, "a national Church is the centre of the national life of a country; and . . . it is responsible as an institution . . . for the social condition at large, as being the first and paramount cause which determines it effectually towards well-being, or towards the reverse" (*CP*, pp. 373f.). He held that the State had rightly recognised the Church of England as the national Church in this sense. What attitude then was he to adopt, or rather what attitude ought the State to adopt, to the other bodies in the land which also professed the Christian faith? There were three possible attitudes, it seemed: persecution, toleration of dissent, and co-ordinate recognition.

Persecution, it need hardly be said, Gladstone always regarded with horror, and in *The State in its relations with the Church* he was at pains to argue that persecution was neither required nor permitted by his theory.[1]

Co-ordinate recognition he had also rejected (with some qualification) on the ground that the State was bound to recognise the Church on the ground of truth, and the claims of two or more Churches with substantially different doctrines could not both or all be true. "The support of religion is not principally a boon to individuals, but a homage to truth . . . and a public acknowledgement of our duty to seek it."[2]

1. See p. 46 *supra*, and pp. 117f. *infra*.

2. *SRC*, ii. 269; cp. i. 121, 124f. Cp. also Dr Carnegie Simpson, who was asked by the Archbishops' Commission on the relations between Church and State, 1935, whether he had any views on concurrent establishment or endowment. He replied: "This is a line strongly to be deprecated. It has no

What Gladstone advocated was then the continued recognition of the Church of England as the national Church on the ground of truth, with complete toleration for dissenters. In any case, he was of course opposed to the coercive imposition of the Christian faith on the people; indeed, he attached great importance to free assent as a condition, though not as the basis, of true religion. It was the duty of a Christian State to secure the presentation and commendation of the Christian faith to the people, but always so that their freedom to accept or reject it was not suppressed. It has been suggested that Gladstone came to see the importance of individual liberty only when he was converted to liberalism. But is this so?

In *The State and its relations with the Church* he had spoken of "the true moral freedom of the individual" as "one of the great conditions of our well-being",[1] and also of "the paramount principle of our private responsibility".[2] Did he need to learn this from modern liberals? His masters, Dante and Butler, will have taught him this. Dante had described freedom of choice as *maximum donum humanae naturae a Deo collatum.*[3] Butler had written strongly of the need for a religious establishment to be accompanied by toleration.

> Liberty, which is the very genius of our civil constitution, and runs through every branch of it, extends its influence to the ecclesiastical part of it. A religious establishment without a toleration of such as think they cannot in conscience conform to it, is itself a general tyranny; because it claims absolute authority over conscience; and would soon beget particular kinds of tyranny of the worst sort, tyranny over the mind, and various superstitions; after the way should be paved for them, as it soon must, by ignorance. . . . A reasonable establishment provides instruction for the ignorant, withdraws them, not in

principle, supporting impartially truth and error. . . . (It is true that such a scheme is practically admitted with regard to Army chaplaincies, etc., but this is no more than an anomalous exception in special circumstances.)"—*Church and State*, ii. 190.

It would appear that Dr Simpson supposes the Church of England still to be recognised by the State on the ground of theological truth.

1. *SRC*, ii. 283; cp. 1st ed., p. 76. On free discussion, *e.g.* of defects and corruptions in the Church, as an essential element of our social life, see *CP*, p. 460.

2. *SRC*, i. 80.

3. *De Monarchia*, i. 12.

> the way of force, but of guidance, from running after those kinds of conceits (viz. superstition and enthusiasm).[1]

Again, Burke had been one of his early masters, and Burke had said of his own opinions that they "come from one, almost the whole of whose publick exertion has been a struggle for the liberty of others; from one in whose breast no anger durable or vehement has ever been kindled, but by what he considered as tyranny".[2]

Gladstone's ideal, "uniformity and sufficiency of action by the State according to the faith of the Church, with a full toleration to those who are separated from it", was not novel, though he confessed that it had never been perfectly realised.[3]

It is manifest now, and indeed it was manifest at the time when he wrote, that Gladstone could make out a case for the application of his theory under actual conditions only by extreme ingenuity. It did not take him long to discover that he was "the last man in a sinking ship". His departure from the theory on account of its impracticability, and his eventual acceptance of the Liberal system, made it unnecessary for him to reopen the question as to how a State, which recognises the Church on the ground of its truth, should deal with other religious bodies. The State had ceased to recognise the Church on the ground of its truth, and he did not anticipate a time when it would do so again. But the question of the treatment of dissenters by States, which publicly and exclusively patronise a positive dogma, has in the twentieth century again become, with the supersession of Liberal polities in many contemporary States, a living question. Even in England the drift towards religious liberty in the sense of the State's impartiality is being arrested, and perhaps reversed. It will be necessary in the next chapter to return to this question.

Meanwhile, we take note that Gladstone had seen how Christian

1. A Sermon preached before the House of Lords, June 11, 1747. In the same passage Butler says: "A constitution of civil government without any religious establishment is a chimerical project, of which there is no example: and which, leaving the generality without guide and instruction, must leave religion to be sunk and forgotten amongst them; and at the same time give full scope to superstition, and the gloom of enthusiasm; which last, especially, ought surely to be diverted and checked, as far as it can be done without force."

2. "Reflections on the Revolution in France": *Works* (1826 ed.), v. 438.

3. *SRC*, ii. 283.

disunion, when it reaches a certain point, becomes an insuperable obstacle to the maintenance of a true marriage between Church and State. For a true marriage requires there to be one, visible Church for the State to recognise. For this reason, as well as for other reasons, Gladstone was an eager advocate of Church unity.[1] When he wrote *Church Principles*, it was the Church at home that he had chiefly in mind; he did not contemplate the effects that the missionary expansion of the nineteenth century was to have either on the need for, or on the prospects of, reunion. It was the possibility of a single national Church that most concerned him, and, although the problem of Church unity has much wider and more complicated aspects, this possibility is one that continues to be canvassed.

Gladstone believed that the Church of England was "placed in a position eminently fitted to become a centre of union to Christians at present diverging on this side and on that".[2] He hoped that both Romanists and Protestant dissenters would come to see that Scriptural and Catholic principles were more adequately expressed and safeguarded in the Anglican system than in their respective systems. This is a hope which has been, and perhaps still is, shared by other Anglicans, though it is not always this that is intended when the Church of England is advertised as "a bridge church". It is less evident that the hope is shared by Christians "on this side and on that".

On the side of Rome, things have not stood still during the last hundred years. The Roman Church has strengthened its hold in England, through secessions from the Church of England (the most serious of which took place five years after Gladstone wrote *Church Principles*), through the so-called "Papal Aggression", and through Irish immigration. Moreover, the Vatican Council has

1. "I ardently desire the full and effective action of the State for the promotion of religion; and yet more ardently, that general and free coincidence of my fellow-citizens in the principles of Catholic unity, through which alone, as I believe, the former object is attainable".—*SRC*, ii. 403.

Cp. Thomas Chalmers, *Select Works* (1857), xi. 219: "Only by an undivided Church, only by the ministers of one denomination, can a community be out and out pervaded, or a territory be filled up and thoroughly overtaken with the lessons of the gospel."

2. *CP*, p. 504. Cp. *Remarks on the Royal Supremacy* (1850), p. 87; and Gladstone's letter to Hope, in R. Ornsby's *Memoirs of J. R. Hope-Scott* (1884), ii. 69f.

hardened the causes of separation between Anglicanism and Romanism, as Gladstone himself, prominently and somewhat extravagantly, asserted shortly afterwards.[1] These circumstances have made unity on that side a more remote prospect. Although it is still remote, there has been a considerable softening in the relations between the two Churches in recent years.

On the side of the Protestant dissenters, things have changed too. They are now commonly described as the "Free Churches". In the era of *laissez faire* they gained much ground, especially among the classes where the Church of England had few roots. But their present state is apparently fluid, and no reliable forecast of their future relations with one another or with the Church of England is possible. If Gladstone's hope on this side is to be realised, it will probably be through the development among the Free Churchmen of such a theological temper as was shown, for example, by P. T. Forsyth, the distinguished Congregationalist theologian, who has already been referred to more than once in these pages.

This temper, which though still rare is less rare now than it was a quarter of a century ago, may be illustrated by one or two sayings of Forsyth in his book, *The Church and the Sacraments* (1917):

> The first condition of religion is authority. It is an authority before it is a liberty (p. 11).
>
> Wherever (the) Gospel is taken seriously, and duly, and statedly, there is the Church. It is the living organism . . . of the worshippers of Christ, created by His redeeming Gospel in

1. See *The Vatican Decrees in their bearing on civil allegiance: a political expostulation* (1874) and *Vaticanism: an answer to replies and reproofs* (1875). He retained, however, as he wrote elsewhere at about this time, his hopeful view as to the position of the Church of England with reference to Christendom at large; see his art. on "Is the Church of England worth preserving?" in *The Contemporary Review* (July, 1875), p. 207:

> Besides her national office and capabilities, the Church of England, in her highest character as a form of the Christian religion, has a position at once perilous and most precious . . . with reference to Christendom at large. She alone, of all Churches, has points of contact, of access, of sympathy, with all the important sections of the Christian community. Liable, more than any other communion, to see her less stable or more fastidious members drop off from her now in this direction and now in that, she is, nevertheless, in a partial but not an unreal sense, a link of union between the several fractions of the Christian body. At every point of her frontier, she is in close competition with the great Latin communion, and with the varied, active, and in no way other than respectable, forms of Nonconformity. . . ."

Word and Sacrament. There is therefore but one way of recovering the idea of the Church. It is by regaining, on a scale worthy of it, the evangelical faith which made and makes the Church always. To lose that is often too easy. But it is a very hard thing to regain (p. 31).

The day of the sects as sects is over. The day of the denominations is passing. The commanding Church idea returns. We look forward to an ecumenical Christianity composed not of national Churches but of national types of Christianity; and, within each national type, a variety of cohesive and co-operant bodies, which shall be (what we are not now) at least as much concerned about their unity as about their variety (p. 102).

It would be foolish to suggest that Forsyth's Ecclesiology can be completely reconciled with Gladstone's. But if English Nonconformity becomes thoroughly animated by such a temper, Gladstone's hope of a united Church in England will become less visionary. Ideally and *prima facie* it might seem that the Church of England and Christianity in England were very favourably placed, under the providence of God, for working out a synthesis of both the Catholic and Reformed traditions with the new insights that have come to European man through the Renaissance, the Enlightenment, and the achievements of science and technics. Unhappily a realistic contemplation of the actual state of the Church of England and of the other Churches in England does not at present afford much encouragement to those who want to see the realisation of such a hope.

Gladstone was far from idealising the Church of England. In *Church Principles* he freely acknowledged its manifold defects, and by contrast the strong features of the Roman Catholic and Protestant systems. In the case of the latter he went a good deal further in recognising their claims than most of the Tractarians and some of their successors to-day.[1] He had no sympathy, then or later,[2] with undenominationalism, even though as a Liberal

1. The striking article on "The Place of Heresy and Schism in the Modern Christian Church" which he contributed to *The Nineteenth Century* in August, 1894, is in line with, and represents a mature development of, what he had said in *CP* over fifty years earlier; see especially *The Nineteenth Century* (*loc. cit.*), pp. 165f.

2. In the article, to which reference is made in the preceding note Gladstone warned Christians against the trend to an undenominational British Christianity:

If the State should think proper to frame new creeds by cutting the old

statesman he had to countenance it. He always regarded church systems as of fundamental importance. But he adopted a positive, appreciative, and (as far as his principles admitted) an inclusive, attitude to other Christian communions. He rejected for instance the theory of "uncovenanted mercies" by means of which some Anglicans have tried to explain away the palpable evidences of nonconformist churchmanship (*CP*, p. 417). But he would never abandon the principle that in the purpose of God the Church of the Scriptures is one body, and that, if it acquiesced in degenerating into a sect or a collection or federation of sects, it would be confounding its charter.

ones into pieces and throwing them into the caldron to be reboiled, we have no remedy, except such as may lie hidden among the resources of the providence of God. It is fair to add that the State is in this matter beset by severe temptations; the vehicle through which these temptations work will probably, in this country at least, be supplied by popular education.

"The Church, disabled and discredited by her divisions, has found it impracticable to assert herself as the universal guide. Among the fragments of the body, a certain number have special affinities, and in particular regions or conjunctures of circumstances it would be very easy to frame an undenominational religion much to their liking, divested of many salient points needful in the view of historic Christendom for a complete Christianity. Such a scheme the State might be tempted to authorise by law in public elementary teaching, nay, to arm it with executive and prohibitory powers as against other and more developed methods. . . . It is in this direction that we have recently been moving, and the motion is towards a point where a danger signal is already lifted."—*The Nineteenth Century* (August, 1894), pp. 170f.

With this it is interesting to compare what the Attorney-General for Ireland wrote to Peel in 1813 with regard to a project, that was then being canvassed for undenominational schools in Ireland: "The establishing—even for the education of the lower orders of the people—an abstract form of Christianity, that shall avoid what is peculiar to each sect and yet preserve what shall be essential, looks very like making a new religion for the country, and establishing by law a precedent for a schism by consent from all churches and sects."—C. S. Parker, *Sir Robert Peel* (1891), i. 91. Gladstone, in his copy of this book (*SDL*), marked the foregoing passage with an *N.B.*

In 1824 a similar project was still under consideration, and in the course of a letter Peel wrote: "I sincerely hope that the Commissioners will not be induced by any consideration to give up the use of the Scriptures on the five days; let every passage which touches upon the mysteries of religion be excluded, but insist that all the children shall take at least one daily draught from the common fountain of their religious creeds"; *ibid.*, i. 344. Gladstone marked his discontent with the middle clause by inscribing *ma* against it in the margin.

For Gladstone's attitude to proposals for religious education at various stages in his career, see *CCR*, vol. ii. chap. 4.

CHAPTER SIX

TRUTH, TOLERANCE, AND TIME

I

The main question that is raised by Gladstone's theory of the relations of the State with the Church is whether the State (as the legal organisation through which the nation finds itself or expresses itself) is under a moral obligation to recognise truth and, if so, what form this recognition ought to take. In maintaining that the State is morally bound to acknowledge truth, not only the truths of "natural reason" and the "moral law of nature", but revealed truth, as and when presented to it through the Church of Christ, Gladstone was drawing out and making explicit with clear discrimination a doctrine which had on the whole been taken for granted in the Christian tradition. It was certainly not a novel doctrine in the Anglican tradition,[1] but had been taught, for example, by Hooker, though, as Gladstone held, with inadequate discrimination.[2]

In the *Laws of Ecclesiastical Polity* Hooker wrote:

> We agree that pure and unstained religion ought to be the highest of all cares appertaining to public regiment: as well in regard of that aid and protection which they who faithfully serve God confess they receive at his merciful hands; as also for the force which religion hath to qualify all sorts of men, and to make them in public affairs the more serviceable, governors the apter to rule with conscience, inferiors for conscience' sake the willinger to obey. It is no peculiar conceit, but a matter of sound consequence, that all duties are by so much the better performed, by how much the men are more religious from whose abilities the same proceed. For if the course of politic affairs cannot in any good sort go forward without fit instruments, and

1. John Keble could write in 1839: "We have never met with, we have never read of, any set of persons admitting the divine origin and paramount claims of the Apostolical Church, yet denying the obligation of the civil magistrate to enter into relations with it." See reprint (1869) of his review of *SRC*, p. 14. Cp. Keble's *Sermons Academic and Occasional* (1847), pp. 157f.; and Bishop Butler, quoted p. 101, n. 1 *supra*.

2. See *SRC*, i. 15.

that which fitteth them be their virtues, let Polity acknowledge itself indebted to Religion; godliness being the chiefest top and wellspring of all true virtues, even as God is of all good things.

So natural is the union of Religion with Justice, that we may boldly deem there is neither, where both are not. For how should they be unfeignedly just, whom religion doth not cause to be such; or they religious, which are not found such by the proof of their just actions? If they, which employ their labour and travel about the public administration of justice, follow it only as a trade, with unquenchable and unconscionable thirst of gain, being not in heart persuaded that justice is God's own work, and themselves his agents in this business, the sentence of right God's own verdict, and themselves his priests to deliver it; formalities of justice do but serve to smother right, and that, which was necessarily ordained for the common good, is through shameful abuse made the cause of common misery (V. i. 2).

What more savage, wild, and cruel, than man, if he see himself able either by fraud to overreach, or by power to overbear, the laws whereunto he should be subject? Wherefore in so great boldness to offend, it behoveth that the world should be held in awe, not by a vain surmise, but a true apprehension of somewhat, which no man may think himself able to withstand. This is the politic use of religion (V. ii. 3).[1]

1. Cp. p. 16 *supra*. See also John Jewel, *The Defence of the Apology*, Parker Soc. ed., p. 976: "Thus we say, the prince is put in trust, as well with the first as with the second table of the law of God, that is to say, as well with religion as with temporal government; not only to keep and perform the contents of both tables in his own person (for so much every private man is bound to do), but also to see that all others his subjects, as well priests as laymen, each man in his calling, do duly keep them."

Cp. Dr Arnold's letter to W. W. Hull, in Stanley's *Life and Correspondence of Thomas Arnold*,[2] i. 376.

In the prayer for the Church militant in its communion service the Church of England prays that the King and *all that are put in authority under him* "may truly and indifferently minister justice, to the punishment of wickedness and vice, and to *the maintenance of thy true religion*, and virtue".

Dr G. Leibholz, in a *Christian News-Letter* supplement (December 2, 1942) on "Christianity, Justice and Modern Society", writes: "The Christian realises that the appearance of Christianity in history was the supreme revolutionary event which had a final and irrevocable effect also in the political sphere. From that time onwards the political order stands under the judgment of God. This development cannot be undone. The political order can no longer claim as in ancient times to be by its very nature in accord with true religion and ultimately with justice and the universal principles of law; it cannot claim of itself to be a just order and, by implication, to comply with the demands of divine justice."

In the time of Hooker this doctrine could be held without apparent incongruity, not only because religion was represented in England by one visible Church which was virtually coextensive with the commonwealth, but because the State, which operated through the government and, above all, through the monarch, was unequivocally Christian and churchly in its profession. R. W. Church, in an article which he contributed on "Church and State" to *The Christian Remembrancer* in April, 1850, pointed out that the union of Church and State in the Middle Ages and after the Reformation was tolerable, and indeed welcome, to the Church, because the King, who then represented in fact as well as in theory what we now mean by the State, "was a person, not a mere state, or government—a person, having a conscience, owning personal responsibility, and one with her in faith, in practice, in sentiment, in purpose, acknowledging her laws, sympathising with her objects".[1]

By the nineteenth century, although the vestiges of this relationship still survived, conditions had so changed that it was only by a *tour de force* that the doctrine which it implied could be revived. Nevertheless, Gladstone attempted to revive it in a new form. He did not locate the personality of the State in the person of the monarch. But he saw that, unless the State is in some sense "a person", or makes itself articulate in "a person", it cannot be capable of acknowledging, or be bound to acknowledge, truth; it cannot be said to have a conscience. He therefore analysed the idea of the State, and examined the sense in which it could, and ought to be, regarded as "a moral person". It seems that he was right in supposing that there cannot be what we have called a true marriage [2] between Church and State, unless the State is either represented in an individual person or has in itself somewhere so much of the attributes of personality as enable it to fulfil the requisite conditions, *i.e.* to be a proper subject of moral obligation and a proper party to a moral relationship.

1. *Op. cit.*, p. 48. Cp. Gladstone, *Remarks on the Royal Supremacy* (1850), p. 67. Miss M. P. Follett in *The New State*, p. 217, writes: "In the past the monarch got his power from the fact that he represented the unity of his people—the tribal or national consciousness. In the so-called democracies of England and America we have now no one man who represents a true collective consciousness."

2. See p. 94 *supra*.

We have discussed Gladstone's doctrine of personality in the State with reference to subsequent thought on the subject. The conclusion reached was not as clear or definite as could have been wished. This was due, it may be, not only to the reason then given,[1] but also to the circumstance that the State in England now appears to be in a fluid or transitional condition. While Gladstone did not identify the State with the government, it must be remembered that he was a member of Parliament, and he regarded the personality of the State as, so to speak, focused in the legislature. Hence the legislature's recognition of the Church seemed to him to be of crucial importance.[2] Thus, though it was no longer possible to locate the personality of the State in the monarch alone, it was possible to locate it in the whole legislature. The legislature, *i.e.* the monarch and the two Houses of Parliament, was then felt by the whole people to be its representative organ;[3] for even those classes which were not yet directly represented in Parliament eagerly aspired to be. The House of Commons, in particular, was the place where the national community's awareness of itself as a community found expression; it was there that the national conscience was operative.

Doubtless, it is still so to some extent. But Parliament has changed considerably during the last hundred years, and the national community has changed much more. Except during an emergency like war, the nation is much less aware of itself as a community; nor is interest to the same extent centred in the legislature as the organ of its self-expression. The extension of the franchise was expected to heighten the people's sense of belonging to a community for which all were directly responsible; but it seems to have worked in the opposite direction. The prestige of Parliament as the central organ of the nation's self-expression has declined; but it has not been overtly ousted by some other institution. The organisation of the State has become

1. See pp. 69f. *supra*. 2. See p. 96 *supra*.

3. See Gladstone's description of the relation of the legislature to the nation in *Vaticanism: an answer to replies and reproofs* (1875), p. 93:

> The nation is ruled by a Legislature, of which by far the most powerful branch is freely chosen, from time to time, by the community itself by the greater part of the heads of the families in the country; and all the proceedings of its Parliament are not only carried on in the face of day, but made known from day to day, almost from hour to hour, in every town and village, and almost in every household of the land.

immensely complicated—and the Civil Service, the Employers' organisations, the Trade Unions, the Banks, are widely felt to be more powerful expressions of the national life than Parliament. Moreover, there is a suspicion that there may be more hidden centres of power and influence than those, and that what the public is permitted to see is for the most part window-dressing. A recent Supplement to *The Christian News-Letter* refers to the widespread contemporary belief "that democracy is a sham, that the whole system is manipulated by 'sinister vested interests', that effective power does not lie with a responsible parliament, but with an irresponsible clique of financiers and directors".[1]

In other words, there is a widespread impression that there is a great deal of truth in the gibe that Britain has been a "pluto-democracy". It is not necessary here to inquire precisely what the facts of the case have been; it is not yet possible to say what the facts of the case are going to be. But while this uncertainty exists, we cannot say in what way the "personality" of the State will in future express itself, or what new organs may be developed or old organs revived for the purpose.[2] In the totalitarian States the Single Party (whether communist, fascist or nazi) has so far been the organ or distortion of the State's personality. We may hope that in Britain the need for a centrally planned society, which is determined by technological conditions, may be met in some way that will allow scope for a better form of national self-expression; but we cannot be sure yet that it will be so met,[3] or in any case how the State's personality and conscience will in future operate.

Every society has a dominant class which wields special influence and power, the feudal lords in the Middle Ages, the capitalist class during the capitalist era, etc. If it be true that the coming society is to be "managerial", the dominant class will be the managers, as defined by Mr James Burnham in *The Managerial*

1. *Op. cit.*, September 8, 1943.

2. As Miss Follett said: "We are told—The people should do this, the people should do that, the people must be given control of foreign policy, etc. etc. But all this is wholly useless unless we provide the procedure within which the people *can* do this or that."—*The New State*, p. 4.

3. For notable attempts, among many others not all so notable, to say how the need ought to be met, see M. P. Follett's *The New State* and Karl Mannheim's *Man and Society in an Age of Reconstruction.*

Revolution (1943). He holds that managerial society need not be totalitarian, though it certainly will not be democratic in the capitalist or *laissez-faire* sense. The test will be whether it is able to tolerate minorities, and provide them scope for self-expression.

Only as society develops its new structure, will it be possible to say how the State's obligation to recognise truth can take effect, and how it should be called upon to acknowledge the truth of the Christian revelation, to bear witness to which the Church exists.[1] This uncertainty constitutes one reason why we cannot apply Gladstone's theory of the normative relation between State and Church to present conditions. But it is not only the transitional character of the State that makes this impossible. As we have seen, there is an equal, perhaps a graver, difficulty on the side of the Church. Even if we suppose that the State were able in a new way definitely to express its recognition of truth, and its acknowledgment of the truth of the Christian revelation, how could it do this in view of the disunited condition of the Church?

Not the least important part of Gladstone's doctrine was that Christianity is inseparably bound up with a visible Church, a Church that is one, a recognisable body. But whatever Christian propaganda of this school or that may at present say, it cannot reasonably expect the State in England, still less in Great Britain, to accord exclusive recognition to any actual church as the one visible Church. The most that could happen in this direction—and it is what Gladstone at the end of his life saw might quite easily be going to happen[2]—is the giving of public patronage, through the schools and other parts of a national educational

1. Neither the Archbishops' Committee on Church and State, which reported in 1916, nor the Archbishops' Commission on the relations between Church and State, which reported in 1935, dealt directly with this question. Doubtless, this is because in both cases the main interest was in the question whether or how the Church could acquire more satisfactory means of governing itself. The terms of reference of the 1916 Committee did indeed include the duty of inquiring how "a fuller expression . . . of the national recognition of religion" could be secured (see *Report*, p. 1), but the Committee explained (*ibid.*, p. 2) why it limited its task to what it supposed was chiefly expected of it. The terms of reference of the 1935 Commission did not include any reference to the national recognition of religion.

On the other hand, Mr T. S. Eliot has opened up this question in a most illuminating way in *The Idea of a Christian Society* (1939), esp. chap. ii.

2. See p. 104, n. 2 *supra*.

system, to an undenominational form of C
The objection to this from the side of the Chu
that takes its charter and commission seriou
in this case the State adopts Christianity on i
but that public endorsement is given to the n
doctrine and Christian practice can be separ
the Church as a worshipping community.
deep roots which are not generally understo
concealed by a narrow clerical intransigence.

It is in this connexion that we should recall
in *Church Principles* about the error of ratio
fallen being: his faculties are deranged and
reasoning powers are subject to a distractin
man needs to be restored by the grace of Go
well as man the individual. Thus it is not
the intellect rational propositions about m
about God and the way of salvation through

> Spiritual influence upon the heart is nec
> understanding with those primary perce
> become adequately cognisant of spiritual
> of exercising that faculty with profit upo
> trines at large (*CP*, p. 73).

The language is ponderous, but the thought

This spiritual influence, the grace of the
God's ordinance mediated to men through th
visible Church, by the ministry of the Word
the XIXth Article of Religion says, "The vis

1. Dean Church also anticipated the hard choic
made. In 1870 he wrote to his friend, Dr Asa Gray:

> The difficulty is beginning to be more visible
> a Church with great privileges with the general
> combining a National Church with a Church h
> a religious society, believing in a definite religio
> One of these days, I expect we shall find ourselve
> having to choose between making the Church coex
> called the religion of the whole nation or giving u
> *Life and Letters of Dean Church* (1897), p. 226.

2. "What is worst of all is to advocate Christiani
but because it might be beneficial."—T. S. Eliot, *Th*
p. 58.

3. See pp. 86f. *supra*; cp. *Studies subsidiary to the W*

Revolution (1943). He holds that managerial society need not be totalitarian, though it certainly will not be democratic in the capitalist or *laissez-faire* sense. The test will be whether it is able to tolerate minorities, and provide them scope for self-expression.

Only as society develops its new structure, will it be possible to say how the State's obligation to recognise truth can take effect, and how it should be called upon to acknowledge the truth of the Christian revelation, to bear witness to which the Church exists.[1] This uncertainty constitutes one reason why we cannot apply Gladstone's theory of the normative relation between State and Church to present conditions. But it is not only the transitional character of the State that makes this impossible. As we have seen, there is an equal, perhaps a graver, difficulty on the side of the Church. Even if we suppose that the State were able in a new way definitely to express its recognition of truth, and its acknowledgment of the truth of the Christian revelation, how could it do this in view of the disunited condition of the Church?

Not the least important part of Gladstone's doctrine was that Christianity is inseparably bound up with a visible Church, a Church that is one, a recognisable body. But whatever Christian propaganda of this school or that may at present say, it cannot reasonably expect the State in England, still less in Great Britain, to accord exclusive recognition to any actual church as the one visible Church. The most that could happen in this direction—and it is what Gladstone at the end of his life saw might quite easily be going to happen[2]—is the giving of public patronage, through the schools and other parts of a national educational

1. Neither the Archbishops' Committee on Church and State, which reported in 1916, nor the Archbishops' Commission on the relations between Church and State, which reported in 1935, dealt directly with this question. Doubtless, this is because in both cases the main interest was in the question whether or how the Church could acquire more satisfactory means of governing itself. The terms of reference of the 1916 Committee did indeed include the duty of inquiring how "a fuller expression . . . of the national recognition of religion" could be secured (see *Report*, p. 1), but the Committee explained (*ibid.*, p. 2) why it limited its task to what it supposed was chiefly expected of it. The terms of reference of the 1935 Commission did not include any reference to the national recognition of religion.

On the other hand, Mr T. S. Eliot has opened up this question in a most illuminating way in *The Idea of a Christian Society* (1939), esp. chap. ii.

2. See p. 104, n. 2 *supra*.

system, to an undenominational form of Christian teaching.[1] The objection to this from the side of the Church—of any Church that takes its charter and commission seriously—is not only that in this case the State adopts Christianity on inadequate grounds,[2] but that public endorsement is given to the notion that Christian doctrine and Christian practice can be separated from the life of the Church as a worshipping community. This objection has deep roots which are not generally understood, for they are often concealed by a narrow clerical intransigence.

It is in this connexion that we should recall what Gladstone said in *Church Principles* about the error of rationalism.[3] Man is a fallen being: his faculties are deranged and corrupted, and his reasoning powers are subject to a distracting bias. The whole man needs to be restored by the grace of God, man in society as well as man the individual. Thus it is not enough to present to the intellect rational propositions about moral ideals, or even about God and the way of salvation through Christ.

> Spiritual influence upon the heart is necessary to furnish the understanding with those primary perceptions by which we become adequately cognisant of spiritual objects, and capable of exercising that faculty with profit upon the Christian doctrines at large (*CP*, p. 73).

The language is ponderous, but the thought is profound.

This spiritual influence, the grace of the Holy Ghost, is by God's ordinance mediated to men through the ministrations of the visible Church, by the ministry of the Word and sacraments. As the XIXth Article of Religion says, "The visible Church of Christ

1. Dean Church also anticipated the hard choice that would have to be made. In 1870 he wrote to his friend, Dr Asa Gray:

> The difficulty is beginning to be more visible every day, of reconciling a Church with great privileges with the general set of modern society; of combining a National Church with a Church having the *raison d'être* of a religious society, believing in a definite religion, and teaching it. . . . One of these days, I expect we shall find ourselves put into the position of having to choose between making the Church coextensive with what can be called the religion of the whole nation or giving up our present position.—*Life and Letters of Dean Church* (1897), p. 226.

2. "What is worst of all is to advocate Christianity, not because it is true, but because it might be beneficial."—T. S. Eliot, *The Idea of a Christian Society*, p. 58.

3. See pp. 86f. *supra*; cp. *Studies subsidiary to the Works of Bishop Butler*, p. 25.

is a congregation of faithful men, in which the pure Word of God is preached, and the Sacraments be duly administered according to Christ's ordinance in all those things that of necessity are requisite to the same." This is not to say that the work of grace is confined to the visible Church, but that it is in the visible Church that it has been promised. Can the Christians then fail to object to a plan of religious instruction or of religious influence which is abstracted from the ministry of the Word and sacraments in the visible Church?

Is it not clear that a Christian system of education on a national scale, to be adequately entitled to the Christian name, would involve the training of children, as well as of adults, in the habitual worship of the Church? The Book of Common Prayer supposes that all children will be brought to their parish church to be baptised—that, as soon as they are able to learn, they will be taught the meaning of what was then done—that they will be brought to church to hear sermons—that they will learn the Creed, the Lord's Prayer, and the Ten Commandments, and be catechised concerning the same. In the seventeenth century this was done on a national scale; the exceptions but proved the rule. In this way much more than mere instruction was given to each individual child. The Christian tradition, with its mythology and symbols, appealing to the imagination and emotions as well as to the intelligence, was handed on from generation to generation to the national community as a whole. The pattern of the nation's life was determined by the fasts and festivals of the Christian year; the Christian Scriptures, publicly read and expounded in every parish church, penetrated the nation's imagination with common archetypes and images;[1] the language of the Bible and the liturgy became the common language of the people; the traditional and universal songs of Christendom were national songs. All this was bound up with the visible Church; through all this the grace of God was at work. The national conscience was informed with the Law of God; the prayers of the

1. See a paper by Philip Mairet on "The Gospel Drama and Society" in J. H. Oldham's *Real Life is Meeting* (1942), pp. 52–60; Karl Mannheim on "The Concepts of Christian Archetypes" in his *Diagnosis of our Time* (1943), pp. 117ff.; and H. A. Hodges on "The Problem of Archetypes" in *The Christian News-Letter*, June 2, 1943.

nation were directed for forgiveness, for light, and for power, to the throne of grace.

There is no need to idealise the past, nor to pretend that this Christian system of national education was ever perfectly effective; it always stood in need of much improvement and extension. The point is that recognition of the Church by the State carried with it much more than formal assent to Christian doctrine as true. It meant that the Church, in all the ways that have been mentioned, was accorded the opportunity of fashioning the national life, and of moulding the national tradition. This was but summed up in the decisive place that was occupied by the sacrament of holy communion as a qualification for membership in the legislature.

We asked just now: Can Christians fail to object to a plan of religious education which is abstracted from the ministry of Word and sacrament in the visible Church? It is evident that, if what has been said holds good, they have weighty grounds of objection. On the other hand, we have already pointed out that there is no Church in England at present which can reasonably expect to receive that recognition from the State, which was given to the Church of England in the seventeenth century, or to be accorded the opportunity that was accorded then, but has been wasted since.

In this way, the normative conception of the relations of the State with the Church, although it cannot under these conditions be realised, serves to illuminate the causes of the present predicament. It enables us to see that both the present condition of the State and the present condition of the Church are such as to produce an inevitable dilemma. For both State and Church are in an abnormal or unnatural condition. While the churchmen rightly object to an undenominational scheme of religious instruction, abstracted from the Church, and unrelated to the whole educational system, yet that is the most that the statesmen can reasonably be expected to provide for the nation as a whole. They might indeed provide for education to be given in different denominational schools for all children whose parents desired it. But in that case the State would no more be recognising the Church on the ground of truth than in the former case. The fact is that both churchmen and statesmen have to make the best of a bad job. It does not become churchmen to blame the State; they should blame themselves for the present condition of the Church.[1] Until the Christians have found the way to a recovery of the unity of the visible Church, there can be no true marriage of Church and State in England again.

II

Nevertheless, even if it be granted that a marriage of Church and State is a normative Christian ideal—though such an ideal is consistent with human freedom in theory (at any rate this was the claim of Gladstone's theory), would it prove to be so in practice? The problem of toleration calls for fuller consideration than we have yet given to it.

In the Anglo-Saxon world it is nowadays generally taken for granted that religious toleration or religious liberty is so obviously a good thing that there is no need to examine its implications or to provide a theoretical justification for it. As Dr J. W. Allen says:

> One hears, sometimes, talk about something called "the principle of religious toleration". There seems to be an implication that there is just one "principle" on which legal toleration may rationally be based; but it is not very clear what this is. The phrase appears to be one of those catchwords that are abundant in the structure of what is sometimes strangely referred to as "modern thought", and which are useful in saving people the trouble of thinking.[2]

Again, the distinction between toleration and indifference or

1. Cp. T. R. Birks, *Church and State* (1869), p. 315:

> Where there are in a country many religious sects and bodies of Christians, each claiming superior purity or truth, a national Church becomes, in the view of many, a direct nuisance and injustice, a perpetual source of religious jealousy and social discord. The State is perplexed, because the Church is hopelessly divided, and Christ's new commandment has been practically set aside. Such a condition of things calls for humility and confession of guilt, for shame and sorrow, from all earnest and pious Christians. How can truth be publicly honoured if rulers are only deafened by the war-cries of fifty creeds and religious parties, when they ought to hear from the whole Church one consenting witness to the supreme authority of Christ their Lord?

2. J. W. Allen, *Political Thought in the Sixteenth Century*, p. 78.

neutrality [1] on the part of the State is important, but is generally overlooked.

An idea of the complexity that surrounds the subject can be gained from the three volumes of Dr W. K. Jordan's *The Development of Religious Toleration in England.*[2] At the outset he draws a distinction between "religious toleration" and "religious liberty", though he does not always keep it clearly in view as he proceeds.

> In its legal application the word toleration signifies simply a refraining from persecution. It suggests at least latent disapproval of the belief or practice which is tolerated, and refers to a somewhat limited and conditioned freedom. . . . Toleration, therefore, falls considerably short of religious liberty. It presumes an authority which has been and again may become coercive (i. 17).[3]
>
> Toleration, in the historical and legal sense of the term, represents the withdrawal of external authority from the control over certain ranges of human activity, and is essentially negative (i. 19).

As regards the attitude of the State, the word toleration should be used where a definite religion is officially recognised or established, but where freedom of belief and practice is secured to dissenters,[4] and the word indifference, neutrality or equality

1. Cp. Samuel Wilberforce, speaking about India in the House of Lords on July 23, 1858:

> As to neutrality, what was meant? If, not forcing Christianity by violence but observing our own because we believed in it and were not ashamed of it, well and good. But if neutrality meant that our rulers were to show a happy indifference as between Christianity and heathendom, such neutrality would be false to our religion. One was the line of Christian truth; the other the line of a wicked neutrality.—R. G. Wilberforce, *Life of Samuel Wilberforce* (1881), ii. 383.

2. These volumes contain an invaluable collection of material; the author's interpretation of it, however, is not always illuminating.

3. Cp. *Catholic Encyclopædia*, xiv. 763: "By religious toleration is understood the magnanimous indulgence which one shows towards a religion other than his own, accompanied by a moral determination to leave it and its adherents unmolested in private and public, although internally one views it with complete disapproval as a 'false faith'."

4. Thus Disraeli was using the word correctly when, in 1835, he wrote: "The Establishment which, under Laud, persecuted to obtain conformity, is now certainly our surest, perhaps our only, guarantee of Toleration."—*Whigs and Whiggism*, p. 190.

where all religions are treated in the same way, as equally true or equally false. It is question-begging to describe the latter as "religious liberty".[1] Though the State's indifference may be acclaimed as an ideal,[2] though a State may profess indifference or be accused of indifference, it is doubtful whether real indifference is an actual possibility,[3] and, if it were possible, whether it would be in the interest of any significant form of religious liberty. For, as Lord Acton said,

> religious liberty is not the negative right of being without any particular religion, just as self-government is not anarchy. It is the right of all religious communities to the practice of their own duties, the enjoyment of their own constitution, and the protection of the law, which equally secures to all the possession of their own independence. Far from implying a general toleration, it is best secured by a limited one. In an indifferent State, that is, in a State without any definite religious character (if such a thing is conceivable), no ecclesiastical authority could exist.[4]

The question before us here is then whether recognition by the State of the Church, *i.e.* of one Church, on the ground of truth would be consistent with positive religious liberty. Gladstone, we know, considered that his theory not only permitted but required toleration (cp. p. 46 *supra*). He extolled the blessings of toleration in these words:

> It is well that we should be alive to the real blessings which toleration brings with it. The blessing, that the humble and tender-minded inquirer is not solicited to do violence to his conscience for the relief of his property or his person; the

1. On the many possible meanings of this term, see Morley, "Politics and History" in *Works* (1921 ed.), iv. 6ff.

2. "What is the severance of the Church from the State, whereby the Government declares its entire impartiality in matters of opinion, but the ratification of that freedom of inquiry which, while the results of political revolutions are still doubtful, is the clear and inestimable gain of our modern civilisation?"—Goldwin Smith on "The Question of Disestablishment" in *The Nineteenth Century* (October, 1891), p. 523.

3. E. B. Greene points out that in the U.S.A. where the separation between Church and State is in theory complete, this is in practice subject to several qualifications: *Religion and the State*, pp. 97f. See also H. F. Lovell Cocks, *The Nonconformist Conscience* (1943), p. 93.

4. *The History of Freedom, etc.* (1907), pp. 151f. Cp. Gladstone's definition of religious freedom, p. 89 *supra*.

> blessing, that no class of men is now exposed to the corrupting effects which absolute or coercive power in religion has never failed, upon any large scale of the experiment, to produce; the blessing, that the general consent of a free, intelligent, and conscientious people in the religion of the Church offers a far more illustrious testimony to the truth of God than could be yielded by any such uniformity as should rest upon the power of legal penalities or inducements (*SRC*, ii. 255).

He had already defined "the principle of toleration" as follows:

> The principle of toleration amounts, in its proper form, to this, that civil penality or prohibition be not employed to punish or to preclude a man's acting on his own religious opinions. In the largest sense which can properly be assigned to it, it requires that no privilege or benefit which a person is capable of receiving rightly and of using beneficially be withheld from him on account of his religious opinions as such (*SRC*, ii. 178).

He pointed out that this does not exclude the penalisation of the holders of certain religious opinions *on account of the safety of the State*. The latter is part of the question of political, as distinguished from theological, toleration (*SRC*, ii. 178ff.). For example, anyone who holds the religious opinion that coercion may not be used for the preservation of political order may rightly be prohibited from occupying a position in the government of a State,[1] which can nevertheless tolerate that religious opinion and any small sect that professes it.[2]

So far, so good. But at the time when he expounded his theory, Gladstone does not seem to have plumbed the depths of the problem. His definition of the principle of toleration and his conception of religious liberty were too negative. As Acton said, "religious liberty . . . is the right of religious communities to the practice of their own duties, the enjoyment of their own constitution, and the protection of the law, which equally secures to all

1. "We prate of religious toleration," says J. W. Allen, "as though it rested on some principle of universal validity. But religious toleration may be inconsistent with the maintenance of government."—*Political Thought in the Sixteenth Century*, p. 42.

2. Cp. Gladstone, *SRC*, ii. 384. T. R. Birks, *Church and State*, p. 47, says: "Where the view which condemns all oaths as unchristian is the badge of a small sect only, it may be almost harmless. . . . But if the principle once spreads widely, its evil results will soon appear." See also Jeremy Taylor, *The Liberty of Prophesying*, §§ xix, xx.

the possession of their own independence." But can a State, which recognises one Church on the ground of truth, consistently and deliberately secure such liberty to other religious bodies which *ex hypothesi* reject or contradict the truth that is taught by the Church?

This brings us to the crux of the matter. A Church, which professes itself to be infallible and to be in possession of absolute truth, so that outside it there is no salvation, seems bound to oppose the concession of positive liberty to other religious bodies, nay seems bound to call upon the State to grant it the exclusive security of the law. Such a Church, where it has been in a position to do so, has in the past acted in that way. It was the absolutist claims of the medieval and post-Reformation Churches which not only made them intolerant, but sanctioned all the excesses of persecution. If, in the words of Dr Jordan, "the Christian Faith in its very essence teaches that all men who do not embrace a certain body of truth are lost"[1], how can essential Christianity be compatible with the principle of toleration?

"He that is willing to tolerate any Religion, or discrepant way of Religion, beside his owne, unlesse it be in matters meerly indifferent, either doubts of his owne, or is not sincere in it."[2] So wrote Nathaniel Ward, a puritan divine who emigrated to Massachusetts in the seventeenth century, and that expresses the general Christian standpoint from about the time of St Augustine until the seventeenth century. This explains why up to that time the different Churches believed that it would be wrong for them to tolerate one another. Since the seventeenth century, however, not only has toleration come to be accepted in practice, but there has been an important change in theological assumptions.

Dr H. H. Kramm calls attention to this in *The Significance of the Barmen Declaration for the Oecumenical Church*:

> The various denominations, when they were separated from each other in the sixteenth century, did believe that this schism was necessary for Christ's sake, that the other denomination did not worship Christ, but the devil . . .
>
> It cannot be denied that practically all of us have abandoned

1. *Op. cit.*, i. 16. Cp. A. A. Seaton, *The Theory of Toleration*, p. 10.
2. Quoted by E. B. Greene, *Religion and the State*, pp. 43f.

9

> this attitude—perhaps with the exception of some, not all, Missouri Lutherans, certain Roman Catholics and certain sects. Even if we are most convinced children of our own denomination, we will perhaps say that our denomination represents by far the best and purest understanding of Christ, but we will not deny to the other denominations the name of a Church of Christ.[1]

Not only are Christians for the most part much less exclusive now in their attitude to other Christians who are separated from them by ecclesiastical barriers, but *extra Ecclesiam nulla salus*—the well-known saying of St Jerome [2]—has come to be interpreted even by Roman Catholics in an inclusive sense. Whereas Pius IX, in the Syllabus of 1864, condemned the following propositions:

> Liberum cuique homini est eam amplecti ac profiteri religionem, quam rationis lumine quis ductus veram putaverit.
>
> Homines in cuiusvis religionis cultu viam aeternae salutis reperire aeternamque salutem assequi possunt.
>
> Saltem bene sperandum est de aeterna illorum omnium salute, qui in vera Christi Ecclesia nequaquam versantur.
>
> Protestantismus non aliud est quam diversa verae eiusdem christianae religionis forma, in qua aeque ac in Ecclesia catholica Deo placere datum est.[3]

yet he too was, as Newman pointed out in his reply to Gladstone's attack on Vaticanism,[4] the first pope to give authoritative sanction to the doctrine of invincible ignorance.

1. *Op. cit.*, p. 26. The Anglican divines, however, in the sixteenth and seventeenth centuries generally acknowledged that the Reformed Churches on the continent, were Churches of Christ, however defective, and likewise the Church of Rome, however corrupt, though they were more divided in their opinion about the latter. See W. Palmer, *A Treatise on the Church of Christ* [3] (1842), i. 217, 301.

2. Migne, *P.L.*, xxii. 355. See also the gloss of Boniface VIII in the Bull *Unam Sanctam* (1302): "Porro subesse Romano Pontifici omni humanae creaturae declaramus, dicimus, definimus et pronuntiamus omnino esse de necessitate salutis."—Denzinger, *Enchiridion Symbolorum*,[11] p. 206.

3. Denzinger, *op. cit.*, p. 467.

4. *A letter addressed to His Grace the Duke of Norfolk on the occasion of Mr Gladstone's Recent expostulation* (1875), pp. 122f.; cp. *ibid.*, p. 54: "Though 'Out of the Church there is no salvation', this does not hold in the case of good men who are in invincible ignorance."

This doctrine appears now to have become a Roman Catholic commonplace. A writer in the *Catholic Encyclopædia* says that the saying *extra Ecclesiam nulla salus* "certainly does not mean that none can be saved except those who are in visible communion with the Church" (iii. 752); and another: "The foolish and unchristian maxim that those who are outside the Church must for that very reason be eternally lost is no legitimate conclusion from Catholic dogma" (xiv. 766).[1] As regards the non-Roman Churches, Dr Jordan notices that *extra Ecclesiam nulla salus* was affirmed in the main confessions of the Protestant Reformation, except the Anglican and the Zwinglian.[2] But since the advent of toleration, it has been interpreted liberally, where it has not been ignored. F. D. Maurice, the great Anglican theologian of the nineteenth century, interpreted it as follows:

> The doctrine, *Nulla salus extra Ecclesiam*, sounds the cruellest of all doctrines; it has become so in fact. But consider the origin of it. A man possessed with the conviction that human beings are not meant to live in a world where every one is divided from his neighbour—in which there is no uniting, fusing principle, in which each lives to himself, and for himself—bids them fly from that chaos. For he cries, "There is a universe for you! Nay, more, there is a Father's house open to you. God is not the frowning, distant tyrant the world takes Him to be; not split up into a multitude of broken forms and images; not One to whom we are to offer a cold civil lip-service, by way of conciliating Him or doing Him honour. He is the Head of a family; His Son has proved you to be members of it; His Spirit is given you that you may know Him as He is, not as your hard material hearts represent Him to you. Come into this Ark! Take up your place in this Family! here is deliverance and health! *Nulla salus extra Ecclesiam.* No comfort, no health, no peace, while you count yourselves exiles from God, strangers to your brethren."[3]

1. See also K. Adam, *The Spirit of Catholicism* (1929), pp. 161ff.; M. J. Congar, *Divided Christendom* (1939), pp. 222ff. Adam attributes the saying to St Cyprian, *Ep.* lxxiii. 21; but St Cyprian's phrase there is *salus extra Ecclesiam non est.*

2. *Op. cit.*, i. 324. See however W. Palmer, *op. cit.*, Pt I. ch. iii. For a modern Presbyterian comment on the "Nulla salus" formula, see W. A. Curtis, *Jesus Christ as Teacher* (1943), p. 231.

3. *Theological Essays* (1871), pp. 404f.

We may not be so sure that this was the origin of the doctrine, or that St Jerome would have admitted this interpretation. The fact, however, that it is now interpreted in such a broad manner removes its sting, so far as the question of toleration is concerned.

Ecclesiastical intolerance was broken down slowly, and abandoned reluctantly, and it is by no means certain that, like political intolerance, it would not be revived in its harshest form if it became practical politics, or if religion again became a passionate social concern. As Allen says:

> It does not follow, because we are more tolerant of religious difference, that there has been any marked development of a tolerant attitude. Intolerance manifests itself in connection with things in which people, for whatever reason, are passionately interested or with which personal interests are intimately bound up. At the present day, it is manifested most conspicuously in connection not with religion but with politics.[1]

1. J. W. Allen, *Political Thought in the Sixteenth Century*, p. 77. Cp. Mandell Creighton, *Persecution and Tolerance* (1895), pp. 139f.:

> I do not know that the tolerance which is now praised by the world is very firmly established. It rests at present mainly on an equilibrium of forces which might easily be upset. There is always a temptation to the possessors of power—be they an individual, an institution, or a class—to use it selfishly or harshly. Liberty is a tender plant and needs jealous watching. It is always unsafe in the world, and is only secure under the guardianship of the Church; for the Church possesses the knowledge of man's eternal destiny—which alone can justify his claim to freedom.

Dr Arnold Toynbee in *A Study of History*, vi. 316f., issues a warning that the kind of toleration that has been established since the seventeenth century is insecurely grounded:

> In the course of the seventeenth century this victory of the Principle of Toleration in the religious sphere duly won for several succeeding generations that interlude of moderation which gave an ailing Western World a welcome breathing-space between a first and a second paroxysm of its deadly seizure. . . .
>
> Our modern Western Principle of Toleration has failed to bring salvation after all because (as we must confess) there has been no health in it. The spirits that presided over its conception and birth were Disillusionment, Apprehension, and Cynicism, not Faith, Hope, and Charity; the impulse was negative, not positive. . . .
>
> A Toleration that has no roots in Faith has failed to retain any hold upon the heart of *Homo Occidentalis* because human nature abhors a spiritual vacuum.

See also Reinhold Niebuhr, *The Nature and Destiny of Man*, ii. 246f.:

> It is significant that so much of modern toleration applies merely to the field of religion; and that the very champions of toleration in this field may be exponents of political fanaticism. It is simple enough to be tolerant on issues which are not believed to be vital.

Morley's dictum is never to be forgotten: "Man is born intolerant and of all ideas toleration would seem to be in the general mind the very latest."[1] It is therefore requisite that the positive and enduring grounds, which make toleration a Christian principle, should be plainly and irrevocably declared. The danger of an indiscriminate reaction from liberalism is already a present one. The case against toleration, as easily as the case for it, can strike the mind as obvious. In the words of Thomas Carlyle: "Toleration is miserably mistaken; means for the most part only indifference and contempt. What is bad *is* a thing the sooner the better to be abolished."[2] Let it be acknowledged, with thankfulness and with resolution, that the duty of toleration is a lesson that God has taught His Church during the last three centuries, and that it is a lesson that must never be unlearned. The time has come when it must be shown that the duty of toleration does not depend on the assumptions of *laissez faire*, and that its true grounds lie elsewhere.

It is on grounds such as the following that toleration should be defined as a Christian principle, and they are more extensive than those specified by Gladstone when he originally expounded his theory of the relations of the State with the Church, and more authentically Christian than those with which he subsequently associated himself as a Liberal statesman.

(1) The Gospel of Jesus Christ, to which the Church is commissioned to bear witness, is addressed to persons who are responsible for their acceptance or rejection of it. They have no real or adequate opportunity of rejecting it where the alternative to membership in the Church is persecution or penalisation, *i.e.* where they are coerced into being members, or loss of social security, which is a more subtle form of coercion. The conditions for genuine decision exist only where other religious bodies than the national Church have their liberty secured by law. In a State which recognises the Church on the ground of truth, it will be an interest and a duty of the Church to see that such liberty is secured to dissenters. It will not be enough that, to quote the Dutch writer Uytenbogaert, the magistrates permit and tolerate other kinds of religion than that which they hold to be the only

1. Morley on "Politics and History" in *Works* (1921 ed.), iv. 16.
2. See D. A. Wilson, *Carlyle to the "French Revolution"* (1924), p. 303.

true one "by waye of connivencye; looking upon them, as it were, through the fingers".[1] For as Acton said,

> Religious liberty . . . is possible only where the coexistence of different religions is admitted, with an equal right to govern themselves according to their own several principles. Tolerance of error is requisite for freedom; but freedom will be most complete where there is no actual diversity to be resisted, and no theoretical unity to be maintained, but where unity exists as the triumph of truth, through the victory of the Church, not through the enactment of the State.[2]

The agreement most worth having is that of men who are free to differ, and, as Acton also said, "the most certain test by which we can judge whether a country is really free is the amount of security enjoyed by minorities".[3]

(2) Ecclesiastical intolerance, and the demand that the civil power should support it, were in the past sanctioned by the belief that the Church was in possession of absolute truth. Therefore all dissent from the Church was regarded as damnable. The Church, which has its charter in the Holy Scriptures, must certainly claim to be entrusted with the responsibility of bearing authoritative testimony to the truth about God's saving self-revelation in Christ.[4] It must reject, that is to say, the merely relativist notion that all religions are more or less true, or that it is arbitrary to regard one as true and the others as false. But this is consistent with the confession not only that there is some truth in other religions, and indeed in non-religious systems, but also with the confession that God's self-revelation, so far as any actual Church bears witness to it, is in earthen vessels; the testimony of every Church is conditioned by human fallibility.

> The truth, as it is contained in the Christian revelation, includes the recognition that it is neither possible for man to know the truth fully nor to avoid the error of pretending that he does.[5]

1. See Douglas Nobbs, *Theocracy and Toleration* (1938), p. 34.
2. *The History of Freedom, etc.*, p. 152.
3. *Ibid.*, p. 4.
4. See my contribution to *No Other Gospel* (1943), ed. by J. O. Cobham, pp. 52–63.
5. Reinhold Niebuhr, *The Nature and Destiny of Man*, ii. 225. See the whole chapter.

By demanding that liberty be secured to dissenters, a Church acknowledges before God and reminds itself that its witness is not absolutely true or faithful, and consequently that it is always prone to give occasion for the legitimate refusal of assent.

(3) The Church must acknowledge not only that its testimony is not entirely free from error, but that its institutional life is always subject to the corroding effects of sin.[1] When it is prosperous and at peace, it is liable to become self-satisfied and stagnant. Ecclesiastical government is, like civil government, corruptible by power, and prone to discourage and discharge progressive movements, and to suppress minorities which are sensitive to the need for new applications of the everlasting gospel, whether in the field of thought or of action.

The provision of liberty for dissenters—so far as possible within, but where necessary outside, the Church—will act as a preservative against the baleful effects of an established uniformity or of a merely conservative traditionalism.[2] A Church which knows itself to be in danger of stoning the prophets whom God raises up for its correction and reformation will want to make sure that they are not silenced, even if they must needs speak without its bounds. Clericalism, or priestly dominance, is an enemy always at the gate of the Church, even of a Church which prides itself upon its Protestantism or upon its confession of the priesthood of all believers.[3] In the case of a national Church such clericalism will be checked by the tension with the State, which if it arises, as

1. "The fanatic fury of religious controversies, the hatred engendered in theological disputes, the bitterness of ecclesiastical rivalries and the pretensious claims of ecclesiastical dominion all reveal the continued power of sin in the life of the 'redeemed'; and the use which sin makes of the pretension of holiness."—R. Niebuhr, *op. cit.*, p. 227.

2. What Professor Ernest Barker once wrote with regard to the State applies also to the Church:

> It may be urged that heterogeneity of opinion is a symptom of an imperfect community, which has never thought itself together. It may also be urged that the opposite is true. The pullulation of new organizing and associating ideas is not a sign of poverty of mind. . . . The very attempt of factors which conceive themselves neglected to push themselves forward as absolute wholes on their own account may serve as an incentive to a truer synthesis.—Art. on "The Discredited State" in *The Political Quarterly* (February, 1915), pp. 115f.

3. "Rien n'est dangereux comme un théologien puissant", said A. Vinet. *Essai sur la manifestation des convictions religieuses* (1842), p. 198.

it should, from a sense that both are ordained by God, will prevent either the ecclesiastical or the civil power from having unrestricted course. But the governing elements in a Church, from which there is no secured freedom of dissent in the religious sphere,[1] will be too easily tempted to lord it over God's people.

III

Unless on grounds such as those that have just been indicated, the duty of toleration both by Church and State is clearly defined as a Christian principle, the recognition of the Church by the State on the ground of truth would lead to the suppression of that basic and positive freedom, which it is the task of the State to secure, and also to that ecclesiastical stagnation or obscurantism, which is fatal to a Church. If a marriage of State and Church is to be regarded as a norm, it must be with these essential qualifications. A relationship between State and Church, so qualified, would be different from any that existed in the Middle Ages or in the Post-Reformation Church-States. Such a Christian State would be neither a case of political monism (of a single society)—like the Church-States of the past, nor of mere political pluralism (of a collection of societies and individuals), *i.e.* where the State professes no faith, but limits itself to providing conditions in which competing societies with diverse faiths or ideologies are kept together. On the contrary, it would be a State which professes a definite faith, but deliberately provides full security for dissenting minorities.[2] It would be a State which, to use a phrase of

1. While therefore we may agree with Mr T. S. Eliot that the idea of a Christian society implies "the existence of one Church which shall *aim at* comprehending the whole nation" (*The Idea of a Christian Society*, pp. 53f.; italics his), yet we would add that the fact that it is always unlikely to succeed in doing so is a blessing in disguise, as he would probably agree, see following note.

2. The problem may be envisaged in the form of a question. What ought to be the place of the parish church and of dissenting chapels in future town or village planning? In the old Church-State the parish church normally stood in the centre of a community along with the town hall (my native town of Rye, Sussex, provides an admirable illustration of this). The setting up of dissenting chapels in odd corners was eventually tolerated as a regrettable necessity. In the *laissez-faire* period churches and chapels took their chance along with everything else, and were fitted in wherever room happened to be available, though of course in ancient municipalities the old parish church

Disraeli, "proved the compatibility of sectarian toleration and national orthodoxy."[1]

In England, for the reasons that have been given, the realisation of such a relationship on a national scale seems at present to be no more than a remote possibility, though in certain localities approximations to it may be possible already. It is idle to speculate as to the form which such a national recognition of one Church on the ground of truth might take in detail, since that depends on future ecclesiastical and political conditions which are incalculable. But it is not idle to assert that this is the normative relationship which ought always to be an eventual Christian aim, which therefore must prevent Christians from resting satisfied with any arrangement short of it, and which will make them welcome any present approximations to it that are possible.

The relationship that is likely to exist between the various Christian bodies in England and the State in the near future is not easy to predict, but constant recollection of the norm will serve as a warning against two opposite tendencies which are at present observable. These may be described as (*a*) undenominationalism, and (*b*) denominationalism.

(*a*) On the one hand, there is the tendency for the State, needing as it does some fresh moral inspiration (a need which may well become more insistent when the stimulus of the war is removed), to extend its patronage to an undenominational form of Christianity, abstracted from the creed and worship and ministry of the Church or Churches. This might be a kind of British or Anglo-Saxon Christianity, in some ways analogous to the "German Christianity" that was fostered in Nazi Germany. There the enterprise met with mediocre success, partly because its encouragement was only a secondary aim of the State in the

retained its ancient pre-eminence in appearance. In local communities, such as we desire, a parish church and town hall—symbols of the national Church and the national State—would be planned for in the centre of the town and village, together with other "community centres", but the plan would also deliberately make provision nearer the circumference for the buildings of dissenting societies, religious, political, and cultural.

"A positive culture", says Mr T. S. Eliot, "must have a positive set of values, and the dissentients must remain marginal, tending to make only marginal contributions."—*Op. cit.*, p. 46.

1. *Whigs and Whiggism*, p. 231.

religious sphere, and partly because of the firm opposition to it from the German Confessional Church and from the Roman Catholics. But an Anglo-Saxon Christianity might be presented much more seductively to the Christians in England. The emphasis would be, perhaps, on the need for inculcating the morality which all good men in the Western democracies admire, and on the value of ethics quite apart from divine revelation. A faint flavour of Christian dogma, and a considerable residuum of Christian terminology, could be retained in such a scheme,[1] and this might deceive the very elect.

A correspondent of *The Spectator* writes:

> A firm distinction should be drawn between *doctrine* and *ethics* . . . "Do good to them that hate you . . . give to every one that asketh thee", and the like, are magnificent moral principles in their own right. Let the emphasis be laid on them, not on doctrinal dogmas, which as a whole are entirely unsuitable for young people to tackle. If Christian doctrine must be taught, let it be in a secular and impartial manner and, not as at present, as Divine revelation with which no child must disagree.[2]

The temptation to the representatives of the State to forward a scheme of this kind might become, as Gladstone recognised towards the end of his life, a severe one. Traditional ideas about the Law of Nature might be used to justify it to uneasy Christian minds. Is it not the task of the State to instruct its citizens in the

1. This is not a characterisation of the religious instruction that is at present given in provided schools; still less does it apply to such an admirable undenominational manual as *The Cambridgeshire Syllabus of Religious Teaching for Schools* (1939). The question is of a tendency, which—despite any agreed intentions of ecclesiastics and theologians—may prove congenial to those who will hold political power, and even to educationalists, because it is already congenial to society as a whole.

2. Letter from Mr A. P. Kiely, August 20, 1943, p. 173. Cp. the letter written to *The Times* on August 10, 1943, by Lord Horder and seven other well-known public men, who say:

> We venture to commend to the consideration of all concerned a new constructive proposal for the solution of the religious difficulty in schools. Our suggestion is that all religious instruction in State-aided schools should be directed towards a general knowledge of the common spiritual and ethical elements of the great faiths of the world. . . .
>
> The adoption of our proposal would ensure that in the nation's schools religious instruction in its noblest and broadest sense would be universally given.

Law of Nature, upon which all men can agree apart from the claims of the Christian revelation, and to leave revealed religion to be handled separately by the Church for such citizens as want it? We grant that it is the duty of statesmen, and of Christians as citizens, to foster the moral idealism of the British people, and to harness it to a social purpose that will avert the menace of totalitarianism; but it is the duty of the Church to make it clear that this moral idealism is not Christianity. It is Law, not Gospel.

The relation between the Law of Nature and the Christian revelation is indeed a matter of unresolved disputation among theologians. In the earlier part of his career Gladstone himself had no doubt about the dependence of morality on divine revelation. In a speech at the opening of the Liverpool Collegiate Institution on January 6, 1843, which was afterwards published, he spoke of

> a great and indestructible principle—namely . . . the principle that Education, if it is to be effectual, if it is to be valuable—if it is to be deserving of the name—must be a religious education; and . . . in order to deserve the character of a religious education, it must be founded, not upon those vague generalities which are supposed to be common to all men, or at least to all men who assume the name of Christians, but upon the definite revelation which it has pleased God to give, and whereby each man among us must hope to stand or fall.[1]

While as a churchman he did not move from this position,[2] as a statesman he obviously had to do so,[3] and we find him

1. *Op. cit.*, p. 11; cp. p. 16: "We believe that if you could erect a system which should present to mankind all branches of knowledge, save the one which is essential, you would only be building up to heaven a Tower of Babel, which, when you had completed it, would be the more signal in its fall, and would bury those who raised it in its ruins." See also p. 34, n. 2 *supra*, and *SRC*, ii. 395.

2. *E.g.* see his article on "The Courses of Religious Thought" in *The Contemporary Review* (June, 1876).

3. C. E. Osborne in *Christian Ideas in Political History* (1929), p. 68, quotes Gladstone as having spoken during the China War of 1857 of "the higher ground of natural justice which binds man to man; which is older than Christianity, because it was in the world before Christianity; which is broader than Christianity, because it extends to the world beyond Christianity; and which underlies Christianity, for Christianity itself appeals to it". The quotation, though inexact, is not misleading except that Osborne failed to point out that by "higher ground" Gladstone meant higher than the grounds of municipal and international law. See *War in China; speech of the Rt Hon. W. E. Gladstone, M.P.*, March 3, 1857, pp. 23f.

saying on June 24, 1870, in a speech on the Elementary Education Bill:

> The duty of the State is to make use of them (the Voluntary or Church schools) for the purpose of the secular instruction which they give, but to hold itself entirely and absolutely detached from all responsibility with regard to their religious teaching.[1]

As is well known, it did come to appear in the Victorian era that it was possible to retain the main elements of Christian ethics without Christian dogma. Lord Salisbury, who had a less sanguine temperament than Gladstone, offered an explanation of the fact that the habits of Christian morality survive—as they did, for instance, in the great Victorian agnostics—the decay of Christian faith.

> Christian morality is a blessing which can only be enjoyed by the world as a consequence of Christian faith. . . . This rule is true of a community, but it is not necessarily true of an individual. Some of the brightest examples of what a Christian life should be have been, and still are, men who have renounced all but the mere pretence of Christian faith. The fact in their case is that their morality was formed before their intellect went astray. Virtue had become easy to them before faith had become difficult. Thus it has come to pass that Christianity has been reproached with her own success, and the morality which her preaching has produced has been employed to discredit its truth. . . . Men will not be moral without a motive, and . . . a motive can only be furnished by religious belief.[2]

The force of these prescient observations—they were made in 1865—is more evident to-day than it was then. Moreover, they help to explain how a man like Gladstone was led into being too confident about the future.

1. See *The Times*, June 25, 1870.

2. See Gwendolen Cecil, *Life of Robert, Marquis of Salisbury* (1921), i. 334. Cp. P. T. Forsyth, *Rome, Reform, and Reaction* (1899), p. 138:

> All the ethical world spreads away from the true focus of personal faith in God's forgiving grace in Christ. All the moral order is ruled from this throne. I do not say that morality does not exist apart from religion; it does. But I do say that finally it cannot; in the spiritual and ultimate nature of things the two are not separable, distinguish them as you may. The permanent ethic is Christian ethic; and Christian conduct dies soon after Christian faith.

About the same time (1864) Hort, in a letter to Westcott, said: "I believe Coleridge was quite right in saying that Christianity without a substantial Church is vanity and dissolution."[1] As a churchman Gladstone would of course have agreed, but as a statesman, responsible for introducing a national system of education, how could he consistently act upon this conviction? By undenominationalism we mean the attempt to preserve Christianity in abstraction from a substantial Church. Because, especially in the vitally important sphere of education, under present conditions no other way seems to be open to the State, prescient churchmen are bound to maintain a protest against what they must regard as a lamentable, if necessary, evil. But they are bound also, as we have said, to blame themselves for the weak and divided condition of the Church, which is one cause of that necessity, and earnestly to work so to overcome their divisions that the State may eventually be able to have dealings with a substantial Church, a Church that is both one and visible, and qualified to undertake its appointed responsibility for the spiritual and moral education of the people on a national scale.

(*b*) On the other hand, we said that there is an opposite tendency which must be guarded against, namely "denominationalism". Just as clericalism and anti-clericalism thrive on one another, and indeed account for one another, so undenominationalism breeds denominationalism, and *vice versa*. By denominationalism we mean here what Mr Daniel T. Jenkins has defined by this name in his book *The Nature of Catholicity*, though we mean more than this, or are concerned with implications of it which do not lie within his immediate purview. He writes as follows:

> "Denominationalism" is the attitude of a Church which ceases to scrutinise and reform itself under the Word of God and loses all concern about its catholicity, contenting itself with enjoying and perpetuating its own traditions and distinctive ethos and maintaining itself in separation from other Churches not for theological reasons but because "it prefers its own way of doing things". The attitude is, therefore, by no means confined to the "Free" Churches in England.[2]

We are at this point concerned with the implications of denomi-

1. See A. F. Hort, *Life and Letters of Fenton John Anthony Hort* (1896), ii. 30.
2. *Op. cit.* (1942), p. 129; cp. pp. 125ff.

nationalism for the relations of the Church (or Churches) with the State rather than for the relations of separated Churches with each other. A Church becomes a religious denomination when it looks upon its task in terms of providing for the religious or "spiritual" needs of its members and such other persons as it can persuade to use its services, leaving what is not religious and not directly connected with religion to go its own way. Treachery to the gospel of God's sovereignty over the whole world is most blatant where a Church contents itself, in Jenkins' words, "with enjoying and perpetuating its own traditions and distinctive ethos", but it is also possible for a Church, which professes to be continually reforming itself under the Word of God, to interpret this duty in a narrowly religious sense. As Mr Alexander Miller has said,

> It is unquestionably true that a good deal of theologising which claims the name "Catholic" or "Confessional" or "Reformed" tends towards a pretty barren ecclesiasticism, divorced from any radical concern with Christian obedience in terms of contemporary political and economic facts. No type of theology—or philosophy for that matter—ever devised (*sic*) but was exploited for escapist purposes by those who should have known better. . . .
>
> The return to Biblical and Reformation tradition has sometimes by distortion been used to justify a refusal to face the plain issues of contemporary life.[1]

Unfortunately, the "issues of contemporary life" do not always seem plain. They are in many ways extremely perplexing, and those Christians, who are determined to avoid "wishful thinking", may be pardoned for wondering whether, with the best will in the world, they are likely to bring much influence to bear upon general social change. It may seem to them that the most they can expect is to preserve certain limited areas from the control of social planners. The temptation to restrict their interest to these limited areas will be strong, all the more so perhaps in a State which encourages an undenominational form of Christianity, which cannot be simply negated and which therefore may be regarded with acquiescence, though not with enthusiasm. In these circumstances, Churches might easily degenerate into sects or religious clubs, where they have not done so already.

1. Article in *The Presbyter* (August, 1943), pp. 9f.

It must therefore be said, in season and out of season, that a Church to be worthy of the name,[1] however small a minority it may be in any given society, is charged with the responsibility of bearing testimony to God's sovereignty and God's will before kings and rulers and the whole people. It must declare man's civic duties as well as his ecclesiastical duties. It must teach the Law of God, as well as preach the Gospel of God. It must denounce injustice and sin [2] wherever they are to be found, and call upon all men to repent and return unto the Lord their God by obeying His law in their common life.

In particular, it must be said that a national Church, such as the Church of England, may not relinquish the responsibility for and to the whole people with which God entrusted it in the past, and which, in spite of its failures and the anomalies in its present relation to the State, God has not yet removed from it. But even if in the future the Church of England should be disestablished, it would still have the responsibility, grounded in God's ordinance though no longer acknowledged by the State, of addressing the whole nation, and it would have to set about working towards a re-establishment of right relations between Church and State all over again.

IV

Our conclusion is that, while there is a normative relationship between the Church and the State at which Christians must always be aiming, the extent to which this norm can be realised varies with the changing conditions of history. We can point to no time or place in the past, and say, "That is the form of relationship between Church and State which ought to be established everywhere and at all times, and therefore here and now". For even when there has been a marriage between Church and State in the past, it has always been defective, especially in the matter of willingness to secure toleration for dissenters.

1. "A sect", wrote P. T. Forsyth, "was originally defined as such not merely by theological peculiarities but by its lack of relation to the State. . . . To take the name of a Church is really to assume such a relationship to the nation as cannot be indifferent to the State, nor observe a mere neutrality."—*Theology in Church and State*, p. 237.

2. Reinhold Niebuhr in *The Christian News-Letter* (August 25, 1943) spoke of "the final right which makes the Christian Church in the real sense a Church: the right to mediate the judgment of God upon the sins of a nation".

Involved as we are at present in a process of transition, of which the outcome is incalculable, we are not in a position to say what will be the best possible form that the relations between Church and State can take. This study has, however, brought before us a number of considerations which should guide Christians in the decisions that they will have to make, and which we may now try to sum up.

(1) A Christian doctrine of the State must be correlated with a doctrine of the Church. Both Church and State are ordained by God, who is the creator and redeemer of the world, to serve complementary functions. They are necessary to the well-being of one another. That is to say, a Christian doctrine of the State will include a doctrine of the right or normative relations of the State with the Church. A separation or divorce between Church and State may in some conditions be inevitable, but in the long run it spells evil for both.

The State, which does not recognise the Church as the organ of, or witness to, an absolute and transcendent kingdom of God, tends ineluctably to exalt itself into an absolute and to make transcendent claims for itself. And again, because the State must strive to embody justice but can achieve only a rough justice at the best of times, it needs to recognise and provide scope alongside itself for an institution which will declare the State's own limitations so that it shall neither idealise nor rest content with them. As Dr Reinhold Niebuhr has said in another connexion (for "civilisation" we can read "State" or "nation"):

> A Christian civilisation is one which allows the word of God's judgment to be spoken against it, and which therefore knows itself ultimately dependent upon the mercy of God. A Christian civilisation is one therefore which knows itself not to be Christian in the purely ethical sense in which both critics and defenders of our civilisation have currently used that term.[1]

The State is ordained by God for the maintenance of order, for securing the highest possible degree of justice and freedom, and for providing conditions in which the Church can proclaim and make effective the divine message which alone keeps the State in its

1. Article on "The Idea of a Christian Civilization" in *The Student Movement* (October, 1941), p. 6. Cp. preceding note.

right place.[1] Thus the State requires for its well-being to be in right relations with the Church.[2]

But also the Church needs for its well-being to be in right relations with the State. A Church which is not a national Church, or which is not becoming a national Church, is likely to sink into a sect or a religious denomination, if it is not one already. On the other hand, an Erastian relationship is equally fatal, for then the proper distinction in nature and function between the State and the Church is blurred, and what should be the healthy and uneasy tension between them is obliterated. A true Church will therefore declare to the State both the State's true place in the divine economy, and also the State's obligation to recognise the Church as the bearer of the everlasting, saving and universal gospel of God, and to provide it with the opportunity to carry out its mission. This recognition of the Church's inherent authority alongside that of the State may often be embarrassing to the State on a short view, but in the long run it alone can afford the State a sure foundation. A living and strong Church also needs to have its will-to-power balanced and checked by a strong State. The downfall and demoralisation of the medieval papacy were partly due to the decay of the Holy Roman Empire which, as long as it thrived, checked the power of the papacy, and prevented it from the effective assertion of the more extravagant pretensions which led to its eventual downfall.[3]

1. Professor Karl Barth goes so far as to say: "Apart from the Church, nowhere is there any fundamental knowledge of the reasons which make the State legitimate and necessary."—*Church and State* (English translation, 1939), p. 70. But this is a characteristic over-statement.

2. The Christian Church, said Coleridge, "is the appointed Opposite to them all (*sc.* state, kingdom, or realm of this world), *collectively*—the *sustaining, correcting, befriending* Opposite of the world! the compensating counterforce to the inherent and inevitable evils and defects of the STATE, *as* a State".—*Church and State* (1830), pp. 132f. See also *ibid.*, p. 135: the Christian Church "is objective in its nature and purpose, not mystic or subjective . . . an institution consisting of visible and public communities"; and p. 136: "Her paramount aim and object . . . is *another* world, not a world *to come* exclusively, but likewise *another world that now is.*"

Cp. *The Tablet* (February 8, 1941), p. 104: "The extreme importance of religious bodies, and of the Church in particular, is that they are the hearths and foci of standards of conduct and a view of the meaning of life irreconcilable with any all-embracing State philosophy."

3. See A. J. Toynbee, *A Study of History* (1939), iv. 217.

A Christian doctrine of the State would, then, affirm that State and Church are separate and distinct forms of human society, which are complementary to one another, both of them necessary for the well-being of man, and both of them ordained by God. Though distinct and separate, their provinces overlap.[1] The object of the State is to realise order and justice, of the Church to proclaim truth and to embody love. The characteristic concern of the State is with law, of the Church with gospel—of the State with institutions, of the Church with persons. The method of the State is in the last resort coercion, the method of the Church is in the last resort persuasion.

The Christian man must acknowledge that there is an inescapable dualism in historical existence, which will never be overcome until the Lord comes again at the end of the world. The difference between Church and State is a witness to this dualism,[2] and points beyond itself and beyond history to the consummation of all things in the kingdom of God.

(2) No absolute principles have been revealed or discovered regarding the relations between Church and State which can or must be rigorously applied in all historical situations. There are, however, certain norms, which ought to guide the Christian as he participates in the affairs of State. These are based on the affirmations of the gospel and on the nature of the State, as these can be seen after two thousand years of varying circumstance and experiment. In any attempt to define these norms Gladstone's early teaching deserves the serious attention of Christian men, namely, that (*a*) the State is intended by God to be a "moral person"; (*b*) the State is capable of acknowledging, and is therefore morally bound to acknowledge, truth, when adequately presented to it; and (*c*) a marriage between Church and State is the best possible ideal, which therefore Christians should always have in view.

(3) Nevertheless, the extent to which these and other norms

1. Cp. pp. 45 and 95 *supra*.

2. Cp. the evidence of the Church Self-government League before the Archbishops' Commission on the relations between Church and State, 1935. After quoting the saying in the Epistle to Diognetus that Christians "exist in the flesh, but have their citizenship in heaven", they add: "This is to assert an unmistakable dualism, on the human plane, between the Church and the secular State, a dualism which should ideally express itself in a parallelism, not in a conflict, of loyalties."—*Church and State*, ii. 17f.

can be applied and realised will depend on historical conditions. There are periods and situations, such as the first three centuries of our era, and also the twentieth century in England, not to mention other countries—when a true marriage between Church and State is rendered impossible by conditions which admit of no sudden alteration. The secularisation of society and the disintegrated state of the Church are prohibiting conditions in England at present. At such times Christians must work for the best arrangement that is possible, taking into account the welfare and the divinely appointed task of the State as well as of the Church, but even so they should not lose sight of the norm at which they should be eventually aiming. They must not lose interest [1] in a State, which ceases to be Christian, for it still remains God's ordinance. Doctrinaire idealism is not Christian, and to that extent at least Gladstone was right to modify his teaching.

As we have seen, Gladstone wrote his books, *The State in its relations with the Church* and *Church Principles*, in order to vindicate norms, but he did so just at a time when it was ceasing to be possible to continue the realisation of those norms as they had been established in England. The irresistible pressure of *laissez-faire* liberalism was about to break up, or at least substantially to modify, the traditional union of Church and State. The Christian man must read the signs of the times, as well as learn the lessons of theology, history and political theory.

(4) As soon as he took the measure of the situation, Gladstone abandoned the attempt to maintain the reality of the union, though he still wanted to preserve so much of it as could reasonably be preserved. In 1843 he wrote: "Of public life, I certainly must say, every year shows me more and more that the idea of a Christian politics cannot be realised in the state according to its present conditions of existence."[2] In 1845, in the course of an

1. Like, for instance, Dr Pusey who wrote to Gladstone in 1849: "What the State is to do when it casts off the guidance of the Church, and is to act upon some heathen principle, I know not what; some abstraction or ideal of its own, and to have education theories, etc., of its own, is no concern of mine".—Liddon, *Life of Pusey*, iii. 184; cp. *ibid.*, "Pusey thought that government, like everything else, should be conducted on purely Christian principles. Mr Gladstone replied, 'That any man in any country can in this age of the world give *full* effect to Christian principles in the work of government is, alas! very far beyond my belief'" (p. 176). See also *ibid.*, ii. 27, iv. 199f., 361.

2. Morley, i. 183.

important letter to Newman, he wrote: "My language has always been, 'Here is the genuine and proper theory of government as to religion; hold it as long as you can, and as far as you can'. Government must subsist; and if not as (in strictness) it ought, then as it may".[1]

Although the idea of a Christian politics could no longer be realised,[2] he held that Christians—or at all events he himself as a Christian—still were bound to take part in politics. But it would, he said,[3] be "like serving for Leah afterwards to win Rachel". Everyone knows how persistent and magnanimous his service was. It was said of Sir Robert Peel that, after the passing of the Reform Act of 1832, he laboured "to confute his own predictions of disaster".[4] The same may be said of Gladstone here. Indeed, he engaged in the politics of the Liberal State with such enthusiasm [5] and such success that eventually he seems almost to have

1. *CCR*, i. 72. In the same letter he wrote:

> The State cannot be said now to have a conscience, at least not by me, inasmuch as I think it acts, and acts wilfully, and intends to go on acting, in such a way as no conscience—that is, no personal conscience (which is the only real form of one)—can endure. But the State still continues to act in many ways *as if* it had a conscience. The Christian figure of our institutions still remains, though marred by the most incongruous associations. There are, therefore, actual relations of the State to Religion—I mean to determinate religion—which still subsist and retain much vitality, and offer opportunities of good in proportion to it, however they may be surrounded with violent moral contradictions. For the sake of these opportunities I think that public life is tolerable and, in my case, as it at present stands, obligatory. But it is like serving for Leah afterwards to win Rachel.

In 1860 the author of *The Ultimate Principle of Religious Liberty* was shrewd enough to remark that "Mr Gladstone might give it (his theory) up, as unattainable under certain contingent circumstances of this country, but to expect him to abandon a theoretical belief in its legitimacy, would be to overlook all the traditional and instinctive tendencies of his mind" (p. 142).

2. But for a qualification of this, see p. 96 *supra*.

3. See n. 1 *supra*.

4. C. S. Parker, *Sir Robert Peel*, i. (6).

5. On April 9, 1887, Mandell Creighton wrote to Lord Acton:

> I remember that in 1880 I met John Bright at dinner: he was very cross, apparently a Cabinet meeting has disagreed with him. Among other things he said, "If the people knew what sort of men statesmen were, they would rise and hang the whole lot of them." Next day I met a young man who had been talking to Gladstone, who urged him to parliamentary life, saying, "Statesmanship is the noblest way to serve mankind."

Creighton added: "I am sufficient of a Hegelian to be able to combine both judgments; but the results of my combination cannot be expressed in the terms of the logic of Aristotle."—*Life and Letters of Mandell Creighton*, i. 373.

forgotten Rachel! He thought that *laissez-faire* had come to stay in England. No more than his contemporaries did he understand that its success was due to temporary and local conditions, which could not endure. Moreover, his misgivings about the future of religion were allayed by the continuance throughout the nineteenth century of a diffused Christianity in the State, and by an apparent revival in the Church, which concealed the extent to which society was being secularised and the Church was losing its hold on the people. Politics at home retained a Christian flavour, and in foreign policy too conditions were favourable to Gladstone's high moral tone. A foreign writer has remarked, with a touch of cynicism, that "this Christian-ethical policy was only possible because Gladstone's predecessors had already established the supremacy of England both on sea and land so that it could not be questioned, thus giving Gladstone the luxury of carrying on a moral policy".[1]

1. Erich Marks, quoted by Troeltsch, ii. 938. See also Buckle, *Life of Disraeli*, iv. 403. In the volume on *Nationalism*, published by the Royal Institute of International Affairs in 1940, we read:

> Most Englishmen assume as a matter of course that, in countries where the public conscience appears most active, moral considerations have more influence than elsewhere in determining national policy. But is this assumption justified? May not the function of the public conscience be, not to influence national policy, but to provide a moral basis for policies determined on purely national grounds? . . . The personal sincerity of the individual does not preclude the existence of that more deep-seated unconscious national hypocrisy which instinctively and unerringly produces at a given moment the appropriate moral principles to justify British policy and to condemn that of an opponent. Some years ago an Italian ex-Minister for Foreign Affairs, Count Sforza, wrote of "that precious gift bestowed on the British people—the possession of writers and clergymen able in perfect good faith to advance the highest moral reasons for the most concrete diplomatic action, with inevitable moral profit to England" (pp. 319f.).

In a leading article in *The Times* (November 16, 1940) we read:

> The comparatively liberal system of international trade which flourished in the nineteenth century was built up on British supremacy in the world of industry, commerce, and finance. That supremacy, due to the long start obtained by Great Britain through her early industrial development, could not be indefinitely maintained; and no doubt the British apostles of free trade were open to the charge of preaching a British interest in the guise of a universal ideal.

A view which tried to account for Gladstone's political moralism simply in terms of the unconscious national hypocrisy of Britain would be shallow, and indeed frivolous; nevertheless, those considerations would be pertinent to a discerning estimate of the moral significance of his statesmanship.

The Christian man must acknowledge that all human thought and action are historically and sociologically conditioned, and that this is one reason why not only Christian public opinion errs, but great Christian leaders err as well.

(5) It is as a result of changes which he failed to anticipate that his work on *The State in its relations with the Church* has acquired, a century after its publication, a kind of relevance which neither he nor anyone else in the hey-day of the Victorian era could have imagined. The collectivist State or the planned society of the future will, so far as we can judge, be based on some sort of metaphysical or anti-metaphysical dogma; its ideology will not be *laissez-faire*.[1] The question has to be asked whether the Christian faith can be so re-presented to the State and so recover its hold on the community as to lead to the public acknowledgment of its truth, and so to a new form of marriage between the visible Church and the State. We have had to confess that there are formidable obstacles to any such development in the proximate future. But it will make a great difference if both churchmen and statesmen, when framing the best arrangements that alone are possible in a transitional period, are aware that this is the eventual Christian aim, and that any arrangement short of it must be a provisional and not an enduring solution.

(6) But, lastly, there are no final solutions. Men have here no abiding city; Christian men seek one to come. As AE said, "No country can marry any particular solution and live happily ever afterwards."[2] The cities that men build on earth, the social systems and civilisations that they must be constantly striving to achieve, are impermanent, though great and good men like Gladstone may be deceived as to the immediate prospect and may misread the signs of the times. History seems to show that each solution contains within itself the seeds of its own decay and disintegration.[3]

1. Canon J. S. Bezant writes: "The idea that the State should be stripped of all responsibility for the religious and moral life of the nation is in practice impossible, and anyhow is all wrong."—*The Guardian* (August 20, 1943), p. 276.

2. Quoted by Lewis Mumford, *The Culture of Cities* (1940 ed.), p. 363.

3. "In the mixed combinations of worldly affairs", wrote Gladstone, "even the most needful, and, on the whole, beneficial changes, bear within them the seeds of disorganisation."—*SRC*, ii. 257.

We can see how this has worked out in the case of ancient Rome, in the case of the medieval synthesis of the Papal Church and the Empire, in the case of the post-Reformation marriage of national Churches with national States; and we can see how it is working out now in the case of the tolerated Church in the *laissez-faire* or Liberal State.[1] Doubtless, the same law will apply to the coming collectivist State, whether or not it has a Christian character; and even if it is only beyond that that a new Christendom can be born, that too will sooner or later decay. As Jacques Maritain has said,

> The idea of making this world purely and simply the Kingdom of God is heresy for a Christian. . . .
>
> Worlds which have risen in heroism lie down in fatigue, for new heroisms and new suffering to come in their turn and bring in the dawn of another day. Such is the growth of human history, which is not a process of repetition but of expansion and progress: it grows like an expanding circle, so stretching out to its double consummation—in that absolute from below where man is a god without God, and the absolute on high where he is God in God.[2]

1. "Democracies of the bourgeois liberal type tend to engender their contrary, the totalitarian State."—J. Maritain, *Scholasticism and Politics* (English translation, 1940), p. 95.

2. *True Humanism* (English translation, 1938), pp. 98, 287.

CHAPTER SEVEN

GLADSTONE'S CREED AND CAREER

One upshot of this study has been to assign to Gladstone's early writings and ideas a value and a relevance which have not hitherto been claimed for them.[1] The suggestion has also been made that he did not at bottom abandon the political philosophy which he had thought out as a young man, although he was unable to act upon it. His career as a Liberal statesman did not annul this fact, although it concealed it. His early writings and ideas have been for so long ignored, or at least depreciated, that the present estimate of them may well cause surprise, and call for some further justification than has already been offered.

I

Gladstone was aware, when he wrote *The State in its relations with the Church*, that he was setting himself against the spirit of the age. "It is very clear", he said, "that these later times have been parents to an opinion, that government ought to exercise no choice in matters of faith, but leave every man without advice, or aid, or influence, from that source to choose for himself" (*SRC*, i. 146). If this opinion prevailed, it would from the Christian standpoint be a case of retrogression, and not of progress. Christianity in its pristine days brought to an end the indiscriminate toleration and the utilitarian exploitation of religions by the State; for indifference to the truth of religions cannot subsist with belief in divine revelation.

> Rome, the mistress of state-craft, and beyond all other nations in the politic employment of religion, added without stint or scruple to her list of gods and goddesses, and consolidated her military empire by a skilful medley of all the religions of the world.
>
> Thus it continued while the worship of the Deity was but a conjecture or a contrivance; but when the rising of the Sun of Righteousness had given reality to the subjective forms of faith, had made actual and solid truth the common inheritance of all

1. The German writer, Rudolf Craemer, is exceptional in his recognition of their importance as a key to Gladstone's outlook; see his *Gladstone als christlicher Staatsmann* (1930), *e.g.*, pp. 492f.

men, then the religion of Christ became, unlike other new creeds, an object of jealousy and of cruel persecution, because it would not consent to become a partner in this heterogeneous device, and planted itself upon truth, and not in the quicksand of opinion; and in the same natural order, when Christianity became the religion of the State, it excluded every other system from public patronage. . . . Should the Christian faith ever become but one among many co-equal pensioners of a government, it will be a proof that subjective religion has again lost its God-given hold upon objective reality; or when, under the thin shelter of its name, a multitude of discordant schemes shall have been put upon a footing of essential parity, and shall together receive the bounty of the legislature, this will prove that we are once more in a transition-state—that we are travelling back again from the region to which the Gospel brought us, towards that in which it found us (*SRC*, i. 124f.; cp. Disraeli, *Lord George Bentinck*, 1905 ed., p. 331).

This solemn and prophetic warning fell on deaf ears when it was uttered, but to-day, after the interval of a hundred years, it may be deemed worthy of consideration. In the interval the opinion that governments ought to exercise no choice in matters of faith steadily gained ground, until those, for whom it was becoming almost axiomatic, were rudely awakened through the adoption by an increasing number of States of new faiths, which they imposed by all the mechanics of totalitarianism. In England the *laissez-faire* axiom was never acted upon with logical consistency; nevertheless, it was becoming axiomatic.

It was by a strange irony that Gladstone, who, as a young man, had these profound forebodings as to its significance and its outcome, should himself as a Liberal statesman have taken a leading part in promoting the constitutional changes from which at first he anticipated such grave consequences. Was his first instinct right, or did years and experience lead him to a yet deeper wisdom? The answer has been taken for granted for so long, that it may not be easy to realise that the question is again open.

Throughout his life Gladstone continued to have serious forebodings about the future battle for Christian belief, but his eventual conversion to political liberalism was apparently unshaken. He never formally reasserted the general principles of *The State in its relations with the Church;* neither, however, did he formally retract them. *A Chapter of Autobiography*, published in

1868, is indecisive on this score.[1] The noteworthy fact is that he never worked out an alternative theory of the State in its relations with the Church to replace his first theory, nor did he reopen the question *au fond*. It may have to be admitted that as a Liberal he had no clearly thought-out political philosophy. This suggestion, at least, is not altogether novel.

Goldwin Smith wrote:

> Gladstone's multifarious reading does not seem to have included a large proportion of history or political philosophy. He has left among his writings nothing of importance in the way of political science, nor does he seem even to have formed any clear conception of the polity which he was seeking to produce. His guiding idea, when once he had broken loose from his early Toryism, was liberty, which he appeared to think would of itself be the parent of all good.[2]

With this, the more sympathetic testimony of Viscount Bryce should be compared:

> All (Gladstone's) political writings, except the books on *The State in its Relations to* (*sic*) *the Church* and *Church Principles considered in their Results*, belong to the class of occasional literature, being pamphlets or articles produced with a view to some current crisis or controversy. They are valuable chiefly as proceeding from one who bore a leading part in the affairs they relate to, and as embodying vividly the opinions and aspirations of the moment, less frequently in respect of permanent lessons of political wisdom, such as one finds in Machiavelli or Tocqueville or Edmund Burke. Like Pitt and Peel, Mr Gladstone had a mind which, whatever its original tendencies, had come to be rather practical than meditative. He was fond

1. See p. 97, n. 2 *supra*. The fragmentary notes of 1894, headed "Some of my Errors", quoted by Morley, i. 179f., are also indecisive.

Lord Selborne's *A Defence of the Church of England against Disestablishment* (1886) contains an introductory letter to Gladstone, which opens as follows: "To whatever extent you may retain or may have relinquished your early views of the proper relations between Church and State, the subject (I am persuaded) is one to which you are not and cannot be indifferent. If your later public utterances concerning it have been (as must be confessed) uncertain and enigmatical, this may be due to the exigencies of a political position to which it would be hard to find a parallel in the history of this, or perhaps of any other country." In his copy of this book (*SDL*) Gladstone put a mark of agreement against the description of his later public utterances.

2. *My Memory of Gladstone* (1904), pp. 37f.

of generalisations and principles, but they were always directly related to the questions that came before him in actual politics; and the number of weighty maxims or illuminative suggestions to be found in his writings and speeches is small in proportion to the sustained vigour they display.[1]

Dr E. Wingfield-Stratford has passed a more trenchant verdict:

> His will and not his philosophy was his guide; the latter was, in fact, mostly a matter of high-sounding generalisations about social forces moving onwards in their might and majesty, the freedom of nations and so forth, generalisations that he was invariably capable of qualifying to admit of any concrete application, or none, as the spirit moved him.[2]

These observations, except for the concluding part of the last (though that too is not altogether wide of the mark), appear on the whole to be just. In the latter part of his career Gladstone talked a good deal about the principles of liberalism, but these "principles", if a clear definition of them is sought for in his writings and speeches, turn out to be vague and elusive, or else not to be principles; for such policies as free trade and an extension of the franchise are hardly to be termed "principles". "Current Liberalism in the middle of the last century", it has been said, "was still largely founded in the idealism of Locke".[3] Is it likely that Gladstone, who till the end of his life held with de Maistre that contempt for Locke is the beginning of knowledge,[4] was in any accepted or representative sense a believer in Liberal principles?[5] It is significant that the chapter on

1. *Studies in Contemporary Biography* (1903), p. 465; cp. *ibid.*, pp. 439f.

2. *The History of British Civilisation* (1938), p. 1026. G. E. Buckle in vol. v. of the *Life of Disraeli* observes, with reference to the latter part of Gladstone's career, that he "seldom or never played with political ideas which could not be enclosed within the compass of a Bill" and that this fact "explains his diminishing hold on the present generation". May it not be that, if he regains a hold, it will be through attention to the earlier period when he did "play with political ideas which could not be enclosed within the compass of a Bill"?

3. J. H. Muirhead in an article on "Recent Criticism of the Idealist Theory of the General Will" in *Mind* (1924), xxxiii. 168.

4. See Morley, iii. 476f; cp. ii. 179.

5. C. R. L. F[letcher] in *Mr Gladstone at Oxford*, 1890, reports "T. R." as saying: "I fancy that there were indeed many Liberal principles which he (Gladstone) had adopted without assimilating" (p. 13); and again: "What struck me was that he spoke not as a Liberal, but as an Oxford man who had

"Liberalism" in Professor G. H. Sabine's *History of Political Theory* (1939), although it is concerned almost entirely with English Liberalism in the nineteenth century, contains no allusion to Gladstone.

On November 5, 1884, Gladstone delivered a characteristic speech on liberalism at the laying of the foundation stone of the National Liberal Club. Amid cheers he eloquently likened "Liberal principles" to "that solid and massive stone which it has been permitted to me this day to lay". "What, gentlemen", he asked, "are Liberal principles, and what part have they played, do they play, and will they play in the public life of this country?" But the speech contains no clear answer to the first part of the question; all it amounts to is a rhetorical expansion of the claim that "the legislation of the last half century has been in general Liberal legislation . . . and that Liberal legislation has been beneficial to the country".[1]

The fundamentally conservative cast of Gladstone's mind has in fact often been remarked upon, though there is no reason to suppose that those who have remarked upon it have thought it worth while to attend to the book in which he gave expression to his original political philosophy. Gladstone, said Professor L. Susan Stebbing, who was not given to making loose statements, "entered Parliament as a High Church Tory, and he was by

gone into the Liberal party because the Tory party was under *influences* . . . no doubt Protectionism and Disraeli were in his mind" (p. 17).

Cp. J. A. R. Marriott, *Queen Victoria and her Ministers* (1933), p. 144: "Although his career as Prime Minister synchronized with the advent of Democracy, Gladstone himself was more of a demagogue than a democrat. In some respects, indeed, the man who had opposed the Reform Bill of 1832 remained to the end of his long life a Tory."

On Gladstone's "inequalitarianism", see Mary Drew, *Acton, Gladstone and Others* (1924), p. 19.

1. See *The Times*, November 6, 1884.

But in private Gladstone sometimes expressed doubts about the beneficial results of Liberal legislation. Sir Henry Ponsonby has left a description of a conversation that he had with Gladstone at Balmoral in 1873. Gladstone had been speaking about the effect of reform on the House of Commons. "'But', I said, 'that sounds as if the Reform Bills have done more harm than good'. So they have undoubtedly as far as the composition. Statesmen on the old lines are becoming impossible. We have scarcely any rising young men in the House now", replied Gladstone.—Arthur Ponsonby, *Henry Ponsonby: Queen Victoria's Private Secretary* (1942), p. 251.

temperament a High Church Tory to the end."[1] His son, Viscount Gladstone, wrote:

> Lord Morley is in a general sense right in saying that Mr Gladstone remained in the citadel of Tradition—or as I should prefer to put it, of Authority. Mr Gladstone's principle was to uphold all institutions, tenets, practices, dogmas, whether social, political, or religious, established by the work and views of the best and greatest authorities of the past, until weakness or error were demonstrated.[2]

The secondary, and almost accidental, character of Gladstone's liberalism is borne out by the circumstances in which he became associated with the Liberal party. There was no sudden conversion; no clear or clean adoption of one political philosophy in the place of another. As Bryce said, "It took fourteen years, from 1846 to 1860, to carry him from the Conservative to the Liberal camp."[3] Had it not been for the position that had already been occupied by Disraeli in the Conservative party, it is a reasonable conjecture that Gladstone might have occupied that place instead. Bryce may even underestimate the period of transition. Until late in the 'sixties the question was still open whether Gladstone would be known as a Conservative or as a Liberal statesman; his final association with the Liberal party was more the result of personal and accidental circumstances than of natural affinity.[4]

1. *Ideals and Illusions* (1941), p. 108, n. 2. Cp. Algernon Cecil: "The greatest Liberal in Britain had been formed in a school of theology and politics highly conservative and even in some respects medieval."—*Metternich* [2] (1943), p. 9. Cp. B. Holland, *Life of the Eighth Duke of Devonshire* (1911), i. 280f.; ii. 51, 58.

T. S. Eliot in *The Idea of a Christian Society* (p. 17) says: "In the nineteenth century the Liberal Party had its own conservatism, and the Conservative Party its own liberalism; neither had a political philosophy."

2. *After Thirty Years* (1928), p. 80. In the case of his theory of the relations of the State with the Church, we may add, it was the demonstration rather of weakness than of error that led Gladstone to abandon it in practical politics.

3. Bryce, *op. cit.*, p. 414.

4. On April 8, 1855, Bishop Samuel Wilberforce noted in his diary that Gladstone, in the course of a conversation with him, had said that his "sympathies" were "with Conservatives, his opinions with Liberals". In his copy of the *Life of Wilberforce* (*SDL*) Gladstone has written against this *true then*. Again, on November 4, 1856, recording another conversation with Gladstone, Wilberforce noted: "Manifestly Gladstone leans to a Conservative alliance.

There was always, as Mr J. L. Hammond has pointed out, a wide divergence between Gladstone and the intellectual Liberals. "His liberal views were not a body of truth acquired from the study of masters like Locke, Bentham and Mill; they were the effect of experience on a mind nursed on Aristotle, Augustine, Dante and Butler."[1]

> Most persons would agree that the masters of Liberalism as an intellectual force in the days of Gladstone's ascendancy were Locke, Adam Smith, Bentham and Mill. For how much (apart from Adam Smith's *Free Trade*) did they count in Gladstone's development? For nothing of which Gladstone was conscious. . . .
>
> His fellow Liberals found him difficult to understand, not merely because of the subtlety and mystification of his language, but because his opinions were derived from sources so different and in some aspects so hostile.[2]

It would be untrue to say that Gladstone abandoned his original political philosophy and embraced its opposite. He ceased to advocate, or to try to act upon, the position that he had taken up in *The State in its relations with the Church*, not because he became convinced that it was in principle wrong, but because he came to see that it was in practice impossible. He wrote that book at a time when, in the words of Samuel Wilberforce, Church and State were "at the fag-end of an old alliance".[3] As Gladstone explained in *A Chapter of Autobiography*, he was deceived by the Church revival in the 1830's into supposing that the alliance might yet be renewed in its old form. It must be remembered

The Conservative the best chance for the Church"; and again two days later: "About parties. He evidently inclines to the Conservative." In February, 1865, Wilberforce wrote to a friend: "What Gladstone is to head is all uncertain. Walpole still thinks that, having gone a certain way with the Radicals, he will on some Church measure wheel round and break wholly with them."—*Life of Wilberforce*, ii. 283, 335f.; ii. 158.

See also D. C. Somervell, *Disraeli and Gladstone*, pp. 116f.; and Buckle, *Life of Disraeli*, iv. 117, 159.

Mr A. Tilney Bassett writes of Gladstone's speech on the Reform Bill of 1866 as being the first occasion on which he "definitely adopted the creed of the Liberal Party".—*Gladstone's Speeches* (1916), p. 343.

1. *Gladstone and the Irish Nation* (1938), p. 535.

2. Hammond, *op. cit.*, pp. 533f. See the whole passage. Sir Henry Slesser, in *A History of the Liberal Party* (1944), says of Gladstone: "It is remarkable that no biographer has ever succeeded in making the character of the founder of Liberalism really intelligible" (p. 95).

3. *Life of Wilberforce*, i. 265.

that he formulated his Church and State theory when the Anglican revival was still full of great promise,[1] before the debacle caused by the secessions to Rome was anticipated.[2]

II

Although his service of Church and State could not take the form for which he had hoped, still he was convinced that he must serve both Church and State in the best way that was possible. Moreover, he was ambitious as well as religious.[3] "I greatly felt being turned out of office", he candidly admitted to Samuel Wilberforce in 1857, "I saw great things to do. I longed to do them. I am losing the best years of my life out of my natural service."[4] Gladstone, wrote Charles Wordsworth, "soon discovered, as he could not fail to do, in his Parliamentary experience, that the *State-conscience* theory, which he had attempted to maintain with so much ability, but with less practical wisdom, *would not work*; and that if he was to succeed in the main object which he proposed to himself for life—viz. to become a great statesman—it must be abandoned".[5] Gladstone, wrote Goldwin Smith, "was ambitious, happily for the country; and he wanted to recover the means of doing great things. His admirers need not shrink from that avowal".[6]

Gladstone himself had written in *The State and its relations with the Church*: "Some men are better fitted to command than others, and therefore . . . their being in places of authority is a benefit, not merely to themselves, which is a secondary question, but likewise to the community at large."[7] Such men, of whom he was obviously one himself, have to come to terms with actual conditions; they cannot wait for congenial conditions. Thus he wrote in *A Chapter of Autobiography*:

> Honour and duty themselves require their loyal servant to take account of the state of facts in which he is to work,

1. In *SRC*, i. 253, Gladstone wrote: "The Establishment has arisen from her torpor, she is awake and has put on strength; and in an age august and venerable, she manifests the vigour of the earliest youth."

2. See *A Chapter of Autobiography*, pp. 47–56. Cp. *Life of Samuel Wilberforce*, i. 135f., and D. C. Somervell, *Disraeli and Gladstone*, pp. 52ff.

3. Cp. p. 25 *supra*.

4. *Life of Wilberforce*, ii. 349.

5. *Public Appeals in behalf of Christian Unity* (1886), p. 21.

6. *My Memory of Gladstone* (1904), p. 28.

7. *SRC*, i. 284.

> and, while ever labouring to elevate the standard of opinion and action around him, to remember that his business is not to construct, with self-chosen materials, an Utopia or a Republic of Plato, but to conduct the affairs of a living and working community of men, who have self-government recognised as in the last resort the moving spring of their political life, and of the institutions which are its outward vesture (pp. 11f.; cp. p. 38).

There is no escape from the fact that, as Disraeli said,[1] "a statesman is the creature of his age, the child of circumstance, the creation of his time". F. S. Oliver made a similar point when he remarked that "an artist, starving in a garret because he had ventured to outrage the popular taste, may yet paint masterpieces; but political masterpieces can only be made by a politician working in energetic partnership with a prevalent opinion".[2]

Contemporary political conditions, rather than an interior change of fundamental convictions—his career rather than his creed, carried Gladstone from the Conservative to the Liberal camp.[3] The worst of the argument of *The State in its relations with the Church*, as D. C. Somervell says, "was that no practical politician of the Victorian Age now opening could possibly accept it".[4] Gladstone's biographers have noted[5] that he had a flair for actual, as distinguished from ideal, possibilities, in the case of particular problems. "His whole temper and spirit turned to practice", says Morley. "He was of the mind of the Roman emperor, 'Hope not for the republic of Plato; but be content with

1. In *The Crisis Examined* (1834). He continued: "A statesman is essentially a practical character; and when he is called upon to take office, he is not to inquire what his opinion might or might not have been upon this or that subject—he is only to ascertain the needful and the beneficial, and the most feasible manner in which affairs are to be carried on." See *Whigs and Whiggism*, p. 32. Cp. Coningsby's remark: "The man who enters political life at this epoch has to choose between political infidelity and a destructive creed."—Monypenny, *Life of Disraeli*, i. 118.

2. *The Endless Adventure* (1930), i. 31.

3. For another example of the way in which contemporary political conditions determine a man's change of political profession, see Ernest Barker (*Political Thought in England*, 1915, p. 128) who says of Herbert Spencer's move to the Conservative camp: "It was the change of political conditions which made him the prophet of a different cause."

4. *Disraeli and Gladstone*, p. 34.

5. See Mary Drew, *Acton, Gladstone and Others* (1924), p. 12.

ever so small an advance, and look on even that as a gain worth having'."[1] Indeed, Gladstone noted this propensity in himself. In a general retrospect of his career, which he left among his papers, he wrote:

> I am by no means sure, upon a calm review, that Providence has endowed me with anything which can be called a striking gift. But if there be such a thing entrusted to me, it has been shown, at certain political junctures, in what may be termed appreciation of the general situation and its result. To make good the idea, this must be considered as the simple acceptance of public opinion, founded upon a discernment that it has risen to a certain height needful for a given work, like a tide. It was an insight into the facts of particular eras and their relations one to another, which generates in the mind a conviction that the materials exist for forming a public opinion and for directing it to a particular end.[2]

His aptitude for this kind of discernment may throw light, not only on his attitude to particular problems, but on the main change in his whole career.

"Mr Gladstone", wrote Walter Bagehot, "is essentially a man who cannot impose his creed *on* his time, but must learn his creed *of* his time."[3] And in the same essay he quotes Gladstone's own remarks "on the case of the orator":

> His work, from its very inception, is inextricably mixed up with practice. It is cast in the mould offered to him by the mind of his hearers. It is an influence principally received from his audience (so to speak) in vapour, which he pours back upon them in a flood. The sympathy and concurrence of his time, is, with his own mind, joint parent of his work. He cannot follow nor frame ideals; his choice is, to be what his age will have him, what it requires in order to be moved by him, or else not to be at all.[4]

1. Morley, i. 206f.
2. *The Gladstone Papers* (1930), pp. 29f.
3. *Biographical Studies* (1881), p. 112.
4. *Ibid.*, p. 94. Bagehot does not give the reference for this passage; it occurs in Gladstone's *Studies on Homer and the Homeric Age* (1858), iii. 107. In *Juventus Mundi* (1869) it reappears in the following form:

> Great speeches cannot be made, except in an age and place where they are to be understood and felt. The work of the orator is cast in the mould offered him by the mind of his hearers. He cannot follow nor frame ideals at his own will; his choice is to be what his time will have him, what it requires in order to be moved by him, or not to be at all (p. 433).

11

The age would have Gladstone be a Liberal statesman, in the sense of a promoter of *laissez-faire*; however little this role at first appealed to him, he came to see that he could not "change the profound and resistless tendencies of the age"; it was his business "to guide and control their application".[1]

Gladstone, said Bryce, "was accustomed to say that the capital fault of his earlier days had been his failure adequately to recognise the worth and power of liberty, and the tendency which things have to work out for good when left to themselves".[2] His enthusiasm for liberty gathered force with the years and with public opinion, and finally came to rest in an optimism which subsequent events have shown to be unwarranted.[3] We may note the contrast between his language concerning religious liberty in 1847 and in 1883. In the preface to his published speech on the Jewish Disabilities Bill of 1847, Gladstone's language is carefully qualified by allusion to the contemporary political conditions, which had necessitated his change of attitude.

> My own language of late years has . . . been, that as citizens and as members of the Church we should contend manfully for her own principles and constitution, and should ask and press without fear for whatever tends to her own healthy development by her own means and resources, material or moral, but should deal amicably and liberally with questions either solely or mainly affecting the civil rights of other portions of the community. Disclaiming every forced construction of the principle of such conduct, declining to be tied to it as a set

1. See Morley, i. 413.
2. Bryce, *op. cit.*, p. 416.
3. Gladstone, says Mr Tilney Bassett, "was by nature an optimist, apt to be unduly sanguine in his estimate of the forces which move public opinion".—*Gladstone's Speeches* (1916), p. 553. Cp. Lord Selborne, *Memorials Personal and Political* (1898), ii. 212, 318, 350.

In Burke's *Reflections on the Revolution in France* (*Works*, 1826 ed., vol. v), p. 433, these two passages occur:

> What is liberty without wisdom, and without virtue? It is the greatest of all possible evils; for it is folly, vice, and madness, without tuition or restraint.
>
> Grand swelling sentiments of liberty, I am sure I do not despise. They warm the heart; they enlarge and liberalize our minds; they animate our courage in a time of conflict.

In his copy (*SDL*) Gladstone has written *ma* against the first, and a mark of approval against the second.

For his optimism as regards the Church, see his Midlothian address of September, 1885, quoted by Selborne, *op. cit.*, p. 266; also *CCR*, i. 329.

theory, far less as a calculating machine, asserting a perfect freedom to judge of its application to each particular case upon its own merits, I think it reasonable in itself, and well adapted to the spirit of our institutions, and to the genius of the people, as well as *to the exigencies immediately connected with our divisions in faith and in communion*, and *to the political temper of the age*. This I regard as our appointed function: in this, as I think, the duties of churchman and of patriot are harmonised *under the conditions of the time in which we live*, and *for which we are to consult and labour.*[1]

By 1883 his language has become much more general, absolute and simple:

I am convinced that upon every religious, as well as upon every political ground, the true and the wise course is not to deal out religious liberty by halves, by quarters, and by fractions; but to deal it out entire, and to leave no distinction between man and man on the ground of religious differences from one end of the land to the other. . . . I have no fear of Atheism in this House. Truth is the expression of the Divine mind; and however little our feeble vision may be able to discern the means by which God will provide for its preservation, we may leave the matter in His hands, and we may be quite sure that a firm and courageous application of every principle of justice and of equity is the best method we can adopt for the preservation and influence of truth.[2]

Whereas in 1847 Gladstone could still speak as a churchman and a statesman, as it were, in one breath, he came in the end to speak with two voices. This was inevitable, for he never thought out a doctrine of the relations of Church and State to take the place of his original one. His faith as a churchman remained what it had been—as definite and dogmatic as ever: "The fundamentals of Christian dogma", said Morley, "so far as I know and am entitled to speak, are the only region in which Mr Gladstone's opinions have no history."[3] But as a statesman his ideas were

1. *Substance of a speech on the motion of Lord John Russell for a committee of the whole House, with a view to the removal of the remaining Jewish Disabilities; delivered in the House of Commons, on Thursday, December* 16, 1847. *Together with a preface* (1848), p. 22. Italics mine.

Cp. Gladstone's *Letter to the Right Rev. William Skinner, D.D., Bishop of Aberdeen and Primus, on the Functions of Laymen in the Church* (1852), pp. 9f.

2. Bassett, *Gladstone's Speeches*, pp. 596, 600.

3. Morley, i. 207.

continually moving and adapting themselves to fresh situations. But he thought *laissez-faire* had come to stay. He did not suspect that the tide would turn. His limitations as a statesman, and as a prophet, were due not to his acceptance of the conditions of the time and place in which his work had to be done, but to his eventual satisfaction with those conditions and to his failure to make allowances for their temporary character and for the extent to which they were the product of non-moral causes. If he had understood that the strength of *laissez-faire* England depended on favouring circumstances that in the nature of the case would pass away, he would have been less optimistic and less moralistic. He would also have left a larger heritage of political wisdom for posterity.

III

His career offers both an example and a warning to Christian citizens. It offers an example, because Gladstone shows that a man, in order to serve God as a citizen, must accept the actual political conditions of his age and throw himself into the conflicts which the history of his own time raises.[1] It is no good taking part in politics half-heartedly. The Christian man, who is looking always towards the heavenly city of God and waiting for that to be unveiled, must meanwhile accept all the responsibilities of which he is capable for the government of the earthly city, which is also God's, though strangely so. There must be no shrinking from the distasteful, and often dreadful, tasks which God's veiled city on earth requires its citizens to undertake.

But Gladstone's career also offers a warning against too naïve and confident an acceptance of current trends, whether economic, cultural or religious. His standpoint as a Christian ought to have given him a deeper insight into the relativity of the Victorian assumptions, so that, while he was immersed in the political struggles of that age, he could remain aware of the transitory character both of his tasks and of his achievements. As it was,

1. Gladstone, says J. L. Hammond, "brought to public life the strength of two powerful impulses not often found together. Politics, however ignoble their evil hours, belonged, as he believed, to man's spiritual nature, and summoned to their duties man's spiritual power. He reached this conclusion by a path of his own; he held it with a passion of his own; he lived by it with a conviction of his own".—*Gladstone and the Irish Nation*, p. 702.

his faith as a Christian and his faith as a statesman were not sufficiently integrated, although his oratory kept a glowing haze over the separation between them.[1] He is a symbol of the fact that no satisfactory doctrine of the relations of the State with the Church or of a Christian politics was found in the Victorian era to take the place of the older doctrines.[2]

Christians to-day need both this example and this warning. Young men and women need to see that their duty in the political sphere is not fulfilled by the doctrinaire advocacy of ideals,[3]—even of normative ideals. It requires them to engage in the actual political struggles with which the history of their own time confronts them. If they have a capacity for political leadership, they must exercise it in terms of the social movements and forces of the period, and accept whatever distasteful,[4] and even dreadful, tasks the conditions may impose. Thus, if there is an inevitable movement towards a planned society, they must aim at taking a leading part in the planning, and not merely deplore, criticise or oppose it. On the other hand, they should remain aware of the dangers and limitations of planning, as Gladstone did not remain aware of

1. Morley (i. 81) speaks of "that double-mindedness, that division of sensibility between the demands of spiritual and of secular life, which remained throughout one of the marking traits of his career". But it was in the latter part of his career that Gladstone was most torn in opposite directions, to retirement from politics, and back from retirement into politics. If his sense of obligation as churchman and statesman had been objectively integrated (and not only "of his own"—see preceding note), there would still no doubt have been this double pull, as there should be in every Christian's sensibility, but there would not have been the same wavering, the uncertainty, the changeableness of intention that marked his case.

2. J. L. Hammond remarks that it seems to be true of Gladstone (and also of Shaftesbury and Manning) that "religion had more effect in giving them courage and devotion than in giving definite shape to their opinions", *i.e.* as regards politics.—*Op. cit.*, p. 719.

3. Paley was not recording a unique experience when he said: "An experience of nine years . . . afforded me frequent occasions to observe, that in discoursing to young minds upon topics of morality, it required more pains to make them perceive the difficulty than to understand the solution."—*The Principles of Moral and Political Philosophy* in *Works* (1825 ed.), vol. iv. p. xiii.

4. "Politics unfortunately abounds in shams that must be treated reverentially by every politician who would succeed. If you are the sort of man whose stomach revolts against treating shams reverentially, you will be well advised to stay out of politics altogether and set up as a prophet; your prophecies may perhaps sow good seed for some future harvest. But as a politician you would be impotent."—F. S. Oliver, *The Endless Adventure*, i. 106.

the dangers and limitations of *laissez-faire*. In particular, they must remember that the well-being of society depends in the long run on right relations between Church and State. The quest for these right relations is an obligation that rests upon Christians in every age. All that is involved in this quest now needs to be re-examined *au fond*. Because no normative solution is practicable at present, it is all the more necessary to regard provisional arrangements from the perspective of what is normative, and not to be contented with any temporary compromise, however well it may seem to work for the moment.

IV

It is tempting to speculate, in conclusion, whether the course of English history would have been substantially different if Gladstone had followed the voice, which prompted him on the threshold of his career, to take holy orders.[1] "For a time", wrote Bryce, "he desired to be ordained a clergyman. Had this wish, abandoned in deference to his father's advice, been carried out, he must eventually have become a leading figure in the Church of England and have sensibly affected her recent history."[2] In that case, instead of the great Liberal statesman, he would surely have become a churchman no less great, a churchman whose genius compassed much of the strength of a Newman, a Simeon and a Tait without their several limitations,[3] and who as Primate

1. On Gladstone's leaning to the clerical calling see, in addition to the references given in Morley, Harry Drew, *Death and the Hereafter*, (1911) p. 110; D. C. Somervell, *op. cit.*, pp. 21, 136; G. W. E. Russell, *The Household of Faith* (1902), pp. 4f.; R. Craemer, *op. cit.*, pp. 58ff.

2. Bryce, *op cit.*, p. 407.

3. If this suggestion seems too presumptuous, we may recall Acton's words about Gladstone in 1879:

> When our descendants shall stand before the slab that is not yet laid among the monuments of famous Englishmen, they will say that Chatham knew how to inspire a nation with his energy, but was poorly furnished with knowledge and ideas; that the capacity of Fox was never proved in office, though he was the first of debaters; that Pitt, the strongest of ministers, was among the weakest of legislators; that no Foreign Secretary has equalled Canning, but that he showed no other administrative ability; that Peel, who excelled as an administrator, a debater, and a tactician, fell everywhere short of genius; and that the highest merits of the five, without their drawbacks, were united in Mr Gladstone.

See Mary Drew, *Acton, Gladstone and Others*, p. 27.

of the national Church might have healed not only the divisions within it but also those outside it, and so have influenced the fate and future of this country, and of Christianity in this country, more fruitfully than any statesman could in such a time.

After all, would not Gladstone's political achievements have been carried out, in one way or another, even if he had not been at the political helm?[1] Whereas, if the Church had been under his leadership, its history might have pursued a very different course, and it might be in a very different condition to-day. As late as 1846 he wrote to Manning concerning the best way to serve the Church:

> It is the essential change now in progress from the catholic to the infidel idea of the state which is the determining element in my estimate of this matter. . . . For I hold and believe that when that transition has once been effected, the state never can come back to the catholic idea by means of any agency from within itself: that, if at all, it must be by a sort of re-conversion from without.[2]

And in 1850, when his career was irrevocably set in politics, he wrote again to Manning:

> In my own case there is work ready to my hand and much more than enough for its weakness, a great mercy and comfort. But I think I know what my course would be, were there not. It would be to set to work upon the holy task of clearing, opening, and establishing positive truth in the church of England, which is an office doubly blessed, inasmuch as it is both the business of truth, and the laying of firm foundations for future union in Christendom.[3]

After quoting this passage, Morley finely adds: "If this vision of a dream had ever come to pass, perhaps Europe might have seen the mightiest Christian doctor since Bossuet; and just as Bossuet's struggle was called the grandest spectacle of the seventeenth century, so to many eyes this might have appeared the greatest of the nineteenth."

1. Cp. p. 23, n. 2 *supra*. J. L. Hammond writes: "Of most of the great reforms of the nineteenth century it might be said that in one sense they were agreed reforms. It is significant that hardly any of them were repealed".—*Op. cit.*, p. 518.

2. Morley, i. 324.

3. Morley, i. 382.

Manning, on the other hand, had once contemplated a political career,[1] and, as G. W. E. Russell said, "though a priest, he was essentially a statesman".[2] If these two men had followed their first inclinations, it is not probable that the political history of England in the nineteenth century would have been very different from what in fact it was. In its social and economic history more might have been done to remedy injustice, for Manning had a deeper sympathy with the lot of the poor than Gladstone.[3] But there might have been an immense difference in its ecclesiastical history, and Gladstone's fame and following to-day might have been much greater than in fact they are.

However, if Bryce could say of the Gladstone that was, "Of no man who has lived in our times is it so hard to speak in a concise and summary fashion",[4] it is very much harder to speak of the Gladstone that might have been, and the speculation is one that it would now be fruitless to pursue.

1. E. S. Purcell, *Life of Cardinal Manning* (1895), i. 70.
2. *William Ewart Gladstone* (Everyman ed.), p. 92.
3. There was warrant enough for what Joseph Chamberlain wrote to Dilke in 1893: "Mr. Gladstone has no real sympathy with the working classes—and a perfect hatred of all forms of Socialism. His concessions are extorted from him and are the price paid for votes". See J. L. Garvin, *The Life of Joseph Chamberlain* (1933), ii. 555. Cp. what Lloyd George said to C. F. G. Masterman: "Gladstone was not really a democrat. He believed in liberty but not in equality, and was very suspicious of all we mean by social reform". Lucy Masterman, *C. F. G. Masterman* (1939), p. 181.
4. Bryce, *op. cit.*, p. 400.

APPENDED NOTE

GLADSTONE AND MACHIAVELLIANISM (see p. 56)

On April 28, 1827, Arthur Hallam wrote to Gladstone: "Have you seen the new *Edinburgh*? An excellent article on Machiavelli by Macaulay . . .".[1] Gladstone's reply does not appear to have survived, but it is unlikely that he would have subscribed to Hallam's opinion without considerable qualification. Gladstone's limitation was of an opposite kind to Macaulay's. He could not easily bring himself to acknowledge the extent to which statesmen, especially in the post-medieval period, did in fact act upon Machiavelli's precepts, however much they might profess to deplore them. The following is an instructive illustration of Gladstone's obstinate moralism in regard to politics.

His friend, Lord Acton,[2] contributed an introduction to a new edition of *Il Principe*, edited by L. A. Burd (1891),[3] in which he wrote:

> No reader of this volume will continue to wonder how so intelligent and reasonable a man (as Machiavelli) came to propose such flagitious counsels. When Machiavelli declared that extraordinary objects cannot be accomplished under ordinary rules, he recorded the experience of his own epoch, but also foretold the secret of men since born. . . . He represents more than the spirit of his country and his age. Knowledge, civilisation, and morality have increased; but three centuries have borne enduring witness to his political veracity. . . . He is the earliest conscious and articulate exponent of certain living forces in the present world. Religion, progressive enlightenment, the perpetual vigilance of public opinion, have not reduced his empire, or disproved the justice of his conception of mankind.[4]

Acton supported these statements with a formidable list of quotations from authorities who had flourished during the intervening centuries in the chief countries of Europe. He abhorred political

1. See *The Gladstone Papers* (1930), p. 50.
2. On Gladstone's friendship with Acton, see Mary Drew, *Acton, Gladstone and Others* (1924), pp. 1–31.
3. Acton's introduction is reproduced in *The History of Freedom and other essays*.
4. *Op. cit.*, pp. xix, xl. Cp. J. N. Figgis, *From Gerson to Grotius*, p. 94.

amoralism as much as Gladstone (and disapproved of Macaulay no less [1]) but he did not allow his own moral fervour to whitewash political realities. If he erred it was in the other direction. Gladstone too, in the light of hard and protracted experience, was sometimes driven to allow the difficulties in the way of applying moral standards to political action,[2] but it was never characteristic of him to make such allowances.

Thus on August 16, 1891, he wrote to Acton, evidently acknowledging a gift of the book that has just been quoted:

> I have to thank you also for the Machiavelli. . . . What a marvellous, what a terrible—I almost add what a detestable—array of authorities you produce. Against such pricks as these I must kick a little. I affirm the identity of all moral laws, though I admit they apply with variations to different subject matters. . . . I won't admit politics to be so bad as all these bigwigs make them, or they could not attract and hold two such men as Frederick Cavendish and the last Dalhousie, two men whose minds were in political action of a truly angelic purity.[3]

Gladstone's copy of the book which Acton gave him is in St Deiniol's Library. His pencil markings upon it, which are confined to Acton's introduction, are in this connexion interesting. For instance, against Acton's quotation of Pascal's saying: *On ne voit rien de juste ou d'injuste qui ne change de qualité en changeant de climat*, Gladstone has pencilled "satire?" Against Acton's comment that Machiavelli "was simply a faithful observer of facts, who described the fell necessity that governs narrow territories and unstable fortunes; he discovered the true line of progress and the law of future society", Gladstone has written *ma.*

1. Mary Gladstone noted in her diary (February 19, 1884) that Lord Acton was "certainly severe" on Macaulay's character—*Diaries and Letters* (1930), p. 302.

2. "Men have no business to talk of disenchantment; ideals are never realised." "The history of nations", Gladstone wrote in 1876, "is a melancholy chapter; that is, the history of governments is one of the most immoral parts of human history."—Morley, iii. 539. But Gladstone rarely admitted so much. His more usual language was: "We may perceive, by every form of instance, how often the wisdom of love, goodness and simplicity wins, against the wisdom of the crafty and astute self-seeking."—"A Modern Symposium" in *The Nineteenth Century* (July, 1878), p. 188.

3. Figgis and Laurence, *Selections from the Correspondence of the First Lord Acton* (1917), i. 257f. (It is lamentable that no further volume of this correspondence has yet been published.)

BIBLIOGRAPHY

In each case the editions specified are those that have been used in the preparation of this book. Articles in periodicals, etc., are not included, except in cases of special importance.

Acton, Lord. *The History of Freedom and other essays.* (1907).

Allen, J. W. *A History of Political Thought in the sixteenth century.* (1928). *English Political Thought* 1603–60. (1938).

Anon. *The Ultimate Principle of Religious Liberty: the philosophical argument with a review of the controversy on grounds of reason and expediency, in the writings of Locke, Warburton, Paley, Dick, Wardlaw, Gladstone, Martineau, and Miall.* (1860).

Aristotle. *Politics.* English translation by William Ellis. (Everyman ed.)

Arnold, Thomas. *Introductory Lectures on Modern History.* ([2]1843). *Fragment on the Church.* 2nd ed. with Appendices. (1845).

Ashwell, A. R., and Wilberforce, R. G. *Life of Bishop Wilberforce.* 3 vols. (1880–2).

Augustine, St. *The City of God.* English translation by J. Healey, with an introduction by E. Barker. (1931).

Badenoch, G. R. *Coronation Service of Queen Victoria.* (1897).

Bagehot, Walter. *Biographical Studies.* (1881).

Balfour, A. J. *The Foundations of Belief.* ([4]1895).

Barker, Ernest. *Political Thought in England from Herbert Spencer to the Present Day.* (1915). Art. on "The Discredited State" in *The Political Quarterly* (February, 1915); reprinted in *Church, State and Study.* (1930). *Reflections on Government.* (1942). *Britain and the British People.* (1942).

Barth, Karl. *Church and State.* (English translation, 1939).

Bassett, A. Tilney (Ed.). *Gladstone's Speeches.* (1916). *Gladstone to his Wife.* (1936).

Birks, T. R. *Church and State; or, National Religion and Church Establishments considered with reference to present controversies.* (1869).

Brown, W. Adams. *Church and State in Contemporary America.* (1936).

Brunner, Emil. *The Divine Imperative.* (English translation, 1937).

Bryce, James. *Studies in Contemporary Biography.* (1903).

Buber, Martin. *I and Thou.* (English translation, 1937).

Bunsen, Frances Baroness. *A Memoir of Baron Bunsen.* 2 vols. (1868).

Burke, Edmund. *Reflections on the Revolution in France* in vol. v of *Works.* ed.).

Butler, Joseph. *Works.* 2 vols. (1849 ed.).

Cambridge Medieval History, The. (1911–36).

Cambridge Modern History, The. (1902–11).

Cambridgeshire Syllabus of Religious Teaching for Schools, The. (1929).

Carlyle, A. J. *The Christian Church and Liberty.* (1924). *Political Liberty.* (1941).

Carlyle, R. W., and A. J. *A History of Mediæval Political Theory in the West.* 6 vols. (1903–36).

Carr, E. H. *Conditions of Peace.* (1942).

Cecil, Lady Gwedolen. *Life of Robert, Marquis of Salisbury.* 4 vols. (19

Chalmers, Thomas. "Lectures on Church Establishments" in vol. xi of *Select Works*. (1857 ed.).

Charles, R. H. *The Decalogue*. (1923).

Chavasse, C. *The Bride of Christ*. (1940).

Church, M. C. *Life and Letters of Dean Church*. (1897).

Church, R. W. Art. on "Church and State" in *The Christian Remembrancer*. (April, 1850).

Church, Community and State. Oxford Conference Series. 6 vols. (1938).

Church and State. Report of the Archbishops' Commission on the relations between Church and State. 2 vols. (1935).

Clark, G. Kitson. *Peel and the Conservative Party*. (1929).

Cobham, J. O. (Ed.). *No Other Gospel*. (1943).

Coleridge, S. T. *On the Constitution of the Church and State with aids to a right judgment on the late Catholic Bill*. (1830). *On the Constitution of Church and State according to the Idea of each*. (1839).

Cook, S. A. *The Rebirth of Christianity*. (1942).

Craemer, R. *Gladstone als christlicher Staatsmann*. (1930).

Creighton, Louise. *Life and Letters of Mandell Creighton*. 2 vols. (1904).

Creighton, Mandell. *Persecution and Tolerance*. (1895). *The Church and the Nation*. (1901).

Cunningham, W. *Christianity and Politics*. (1916).

Dalby, J. *The Catholic Conception of the Law of Nature*. (1943).

Dante. *De Monarchia*. (Temple Classics ed.).

Dawson, Christopher. *Religion and the Modern State*. (1935). *Beyond Politics*. (1939). *The Judgement of the Nations*. (1943).

Demant, V. A. *Christian Polity*. (1936).

Denzinger, H. *Enchiridion Symbolorum*. ([11]1911).

Disraeli, B. *Whigs and Whiggism*. Ed. by W. Hutcheon. (1913). *Lord George Bentinck: a Political Biography*. (1905 ed.).

Dostoevsky, Fyodor. *The Brothers Karamazov*. 2 vols. (Everyman ed.).

Drew, Harry. *Death and the Hereafter*. (1911).

Drew, Mary (*née* Gladstone). *Catherine Gladstone*. (1919). *Acton, Gladstone and others*. (1914). *Diaries and Letters*. (1930).

Edinger, G., and Neep, E. J. C. *The Grand Old Man: a Gladstone Spectrum*. (1936).

Ehrenström, Nils. *Christian Faith and the Modern State*. (1937).

Eliot, T. S. *The Idea of a Christian Society*. (1939).

Eyck, Erich. *Gladstone*. (English translation, 1938).

Figgis, J. N. *Studies of Political Thought from Gerson to Grotius*, 1414–25. (1907). *Churches in the Modern State*. ([2]1914). *The Political Aspects of S. Augustine's "City of God"*. (1921).

and Laurence, R. V. *Selections from the Correspondence of the First Lord Acton*. Vol. i. (1917).

F[letcher], C. R. L. *Mr Gladstone at Oxford*, 1890. (1908).

Follett, M. P. *The New State: group organisation the solution of popular government*. English ed. with introduction by Lord Haldane. (1920).

Forsyth, P. T. *Rome, Reform, and Reaction*. (1899). *Theology in Church and State*. (1915). *The Justification of God*. (1916). *The Christian Ethic of War*. (1916).

Froude, J. A. *The Earl of Beaconsfield.* (Everyman ed.).

Galichet, Pierre. *L'Eglise Anglicane et l'Etat.* (1909).

Garratt, G. T. *The Two Mr Gladstones.* (1936).

Gavin, F. *Seven Centuries of the problem of Church and State.* (1938).

Gierke, O. *Political Theories of the Middle Ages.* English translation with intro duction by F. W. Maitland. (1900). *Natural Law and the Theory of Society.* English translation with introduction by Ernest Barker. 2 vols. (1934).

Gladstone, Viscount. *After Thirty Years.* (1928).

Gladstone, W. E. *The State in its relations with the Church.* 1st ed. 1838; 4th ed. 2 vols. 1841. *Church Principles considered in their results.* (1840). *Remarks on the Royal Supremacy* (1850); reprinted in *Gleanings*, vol. v. *Letter to the Right Rev. William Skinner, D.D., Bishop of Aberdeen and Primus, on the Functions of Laymen in the Church* (1852); *reprinted in Gleanings*, vol. vi, where the date of its first publication is given as 1851. *Studies in Homer and the Homeric Age*, vol. iii. (1858). *A Chapter of Autobiography* (1868); reprinted in *Gleanings*, vol. vii. *Juventus Mundi.* (1869). *The Vatican Decrees in their bearing on civil allegiance: a political expostulation.* (1874). *Vaticanism: an answer to replies and reproofs.* (1875). *Gleanings of Past Years.* 8 vols. (1879–97). *The Impregnable Rock of Holy Scripture.* (1890 ed.). *Studies subsidiary to the works of Bishop Butler.* (1896). (Use has been made of two series of Gladstone's speeches and writings in *SDL*, one consisting of 12 vols., the other of 38 vols.)

Gloyn, C. K. *The Church in the Social Order; a study of Anglican social theory from Coleridge to Maurice.* (1942).

Goudge, H. L. *The Church of England and Reunion.* (1938).

Greene, E. B. *Religion and the State: the making and testing of an American tradition.* (1941).

Halévy, E. *A History of the English People*, 1830–41. (English translation, 1927.)

Hammond, J. L. *Gladstone and the Irish Nation.* (1938).

Hanna, W. *Memoirs of the Life and Writings of Thomas Chalmers.* 2 vols. (1852).

Hoare, F. R. *The Papacy and the Modern State.* (1940).

Hobbes, Thomas. *Leviathan.* Reprinted from the ed. of 1651. O.U.P. ed. (1929).

Hocking, W. E. *Man and the State.* (1926).

Hodgson, L. *The Doctrine of the Trinity.* (1943).

Holland, B. *The Life of Spencer Compton, Eighth Duke of Devonshire.* 2 vols. (1911).

Holland, H. Scott. *Personal Studies.* (1905).

Hooker, Richard. *Works.* Ed. J. Keble. 3 vols. (^{2}1841).

Hort, A. F. *Life and Letters of Fenton John Anthony Hort.* 2 vols. (1896).

Hort, F. J. A. *The Christian Ecclesia.* (1897).

Hudson, C. E., and Reckitt, M. B. *The Church and the World.* 3 vols. (1938–40).

Huxley, Aldous. *Grey Eminence: a study in religion and politics.* (1941).

Huxley, J. S. *The Individual in the Animal Kingdom.* (1912).

Ingham, R. *Church Establishments Considered, especially in reference to the Church of England.* (1875).

Jenkins, C. *Frederick Denison Maurice and the New Reformation.* (1938).

Jenkins, D. T. *The Nature of Catholicity.* (1942).

Jewel, John. *The Defence of the Apology*. (Parker soc. ed.).
Johnson, A. R. *The One and the Many in the Israelite Conception of God*. (1942).
Johnston, G. *The Doctrine of the Church in the New Testament*. (1943).
Jordan, W. K. *The Development of Religious Toleration in England*. 3 vols. (1932–8).
Keble, John. "*The State in its Relations with the Church*": *a paper reprinted from the "British Critic", October*, 1839. With a preface by H. P. Liddon. (1869).
Keller, A. *Church and State on the European Continent*. (1936).
Knox, W. L., and Vidler, A. R. *The Development of Modern Catholicism*. (1933).
Lamennais, F. de. *Essay on Indifference in matters of religion*. (English translation, 1895.)
Laski, H. J. *Studies in the Problem of Sovereignty*. (1917). *The Foundations of Sovereignty*. (1921).
Lathbury, D. C. *Correspondence on Church and Religion of William Ewart Gladstone*. 2 vols. (1910).
Leigh, M. S. (Ed.). *Christianity in the Modern State*. Report of the 65th Church Congress. (1936).
Leonis Papæ XIII Allocutiones. (1887).
Leveson-Gower, Sir George. *Years of Content*. (1940).
Liddon, H. P. *Life of Edward Bouverie Pusey*. 4 vols. (1893–7).
Locke, John. "Letters concerning Toleration" in vol. vi of *Works* (1823 ed.).
Macaulay, Lord. *Critical and Historical Essays*. 3 vols. ([5]1848).
Macdonnell, J. C. *The Life of Archbishop Magee*. 2 vols. (1896).
Machiavelli, N. *Discourses*. English translation by E. E. Detmold. 2 vols. (1882). *Il Principe*. Ed. by L. A. Burd. (1891).
MacIver, R. M. *The Modern State*. (1926).
McIlwain, C. H. *The Growth of Political Thought in the West*. (1932).
Magee, W. C. *The Gospel and the Age*. (1884).
Maitland, F. W. *Collected Papers*. Ed. by H. A. L. Fisher. 3 vols. (1911).
Mannheim, K. *Man and Society in an Age of Reconstruction*. (1940). *Diagnosis of our time*. (1943).
Manning, H. E. *The Vatican Decrees in their bearing on civil allegiance*. (1875).
Maritain, J. *True Humanism*. (English translation, 1938). *Scholasticism and Politics*. (English translation, 1940).
Marshall, C. C. *The Roman Catholic Church in the Modern State*. (1928).
Martineau, James. Art. on "Church and State" in *The Prospective Review* (May, 1845); reprinted in *Miscellanies* (1852).
Maurice, F. *Life of Frederick Denison Maurice*. ([2]1884).
Maurice, F. D. *The Kingdom of Christ*. 3 vols. (1838). *Has the Church, or the State, the Power to Educate the Nation?* (1839). *Theological Essays*. ([3]1871). *The Patriarchs and Lawgivers of the Old Testament*. ([2]1890).
Maynard, T. *Apostle of Charity: the life of St Vincent de Paul*. (1940).
Mersch, E. *Le Corps Mystique du Christ*. 2 vols. (1933).
Mill, J. S. *On Liberty*. (1859).
Monypenny, W. F., and Buckle, G. E. *The Life of Benjamin Disraeli, Earl of Beaconsfield*. 6 vols. (1910–20).
Morley, John. *On Compromise*. (1874). *The Life of Richard Cobden*. 2 vols. (1881). *The Life of William Ewart Gladstone*. 3 vols. (1903). *Works*. 14 vols. (1921 ed.).

Mozley, A. *Letters and Correspondence of John Henry Newman.* 2 vols. (1891).

Mumford, Lewis. *Technics and Civilization.* ([5]1938). *The Culture of Cities.* (1940).

Murray, R. H. *Social and Political Thinkers of the Nineteenth Century.* 2 vols. (1929).

Namier, L. B. *Conflicts.* (1942).

Newman, J. H. *A letter addressed to His Grace the Duke of Norfolk on the occasion of Mr Gladstone's recent expostulation.* (1875). *Correspondence with J. Keble and others,* 1839–45. (1917).

Niebuhr, R. *Beyond Tragedy.* (1938). *The Nature and Destiny of Man.* 2 vols. (1941–3).

Nobbs, Douglas. *Theocracy and Toleration: a study of the disputes in Dutch Calvinism from* 1600 *to* 1650. (1938).

Noel, Baptist W. *Essay on the Union of Church and State.* (1848).

Oldham, J. H. *Real Life is Meeting.* (1942).

Oliver, F. S. *The Endless Adventure.* 3 vols. (1930–5).

Ornsby, R. *Memoirs of James Robert Hope-Scott.* 2 vols. (1884).

Osborne, C. E. *Christian Ideas in Political History.* (1929).

Our Place in Christendom. Nine lectures with a preface by the Bishop of London. (1916).

Paley, W. *The Principles of Moral and Political Philosophy* in vol. iv of *Works* (1825 ed.).

Palmer, W. *A Treatise on the Church of Christ.* 2 vols. ([3]1842).

Parker, C. S. *Sir Robert Peel.* 3 vols. (1891–9).

Patmore, Coventry. *The Rod, the Root, and the Flower.* ([2]1923).

Politics and Citizenship, C.O.P.E.C. Commission Reports. Vol. x. (1924).

Ponsonby, Arthur. *Sir Henry Ponsonby: Queen Victoria's Private Secretary.* (1942).

Purcell, E. S. *Life of Cardinal Manning.* 2 vols. (1895).

Ramsey, A. M. *The Gospel and the Catholic Church.* (1936).

Reckitt, M. B. *As it Happened.* (1941).

Reid, T. Wemyss. *Monckton Milnes, Lord Houghton.* 2 vols. (1890). *The Life of William Ewart Gladstone.* (1899).

Relton, H. M. *Religion and the State.* (1937).

Report of the Archbishops' Committee on Church and State. (1916).

Rivière, Jean. *Le problème de l'Eglise et de l'Etat au temps de Philippe le Bel.* (1926).

Robbins, A. F. *The Early Public Life of William Ewart Gladstone.* (1894).

Robinson, H. W. *The Cross of the Servant.* (1936).

Rousseau, J. J. *The Social Contract.* English translation by H. J. Tozer. (1895).

Russell, G. W. E. *William Ewart Gladstone.* (Everyman ed.). *The Household of Faith.* (1902).

Sabine, G. H. *A History of Political Theory.* (1938).

Seaton, A. A. *The Theory of Toleration under the later Stuarts.* (1911).

Selborne, Lord. *A Defence of the Church of England against Disestablishment.* (1886). *Memorials Personal and Political* 1865–95. 2 vols. (1898).

Setton, K. M. *The Christian Attitude towards the Emperors in the Fourth Century.* (1941).

Significance of the Barmen Declaration for the Oecumenical Church, The. (1943).

Simpson, P. Carnegie. *The Church and the State.* (1929).

Slesser, Sir Henry. *A History of the Liberal Party.* (1944).

Smith, G. Barnett. *Thoughts from the Writings and Speeches of William Ewart Gladstone.* (1894).

Smith, Goldwin. Art. on "The Question of Disestablishment" in *The Nineteenth Century* (October, 1891). *My Memory of Gladstone.* (1904).

Smith, W. O. Lester. *To whom do the schools belong?* (1942).

Smuts, J. C. *Holism and Evolution.* (^{2}1927).

Smyth, Charles. *Religion and Politics.* (1943).

Somervell, D. C. *Disraeli and Gladstone.* (^{2}1938).

Stanley, A. P. *The Life and Correspondence of Thomas Arnold.* 2 vols. (^{2}1844).

Stark, W. *The Ideal Foundations of Economic Thought.* (1943).

Stebbing, L. Susan. *Ideals and Illusions.* (1941).

Sturzo, Luigi. *Church and State.* (English translation, 1939).

Tawney, R. H. *Religion and the Rise of Capitalism.* (1926).

Taylor, Jeremy. *The Liberty of Prophesying* in *Practical Works.* (1838 ed.).

Taylor, Vincent. *Jesus and His Sacrifice.* (1937).

Temple, W. *Church and Nation.* (1915). *Christ in his Church.* (1924). *Essays on Christian Politics and kindred subjects.* (1927). *Christianity and the State.* (1928). *Citizen and Churchman.* (1941).

Thomas Aquinas, St. *Summa Theologica.* English translation by English Dominicans.

Thorndike, H. *The Rights of the Church in a Christian State* in *Theological Works.* (L.A.C.T.).

Toynbee, A. J. *A Study of History.* Vols. i–iii. (^{2}1935). Vols. iv–vi. (^{1}1939).

Trevelyan, G. O. *Life of Macaulay.* 2 vols. (1876).

Troeltsch, Ernst. *The Social Teaching of the Christian Churches.* 2 vols. (English translation, 1931).

Vidler, A. R. *Christ's Strange Work.* (1944).

Vinet, A. *An Essay on the Profession of Personal Religious Conviction and upon the Separation of Church and State.* (English translation, 1843).

Wand, J. W. C. *The General Epistles of St Peter and St Jude.* (1934).

Warburton, William. *The Alliance between Church and State* in vol. vii of *Works* (1811 ed.).

Wardlaw, R. *National Church Establishments Examined.* (1839).

Weiss, J. *The History of Primitive Christianity.* 2 vols. (English translation, 1937).

Whately. *Life and Correspondence of Richard Whateley.* 2 vols. (1866).

Williams, W. E. *The Rise of Gladstone to the Leadership of the Liberal Party.* 1859–68. (1934).

Wilson, D. A. *Carlyle.* 6 vols. (1923–34).

Wingfield-Stratford, E. *The History of British Civilization.* (1938).

Woodhouse, A. S. P. *Puritanism and Liberty: being the Army Debates* (1647–9) *from the Clarke Manuscripts with Supplementary Documents.* (1938).

Wordsworth, Charles. *Public Appeals in behalf of Christian Unity.* (1886).

INDEX OF PERSONS

INDEX OF SUBJECTS

PRINTED IN GREAT BRITAIN BY WILLIAM CLOWES AND SONS, LIMITED, LONDON AND BECCLES